Marking Past Tense
in Second Language Acquisition

Marking Past Tense in Second Language Aquisition
A Theoretical Model

Rafael Salaberry

continuum

Continuum International Publishing Group

The Tower Building   80 Maiden Lane Suite 704
11 York Road   New York
London SE1 7NX   NY 10038

British Library Cataloguing-in-Publication Data
A catalogue record for this book is available from the British Library.

ISBN: 978-1-84706-238-3   (hardback)

Library of Congress Cataloguing-in-Publication Data
The Publisher has applied for CIP data

Typeset by Newgen Imaging Systems Pvt Ltd, Chennai, India
Printed and bound in Great Britain by Biddles, Norfolk

Table of Contents

List of Figures and Tables

Figures

Tables

Foreword

The analysis of the use of past tense verbal morphology has become a central topic in second language acquisition studies. Its importance is predicated not only on the multifaceted nature of tense-aspect meanings (i.e., from lexical to syntactic to discursive), but also on the fact that there have been very insightful hypotheses to account for its development. Like many others, my work on tense-aspect started after I first read the hypothesis put forth by Roger Andersen on the development of tense-aspect marking in L2 acquisition. The work of Kathleen Bardovi-Harlig has been as influential as Roger Andersen's work and continues to shape the research agenda of tense-aspect studies. The original studies of Andersen and Bardovi-Harlig have initiated a significant area of research that is now transcending the purview of the original studies on this topic.

At the moment, however, there is a significant trend towards isolating research agendas according to specific theoretical paradigms. This is not unusual, and it could be argued that it is, in fact, the norm in most areas of L2 acquisition. On the other hand, the very multifaceted nature of tense-aspect phenomena may require, more than with any other topic, to broaden our perspective beyond the specific theoretical 'pocket of research' with which we are associated. I am not impervious to theoretical preconceptions, nor should I be. Despite my own theoretical views, however, I will incorporate into my analysis the discussion of findings from theoretical frameworks alternative to the one I will ultimately support. Far from promoting a confrontational discussion, my intention is not to ignore other views and in so doing, present a richer and more nuanced view of tense-aspect acquisition. As readers will note, the overall view of tense-aspect acquisition that I will present in this book is not necessarily an either–or perspective, but rather a position that considers that different theoretical frameworks provide complementary information. At a minimum, the empirical findings of previous studies provide useful information that cannot be summarily dismissed even if gathered through alternative methodological procedures. As always, readers will have to judge the ideas presented in this book according to their own theoretical views. I hope, however, that the acknowledgement of alternative perspectives will enrich the study of tense-aspect phenomena.

The analysis presented in this book has benefitted from the very detailed feedback provided by Dalila Ayoun, Llorenç Comajoan, Yas Shirai and Jacqueline Toribio. All of them made probing questions about many of the ideas I put forth in this book and in so doing, helped me recast my proposal. I hope I have been able to make good use of their very insightful comments and suggestions. Many other people also contributed to the writing of this book. The graduate students in my course on tense-aspect during the Spring semester 2007 at UT-Austin and in particular, Meaghan Dinan and Cory Lyle helped me think through many of the ideas discussed herein. I am also thankful to all the people who very generously agreed to answer questions I posed to them through email or in personal meetings at conferences or by phone: Marylin Buck, Henriette de Swart, Beatriz Granda, Asun Martínez-Arbelaiz, Laura Michaelis, Silvina Montrul and Lilia Ruiz-Debbe.

I also have an enormous debt of gratitude to the people at Continuum who were willing to go out of their way to address last-minute requests to improve the quality of the book manuscript and who still managed to make sure the book went to press on time. An enormous thank you to Colleen Coalter, Jennifer Lovel and Gurdeep Mattu. Finally, I want to thank my family. I would not have finished this book without the moral and emotional support of María José, Julián and Lucas. This book was written in between trips to the park, the museum, the zoo and the doctor. I could not have imagined a better way of writing it.

Foreword

Dalila Ayoun

This ambitious volume systematically and thoroughly examines the theoretical and applied issues that the study of Spanish past tense and aspect raises, by questioning and refining – well-known but not always well-understood – theoretical constructs upon which are based second language (L2) acquisition studies. The first chapter provides an overview of the learnability difficulties that English-speaking learners of Spanish face, while Chapter 2 defines the notions of tense and aspect in depth. Chapter 3 examines how the knowledge of tense and aspect develops from a variety of approaches and reviews an impressive body of empirical research. Chapter 4 provides a lexico-discursive definition of tense-aspect acquisition in L2 Spanish, while the last chapter critically delves into methodological issues as a way to evaluate L2 empirical research. The reader is left with a much better appreciation of the theoretical and empirical issues to be addressed in future research to design studies that may contribute to our understanding of the acquisition of tense and aspect in any language.

Chapter 1

Learning Spanish Past Tense Aspect

1. Introduction

The concept of tense-aspect as a theoretical construct has been studied for a long time. Most authors consider that the first known analysis of aspectual concepts is Aristotle's classification of verb types (Binnick, 1991). In contrast, the formal and systematic analysis of the second language (L2) acquisition of tense-aspect has a much shorter history. Shirai (2007) traces back the beginning of the formal and systematic analysis of tense-aspect acquisition to the pioneering work of Roger Andersen in the early 1980s. Andersen's work was eventually implemented as a full-blown research agenda in the 1990s with the work that he and his students conducted at UCLA (Andersen and Shirai, 1994). Those studies focused mostly on the empirical validation of what has become known as the lexical aspect hypothesis (LAH). The LAH has jumpstarted a vigorous research project whose scope has been increasing ever since. In the late 1990s, Kathleen Bardovi-Harlig and her students at Indiana University expanded the study of L2 tense-aspect development with the empirical testing of the discourse hypothesis (DH), focusing on the role of narrative grounding. The majority of studies conducted within the framework of the LAH and the DH can be regarded as representative of what Bardovi-Harlig (2000) labels as form-oriented studies. Thus, most of the studies tracking the theoretical viability of the LAH and the DH use inflectional morphology as their dependent variable.

In contrast, meaning-oriented studies take as a point of departure the analysis of how the meanings of aspectual contrasts are conveyed in the L2 through whatever means are available to learners. For instance, interlocutor scaffolding, calendric references and implicit understandings based on contextual information are all possible means taken into account by meaning-oriented studies. The latter strand of research on tense-aspect acquisition, that is, meaning-oriented studies is mostly represented by studies on temporality conducted by many European researchers during the 1980s and 1990s.

For instance, Dietrich, Klein and Noyau (1995) provide an overview of work carried out by the European Science Foundation Project (ESFP) on the analysis of the morphological and pragmatic marking of temporality in the L2. Among the studies of the ESFP focused on the Romance languages, several have had a great impact on the analysis of tense-aspect development (e.g., Giacalone-Ramat, 1992, 2002; Noyau, 1990; Trévise, 1987; Véronique, 1987). In the United States, the meaning-oriented approach is represented in the early studies of Sato (1990), Schumann (1987) and others. Finally, during the present decade, a number of published studies have tested the acquisition of tense-aspectual knowledge within a syntactic framework of analysis. This latest and very fruitful research agenda, led by the work of Silvina Montrul and Roumyana Slabakova (e.g., Slabakova & Montrul, 2002a, 2002b, 2007), has been carried out within the framework of a generative linguistic theory (i.e., minimalism).

This very brief review shows that the development of tense-aspect meanings is becoming a very fruitful research area in L2 acquisition. In part, this is due to the fact that tense-aspect meanings straddle a wide range of grammatical subsystems: morphology, syntax, semantics and discourse. Thus, findings from the analysis of tense-aspect acquisition can become a very important piece of the puzzle of L2 acquisition. The main thrust of this book is to present a general theoretical framework of analysis of the L2 acquisition of tense-aspect meanings in Spanish in particular, but that framework could, arguably, be extended to other Romance languages. The proposed analysis will be used to bring together various – apparently incompatible – findings gathered through studies conducted among distinct theoretical proposals. The basic question that will guide the discussion throughout the book is whether tense-aspect meanings can be accurately defined as a syntactic-semantic phenomenon or, alternatively, as a semantic-discursive phenomenon. I propose that the latter is the most plausible definition of tense-aspect meanings, and I show that previous empirical findings substantiate the proposed claim. I also argue that future research on the acquisition of tense-aspect phenomena will inevitably start to converge on the definition of tense-aspect phenomena as the most urgent research topic. Indeed, despite a relatively large amount of data on the development of tense-aspect in L2 acquisition, the major discrepancies between theoretical frameworks are predicated on how tense-aspect meanings are defined. More precisely, I believe there are fairly consistent trends in the empirical data from previous studies that can be interpreted differently, mostly due to how we circumscribe the theoretical representation of tense-aspect in grammar.

The book is organized as follows. In the present chapter I describe the main challenge faced by L2 learners in acquiring and developing knowledge about aspectual distinctions, represented primarily in Spanish. In Chapter 2, I summarize previous theoretical analyses of the construct of tense-aspect. In so doing, I specifically concentrate the discussion on the nature of the interaction between lexical classes of verbs associated with particular aspectual values (i.e., lexical aspect) and the marking of aspectual concepts (e.g., boundedness, iterativity, genericity) through inflectional morphology (i.e., grammatical aspect). In Chapter 3, I critically review a selected sample of empirical studies on the development of tense-aspect knowledge among adult L2 learners with access to formal instruction. I primarily discuss the findings from the most recent studies focusing on the role of syntactic structure as well as semantic-discursive structure. I also review in detail the role of L1 transfer effects. In Chapter 4, I outline a theoretical framework of the acquisition and development of tense-aspect knowledge that relies primarily on (1) a definition of tense-aspect meanings that is predicated on a continuum of meanings ranging from invariant to contextualized, (2) the role of the Simple Past as a tense marker in languages such as English and its potential effect on L1 transfer and (3) the role of the Preterite as a default marker of past tense in L2 Spanish and its potential to become a default past tense marker.[1] Finally, in Chapter 5, I describe possible lines of research that can help us refine, modify, expand and ultimately subsume the present specific proposal within a comprehensive model of L2 acquisition in general.

2. The Learning Challenge

One of the most significant challenges faced by adult English native speakers learning Spanish as a second language is the notorious distinction between the Preterite and the Imperfect. For instance, English native speakers confronted with the following sentences may have difficulty ascertaining why the verb in capitals (*saber* = to know) is marked with the Preterite or the Imperfect.

1. SABÍA (IMP) la verdad.
   (S/he) knew the truth.
2. En ese momento, SUPO (PRET) la verdad.
   At that moment, (he) discovered the truth.
3. Siempre SUPO (PRET) la verdad.
   (S/he) always knew the truth.

4. Julián se despertó (PRET) sobresaltado. Finalmente, su larga búsqueda espiritual dio (PRET) resultado. SUPO (PRET) la verdad.
   Julián woke up visibly shaken. Finally, his long spiritual search was fruitful. (He) knew/discovered the truth.
5. Julián se despertó (PRET) sobresaltado. Finalmente, su larga búsqueda espiritual dio (PRET) resultado. SABÍA (IMP) la verdad.
   Julián woke up visibly shaken. Finally, his long spiritual search was fruitful. (He) knew the truth.

In principle, we can rely on a typical rule of thumb provided in most instructional treatments and argue that the verb *saber* is prototypically marked with the Imperfect as shown in (1). We can expand previous analyses to propose that the addition of specific adverbials as shown in sentence (2) triggers the use of the Preterite to indicate the inception point of the state of knowing. This is a commonly used rule of thumb in most instructional treatments. Sentence (3), however, introduces the use of an adverbial that apparently contradicts the rule that accounts for the choice of Preterite in sentence (2). That is, the adverbial *siempre* (always) is supposedly incompatible with the idea of an inception (punctual) point in time. Finally, sentences (4) and (5) show that the same extended contextual set-up may lead to the appropriate use of one or the other marker of past tense in Spanish. Obviously, the use of the Preterite or Imperfect introduces a distinct nuance of meaning that the non-native speaker will have to understand in order to choose the appropriate marker (see discussion of results from García and van Putte, 1988 below). I return to the detailed discussion of these and similar examples in subsequent chapters. Before I discuss specific accounts of the previous uses of the Preterite and Imperfect, I would like to outline the problem space.

In both Spanish and English, temporality is expressed morphologically (e.g., verbal endings), lexically (e.g., time adverbials), syntactically (e.g., periphrastic forms) and contextually (e.g., grounding). There are, nevertheless, some notable differences in the manner in which Spanish and English represent specific notions of temporality such as aspect. That is, the expression of aspectual meanings is represented in different ways in each language. In Spanish, the aspectual contrasts of perfective-imperfective meanings are represented in past tense through the use of the Preterite and Imperfect. English also conveys information about aspectual distinctions as we can see in the contrasts exemplified in, for instance, *he read, he was reading* and *he used to read*. Comrie (1976: 1), however, points out that English, unlike Spanish, does not grammaticalize the perfective-imperfective contrast, but rather the progressive-non-progressive one represented in the distinct meanings conveyed by *he read* versus *he was reading*. Comrie further notes that the progressive-non-progressive opposition is comparable to the perfective-imperfective contrast 'only in relation to a limited set of verbs (non-stative verbs), and then only if habitual meaning is excluded' (p. 7). Note though that the use of periphrastics such as *used to* allow English speakers to convey aspectual meanings (e.g., habituality) that are usually expressed through inflectional morphology (i.e., the Imperfect) in Spanish. In fact, there are several other significant contrasts in meaning conveyed by the Preterite–Imperfect in Spanish that are either not represented in English inflectional morphology (e.g., iterativity-habituality contrast), or that are represented with a variety of means (e.g., habituality).

Given the commonalities in the marking of past tense in English and Spanish, it is apparent that the difficulty of adult learners of Spanish as a second language resides in the representation of aspectual concepts. This assertion is, however, an overstatement, given that English speakers already have a representational knowledge of all the aspectual concepts instantiated in Spanish past tense-aspectual morphology. Where the two languages differ is in how each one maps those aspectual concepts onto language form. Indeed, English native speakers already know a fair amount about aspectual distinctions represented in the Romance languages. For instance, as de Swart and Verkuyl (1999: 134) point out with reference to French, 'the semantic effects of sentences like [(6)/(7) and (8)] are the same, and their DRSs [Discourse Representation Structures] are identical, but only French makes the fact that the state is presented as an event visible in the morphology of the verb, using an aspectually sensitive tense operator'.[2]

6 a. (Soudain,) Jeanne sut la réponse.
   (Suddenly,) Jeanne knew-PS the answer.
7 a. La machine fonctionna (en cinq minutes).
   The machine worked-PS (in five minutes).
8 a. Jeanne d'Arc fut une sainte.
   Jeanne d'Arc was-PS a saint.
6 b. (Suddenly,) Jeanne knew the answer.
7 b. The machine worked (in five minutes).
8 b. Jeanne d'Arc was a saint.

The point made by de Swart and Verkuyl is well taken: English speakers obviously understand the semantic implications of the use of adverbials in the English equivalents of sentences (6a) and (7a). That is, *suddenly* and *in five minutes* bring up the notion of change of state. As de Swart and Verkuyl point out, however, the main challenge for the English speaker is to realize that some (aspectual) meaning contrasts have morphological correlates in the Romance languages that lead to the use of the perfective form (*Passé Simple/Passé Composé* in French), but are effected implicitly in English (i.e., Simple Past has no contrasting imperfective option). On this point, notice that, unlike (6b) and (7b), sentence (8b) is not accompanied by an adverbial and, as such, it provides English speakers with a challenge, given that French (as is the case for Spanish) presents its speakers with two equally acceptable options: one with the perfective form (*Jeanne d'Arc fut une sainte*) as depicted in (8a), and one with the imperfective verbal ending (*Jeanne d'Arc était una sainte*). In other words, the equivalent expression in English (8b) is inadequate to make reference to the meaning conveyed by the use of *Imparfait* with the verb *être* (to be) versus the meaning conveyed by the *Passé Simple* with the same verb.

We need to make reference to actual empirical studies of the acquisition of tense-aspect meanings to address this question. One of the earliest studies on this topic is the one carried out by Coppieters (1987). Given the fact that Coppieters' claim has become a ubiquitous reference in subsequent analyses of the development of tense-aspect meanings, I briefly review his findings here. Coppieters (1987) analysed data from 21 non-native speakers of French who had learned French as adults. His informants were classified as near-native speakers judging by the fact that all of them attained the highest proficiency level of the ACTFL (American Council for the Teaching of Foreign Languages) proficiency scale (i.e., superior) through oral interviews. This classification is not totally surprising when we consider that the sample of near-native speakers gathered by Coppieters had spent an average of 17.4 years living in France (with a range of 5.5–37 years). There was, however, a fair degree of variation in the native language of Coppieters' near-native speakers: English (6), Italian (4), Chinese (3), Spanish (2), Farsi, (2), Portuguese (1), Japanese (1), Korean (1) and German (1). It is interesting to note that 7 of the 21 speakers (one-third of all subjects) were speakers of a Romance language in which the same perfective-imperfective contrast from French is represented. He also analysed data from 20 native speakers of French who were spouses or close colleagues of the near-native speakers selected.

Coppieters investigated the intuitions of native and near-native speakers through a 107-item questionnaire representing a variety of topics of French, among which he included five items testing their knowledge of *Passé Composé* and *Imparfait.* Coppieters also interviewed his informants to gather additional qualitative data about the rationale used for some of the responses. Here are three of the five sentences representing the *Passé Composé* and *Imparfait* contrast:

9. J'ai très souvent mange (*Passé Composé*)/Je mangeais (*Imparfait*) très souvent.
   I ate very often/I would eat very often.
10. Quand j'étais chez ma tante, je racontais (*Imparfait*)/j'ai raconté (*Passé Composé*) plusieurs fois mes aventures.
    When I was at my aunt's, I would tell/I told my adventures many times.
11. En 1885, Victor Hugo mourait (*Imparfait*)/est mort (*Passé Composé*).
    In 1885, Victor Hugo was dying/died.

There are two important findings that I highlight in Coppieters' study. First, notwithstanding Birdsong's (1992) reservation about the decontextualized nature of the prompt sentences used by Coppieters, the responses were more homogeneous among native speakers than near-native speakers. The dependent variable used by Coppieters in the study of all grammatical items was mostly the degree of variation within each group of speakers from the norm for each grammar rule. Across all grammatical items investigated by Coppieters, the native speakers varied from the norm between 5 per cent and 16 per cent, whereas the near-native speakers' responses varied from 23 per cent to 49 per cent. With respect to the analysis of the responses related to the *Passé Composé* and *Imparfait*, the degree of divergence was even more pronounced: almost 40 per cent between each group (from 2 per cent divergence from the norm for native speakers to an average of 41.5 per cent divergence for near-native speakers). Anticipating the (valid) critique of Birdsong, Coppieters acknowledged the liability of the lack of context for his sample sentences to gather any meaningful conclusion, while at the same time pointing out that such outcome shows that

> interpretations were simply constructed on the basis of the forms provided, and they reflect (some aspects of) the conventional meanings associated with each form . . . . No matter how skillful NNSs [non-native speakers] might be at deriving the appropriate interpretation of a sentence in context, their inability to do so in the absence of an explicit context indicates a fundamental difference between their knowledge of the language and that of NS's [native speakers]. (p. 566)

The second most important finding of Coppieters' study was the apparent effect of the L1 (i.e., transfer effects). Coppieters noted that L1 speakers of a Romance language had clear intuitions about the distinctions between the perfective and imperfective renditions of these sentences. As Coppieters mentions, the only participant who was an exception to this trend was a speaker from southern Italy, a region where this aspectual contrast is not marked. On the other hand, speakers of non-Romance languages either chose the wrong option or they acknowledged that they had no clear intuitions about the contrast. Both findings from Coppieters' study substantiate the objective outlined for this book. That is, the analysis of the acquisition of tense-aspect is primarily predicated on (1) a definition of tense-aspect on the basis of a continuum of invariant to contextualized meanings, and (2) L1 transfer seems to be an important independent variable to account for the development of tense-aspect marking in the target language.

3. Tense-Aspect in Context

3.1 Discourse effects

Given Coppieters' claim about the role of context to determine the selection of the perfective-imperfective contrast, the use of the Preterite and Imperfect in sentences (4) and (5) is not very transparent to non-native speakers because, apparently, both markers can be used in the same context. Thus, let us review in more detail one concrete example from a previous L2 acquisition study (to be discussed in more detail in Chapter 3), which may be useful to understand how native speakers may focus on specific features of contextual information. García and van Putte (1988) used the short story '*El muerto*' from the famous writer Jorge Luis Borges as their test instrument to assess potential representational differences of the Preterite and Imperfect among native Spanish speakers and L1 Dutch teachers of Spanish. Both groups were asked to read Borges' story, which was presented to them in the present tense, and rewrite it in the past tense. Although, by and large, the non-native speakers' choices differed little from the ones native speakers made, there were some interesting findings related to selections made by each group. The following is an example that prompted a different choice of past tense marker in each group:

Alguien opina que Bandeira nació del otro lado del Cuareim, ... *Gradualmente*, Otálora *entiende* que los negocios de Bandeira son múltiples y que el principal es el contrabando.

Somebody thinks that Bandeira was born on the other side of the Cuareim, ... *Gradually*, Otálora *understands* that Bandeira's affairs are manifold, and that the chief one is smuggling.

Whereas 60 per cent of non-native speakers marked the verb *entender* (to understand) with the Imperfect, only 14 per cent of native speakers used the Imperfect with the same verb. García and van Putte proposed that non-native speakers chose the Imperfect 'probably motivated by the presence of the adverb *gradualmente* [gradually] which suggests anything but a punctual event'. Essentially, the context surrounding the target verb seems to lead the native speakers towards an interpretation that focuses them on the inception of the state (i.e., the beginning of *entender*). Thus the majority of native speakers selected the Preterite (*entendió* = discovered). From this perspective, the adverb simply refers to the period that leads to the initial moment of understanding. In contrast, non-native speakers seem to prioritize the infor-mation contributed by the adverb and subsume the interpretation of the verb within the one provided by the adverbial. As a consequence, they focused on the state of understanding as a non-dynamic eventuality, rather than the inception of the state. Thus, at first blush, it appears as if L2 learners are not attentive enough to the context in which a particular verb is embedded.

The previous analysis of the effect of context on the use of inflectional markers to convey tense-aspectual meanings is not unique. Güell (1998), for instance, shows results similar to those of García and van Putte with the use of a different test instrument (a fill-in-the-blanks task), administered to learners of various levels of proficiency, among speakers of several L1s.[3] As an example, the choice of Preterite or Imperfect for one specific item rep-resenting the stative verb *pasar* (to happen) revealed important differences across groups. The context surrounding the target item is shown as follows:

> Era un día cualquiera en el centro del pueblo. La gente (1) PASEAR ... El platillo (19) ACERCARSE hasta que (20) ESTAR tan cerca que incluso el perro y el gato (21) DEJAR DE JUGAR para mirar qué *era lo que (22) PASAR*. ...

> It was a regular day on the town square. People (1) STROLL ... The UFO (19) TO GET CLOSER until it (20) TO BE so close that even the dog and the cat (21) STOP PLAYING to see what was that *(22) HAPPEN*. ...

As shown in Table 1.1, Güell reports that whereas native speakers categori-cally selected the Imperfect (i.e., 100 per cent) to mark the stative verb *pasar*, the less-proficient non-native speakers (NN1 and NN2) split their choices between perfective and imperfective marking (i.e.,50 per cent and 43 per cent, respectively), despite the fact that the stative verb *pasar* is preceded by another stative verb already conjugated in the imperfective form (i.e., *era*).

Table 1.1 Selection of past tense marker for the verb pasar (item 22, Task 2)

	NN1 (%)	NN2 (%)	NN3 (%)	NN4 (%)	N (%)
Imperfecto	31	43	84	94	100
Pretérito	50	43	13	6	0
Otros	18	14	3	0	0

Adapted from Table 55 of Güell, p. 439.

The findings summarized in Table 1.1 seem to indicate that the representation of tense-aspectual knowledge cannot be made outside of context. Both the data from García and van Putte and Güell are in line with Coppieters' claim and support his conclusion that 'extracting the precise contribution of an *Imparfait* or *Passé Composé* to the meaning of a given utterance in a given context is a very difficult and complex endeavor. Typically, the context will OVER-determine the meaning of the tense; it will be unclear exactly what the tense expresses by itself' (Coppieters, 1987: 567). Even though I agree with Coppieters' analysis, I argue, however, that L2 learners are not necessarily handicapped to incorporate contextual information to their decision about which past tense marker to use.[4] The claim that ultimate attainment (native-like competence) is restricted to the realm of the discursive domain of tense-aspect meanings (as Coppieters claims) is not incompatible with the argument that tense-aspect meanings are, by definition, discursively determined.

Despite the above-mentioned significance of the effect of contextual information for the proper analysis of tense-aspectual meanings, many analyses restrict their study to a narrow range of features of tense-aspect phenomena. This limitation in many cases reflects a logistical or methodological decision on the part of the researcher, given the increased complexity brought up by the inclusion of discourse factors as determinants of aspectual knowledge and representation. Tenny (1994: 4), for instance, recognizes that 'much, if not most, of the aspectual phenomena to be found in natural language' is not addressed by the aspectual interface hypothesis that she proposes. Thus, Tenny states that the effect of sources of aspectual information such as adverbials and aspectual morphology are not incorporated into her model of representation of aspect. Similarly, Rothstein (2004) explicitly states that the analysis of the interaction of lexical aspect and grammatical aspect lies beyond the scope of her book, *Structuring events: A Study in the Semantics of Lexical Aspect*. It is worth repeating that the limited range of analysis of tense-aspect phenomena in several studies is understandable given the complexity of the topic. I argue, however, that it behooves SLA (second language acquisition) researchers to take a broad view of the phenomenon of tense-aspect marking in order to obtain an accurate picture of the development and ultimate attainment of tense-aspectual knowledge in the target language.

3.2 Lexical and grammatical aspect

A second problem in the analysis of aspectual meanings is that, in general, theoretical definitions of aspect have been vague about (1) the classification of lexical aspectual classes (e.g., states, activities, accomplishments, achievements), and (2) the distinction between lexical and grammatical aspect (e.g., type shifts, coercion, etc.). For instance, in sentences (1)–(5) mentioned earlier, the same verb seems to change categorical status from a stative to a dynamic event not only due to sentential information (adverbial modifiers) as shown in sentences (2) and (3), but also due to extrasentential information (context) as shown in sentences (4) and (5). At this point, one crucial question arises: what is the 'upper limit' of linguistic information that will contain the range of information conveyed by lexical aspect? Is it at the level of the verb phrase containing the verbal predicate along with its internal arguments (i.e., *saber la verdad*)? Should we also include adjuncts (e.g., *En ese momento*)? What about textual information beyond the sentence level (e.g., *Julián se despertó* . . .)? On the other hand, if we argue that the lexical aspectual category does not change, but rather that grammatical aspect (e.g., Preterite and Imperfect) imposes a different viewpoint of the situation (cf. Smith, 1997), we are confronted with a different, but not less-puzzling dilemma: if grammatical aspect determines the aspectual meaning of the situation – irrespective of the inherent lexical aspectual meaning of the verb and its argument – why do we need to posit the existence of two separate layers of aspectual information (i.e., lexical and grammatical aspect)?

Most researchers subscribe to a two-component theory of aspectual meaning that distinguishes lexical aspect from viewpoint or grammatical aspect. There is a big discrepancy, however, on where to draw the boundary between these two components (i.e., lexical aspect and grammatical aspect), or, alternatively, whether each component can be assessed or classified independently from the effect of the other one. Typically, researchers start out with a delimitation of the concept of lexical aspect or situation type. In this respect, the most conservative position considers that only verbs plus internal arguments (i.e., the object of a sentence) determine lexical aspectual classes (e.g., Tenny, 1994). A second major line of research expands the previous position by including the effect of external arguments (i.e., the subject of the sentence) as well as predicates and internal arguments (Smith, 1997; Verkuyl, 1989, 1993). For instance, Smith (1997: 2) proposes that the verb constellation (or situation type) is defined 'as a main verb and its arguments, including subject'. A third, more expansive definition of lexical aspect includes the effect of adjuncts (such as adverbials) as well as predicates and internal and external arguments (e.g., Chung and Timberlake, 1985; Croft, 1998; Klein, 1994; Mourelatos, 1981). The most comprehensive of all approaches are the ones that include the effect of discursive factors above the sentence level (e.g., Silva-Corvalán, 1983, 1986).

The theoretical dilemma about the classification of lexical aspectual classes, on the one hand, and the distinction between lexical and grammatical aspect on the other hand, is even more problematic in studies in L2 acquisition. That is, the vagueness about the description and classification of the theoretical construct inevitably leads to a concomitant degree of imprecision at the level of methodological procedures of the research design of empirical studies. Most important in this respect are inaccuracies in the determination of lexical aspectual classes given that the marking of grammatical aspect as an overt category is, by definition explicit, thus not subject to researchers' possible misclassifications. That is, in general, it is quite evident whether a verb is marked with Preterite or Imperfect, even in cases in which accuracy of form is not totally on target as Lafford (1996) shows with her analysis of verbs stressed on the final vowel (e.g., *comó* instead of *comió*). On the other hand, lexical aspectual classes are a covert category (Binnick, 1991; Salaberry, 2000a). For instance, in Salaberry (2002) the verb *saber* (to know) in the context of the cloze passage in which it was embedded (reproduced as example (12)) was classified as the inception of the state of knowing (i.e., an event). In English, the use of the Preterite with *saber* in this case would be equivalent to *discover* or *find out*. One wonders, however, whether the verb *saber* in the context of (12) should be classified as a prototypical state or as an event as proposed by Salaberry (2002).

12. Porque las palabras que había oido – entonces lo _____ (saber) –
    no _____ (tener) ningún sonido, . . .
    Because the words (s/he) had heard – then _____ (to know) it –
    (they, not) _____ (to have) any sound, . . .

The classification of *saber* as a state or telic event (i.e., with an inherent end point) in (12) is of great significance if, for instance, we would like to claim that the inherent semantic value of lexical aspectual classes is to have an effect on the selection of grammatical markers of past tense (cf. the LAH).

In fact, the significance of the determination of the lexical aspectual class of the verb *saber* is not restricted to hypotheses that pose the value of lexical aspect as an independent variable. Indeed, it is equally significant for hypotheses that leave out of the categorization of lexical aspect the role of adverbials (cf. minimalism), or the ones that focus on the relevance of contextual information (cf. the DH). In Chapter 2 I will summarize and critique various perspectives on the basic components that make up a definition of knowledge of tense-aspect meanings, and I will assess the relevance of contextual information to adequately represent tense-aspect knowledge.

4. Acquisition Hypotheses

There have been several hypotheses proposed for the analysis of the development of tense-aspectual meanings in L2 acquisition spanning a range of explanatory phenomena covering semantic, discursive, cognitive and syntactic factors. For instance, the LAH (Andersen, 1986, 1991) states that in early stages of acquisition, verbal morphology encodes only inherent semantic aspectual distinctions (i.e., it does not encode tense or grammatical aspect). In contrast, the DH (Bardovi-Harlig, 1994: 43) predicts that 'learners use emerging verbal morphology to distinguish foreground from background in narratives'. In turn, the default past tense hypothesis (DPTH) predicts that during the first stages of L2 development, learners will attempt to mark tense distinctions relying on a default morphological marker (most typically the perfective form), whereas inherent semantic aspect and discursive factors are expected to have an increasing effect as learners' proficiency improves throughout time (e.g., Salaberry, 1999, 2002, 2003, 2005, forthcoming; Wiberg, 1996). Finally, within a strictly grammatical theory such as minimalism, the transfer of feature values of the Aspectual Phrase (AspP) are hypothesized to account for differences across languages: in English, the feature [+ perfective] is associated with the Simple Past, whereas in Spanish, both the [+ perfective] and [- perfective] features are instantiated in past tense morphology (associated with Preterite and Imperfect respectively) (e.g., Montrul and Slabakova, 2002, 2003; Slabakova and Montrul, 2002a, 2002b, 2003).[5]

The fact that there are several hypotheses about the acquisition and development of tense-aspect in a second language is a clear indication that each hypothesis has some limitations. For instance, the LAH does not account for the selection of grammatical past tense markers (i.e., Preterite–Imperfect) that do not correlate with lexical aspectual classes (e.g., Preterite with states). This theoretical constraint has important consequences for the analysis of the representation of tense-aspect meanings. For instance, in the narrative text used by Güell (1998: 386–7), the verb *mirar* in item (3) in the following excerpt was marked with the Imperfect by 100 per cent of native speakers, whereas the same verb in the context of item (12) was marked with the opposite marker, the Preterite, by 100 per cent of native speakers as well.

> Era un día cualquiera en el centro del pueblo. La gente (1) PASEAR de aquí para allá, nada (2) PARECER especial. Un perro (3) MIRAR un gato fijamente . . . . Inmediatamente todos se agolparon y (12) MIRAR al cielo.

> It was a day as usual in the downtown area. People (1) STROLL with no specific direction. Nothing (2) SEEM particularly unusual. A dog (3) LOOK AT (stare) a cat in the eyes . . . . All of a sudden, everyone got together and (12) LOOK AT the sky.

Thus, native speakers' choices of grammatical markers of past tense in Spanish show that the inherent lexical aspectual value of the verbal predicate alone is not enough to determine the selection of Preterite or Imperfect. In essence, lexical aspect and grammatical aspect are not coterminous. That is, the specific choice of grammatical aspect (Preterite or Imperfect in Spanish) assigned to any given verbal predicate may support or contradict the specific semantic features of a given verbal predicate (i.e., prototypical and non-prototypical markings).

Interestingly, more recent hypotheses framed within language theories such as minimalism are also constrained to make predictions about the acquisition of tense-aspect meanings represented in prototypical combinations of lexical and grammatical aspect only. For instance, Slabakova (2002: 185) maintains that the '. . . "prototypical" combinations are interpretable only using the syntactic module of grammatical competence but the nonprototypical combinations necessitate pragmatic competence over and above the syntactic competence, . . .' In other words, a common thread across various hypotheses about the acquisition and development of tense-aspect knowledge is that they seem to rely on a fairly decontextualized definition of aspectual meanings. That is, only combinations of lexical and grammatical aspect in which there is a match up of semantic features are regarded as appropriate targets for analysis. The hypothesis most likely to take into account the information provided by the context above the verb phrase is the DH.

Despite the fact that there is no overarching theory about the acquisition of L2 tense-aspect marking, I analyse possible expansions of available hypotheses in order to develop a more plausible account of the representation of tense-aspect knowledge among adult L2 learners. The theoretical framework to be presented in Chapter 4 provides a first step towards the development of a research agenda. In particular, I argue for the strong effect of L1 positive transfer. More specifically, I claim that L1 English speakers use knowledge about aspectual distinctions in their native language as a heuristic 'device' to analyse and process the use of aspect-bearing past tense inflectional morphology in L2 Spanish. For instance, English speakers already mark aspectual meanings in their own L1 with the Past Progressive in contrast with the Simple Past, with the use of periphrastics such as *used to* in contrast with the Simple Past, with the use of narrative grounding, and so on. Thus, it would be quite natural (or, at a minimum, efficient) for English speakers to use previous semantic contrasts to mark aspect in their L1 to guide their understanding of parallel contrasts in the L2. Furthermore, given that the English Simple Past is a straight tense marker (i.e., it does not mark aspect), English speakers are likely to rely on the use of a default past tense marker (cf. the DPTH). Furthermore, the reliance on the use of the Preterite as a default marker of past tense in L2 Spanish among native English speakers is substantiated by at least four different factors (see Chapter 3): (1) only tense is represented in English past tense inflectional morphology (i.e., Simple Past), (2) the Preterite is the basic past tense marker in Spanish, (3) distributional biases in the L2 and (4) specific teaching paradigms that highlight the use of the perfective form as a carrier of tense.

5. Contextualized Meanings: A Lexico-discursive Framework

In a state-of-the-art chapter, Andersen (2002) presented an expanded version of the LAH originally proposed by him in the 1980s. Following up on his assessment, Andersen argued that the relevant research questions about the L2 acquisition of tense-aspect meanings can be fruitfully addressed by a 'discourse-functional account' that includes 'the notion of prototype and a set of cognitive processing strategies such as the one to one principle and the congruence principle . . .' (p. 102). The argument I develop in this book broadly follows the position advocated by Andersen. It also builds on the claim advanced by Coppieters that contextual information is crucial for a definition of tense-aspect meanings.

I argue, however, that a discursive-functional account is not incompatible with the notion of the representation of aspectual concepts as having both invariant meanings (e.g., aspectual concepts such as boundedness, iterativity) and contextualized meanings (e.g., bounded–unbounded, iterative–habitual). I also argue that a discursive-contextual definition of tense-aspect is not incompatible with the proposal of default lexical aspectual classes (verbal predicates) that can be further specified in context. The idea of invariant meanings is based on Binnick's (1991) and Doiz-Bienzobas's (1995, 2002) argument that the inherent conceptual meanings conveyed by past tense markers (e.g., boundedness, iterativity, genericity) represent their general characterizing meaning or invariant meaning. On the other hand, the notion of default lexical aspectual classes is based on Klein's (1994) maxims of minimality and contrast. Both of these arguments (invariant meanings of aspect and default lexical aspectual classes) will be progressively developed in Chapters 2–4.

To place this argument in context, it should be noted that the claim that tense-aspect meanings can be represented at two different levels (e.g., invariant and contextualized) is not new. Larsen-Freeman (2003: 34), for instance, defines 'the morphological and syntactic subsystems as a resource for making meaning in a context-sensitive manner'. Larsen-Freeman further identifies three dimensions of language: form, meaning/semantics and use/pragmatics. As acknowledged by Larsen-Freeman, however, it is not easy to make a clear-cut distinction between meaning attributed to semantics as opposed to meaning associated with pragmatics. The important question for studies focused on the development of tense-aspect is: Where can we locate the representational meaning of tense and aspect inflectional morphology? The principled answer to this question is determined by the definition of tense-aspect meanings. As I stated, I propose that tense-aspect forms have both invariant and contextualized meanings. The latter distinction is, nevertheless, not necessarily equivalent to the contrast of semantics and pragmatic information described by Larsen-Freeman.

Whether we adopt a definition of tense-aspect meanings that cuts across a semantic-pragmatic contrast (e.g., syntactic theories), or one that spans a continuum of invariant to contextualized meanings has important consequences for the development of theoretical claims regarding the acquisition of L2 competence. For instance, some L2 acquisition proposals are based on the argument that aspectual information conveyed by means of Spanish Preterite–Imperfect is represented separately as syntactic and pragmatic phenomena (e.g., Montrul and Slabakova, 2002; Slabakova, 2002; Slabakova and Montrul, 2002a, 2002b, 2003, 2007). Thus, Montrul and Slabakova (2002: 141) argue that their findings indicate that 'the formal features associated with the functional category AspP are fully acquirable and "unimpaired" in SLA'. In contrast, Slabakova and Montrul (2002a: 387) contend that '. . . pragmatics is outside of Universal Grammar, and acquisition of pragmatic contrasts are not guided by the same principles that guide the acquisition of the viewpoint contrast'. It is interesting to note that Coppieters may have made the same or the opposite claim advanced by Montrul and Slabakova depending on how we define tense-aspect phenomena. That is, Coppieters argues that L2 learners cannot reach native-like competence on tense-aspect knowledge (thus disagreeing with Montrul and Slabakova). On the other hand, Coppieters places the representation of tense-aspect meanings outside the realm of Universal Grammar (UG) (i.e., a discursive component). Thus, from the latter perspective, Coppieters agrees with Montrul and Slabakova insofar as phenomena outside of the realm of UG may not be acquirable.

The position I argue for in this book will be unlike the claims advanced by Coppieters or Montrul and Slabakova because I propose that the representation of tense-aspect meanings can only be described as a continuum of invariant-contextualized meanings. Furthermore, I propose that learners are able to progressively learn the meaning of the Preterite–Imperfect distinction in the context of discourse broader than the sentence, but they are unable to formally represent the conceptual (invariant) meaning of the Preterite–Imperfect morphology (e.g., boundedness, iterativity). I argue that this asymmetrical outcome in development is directly related to the fact that although English does not convey a representation of aspectual meaning through inflectional morphology (as Spanish does), it does convey aspectual contrasts at the discursive level in a similar way to Spanish. In essence, I propose that the lack of native-like attainment in the area of invariant meanings is not necessarily predicated on the understanding of the aspectual concepts per se. More specifically, English native speakers continue to have a representation of past tense morphology only as a carrier of tense, not as a carrier of both tense and aspect meanings. As a consequence, L2 learners fail to map their representational knowledge of the characterizing meaning of tense-aspect distinctions (e.g., boundedness, iterativity, etc.) on inflectional markers of past tense in Spanish. A corollary of this proposal is that L2 learners are not able to create a second linguistic system independent from their L1 system. In other words, English speakers are constrained in their development of past tense aspectual meanings in L2 Spanish by the representation of tense-aspect already available in their native language.

Finally, I argue that the theoretical framework of Cognitive Grammar (e.g., Langacker, 1982, 1987, 1999) is especially useful to provide a comprehensive account of the representation of knowledge about tense-aspect marking in which contextual factors larger than the verb and the sentence are determinants of choices of tense-aspect grammatical markers. For instance, Doiz-Bienzobas (1995: 259) claims that the 'understanding of grammar and meaning rely on viewing, where the latter represents a conceptualization of perception'. Doiz-Bienzobas' argument – framed within the work of Cognitive Grammar – brings together the two separate components of Smith's (1997) two-component theory of aspect. That is, Smith's framework of analysis proposes the existence of a general cognitive factor (cf. situation aspect), and a discursive-pragmatic component (cf. viewpoint aspect). Doiz-Bienzobas' proposal entails that viewpoint aspect is, essentially, a basic cognitive phenomenon. That is, there is a lexically based continuum ranging from lexical aspect to narrative grounding that serves to contextualize and ultimately define tense-aspect meaning at a conceptual level.

6. Conclusion

Despite the fact that there is no overarching theory about the acquisition of L2 tense-aspect marking, there is a large body of theoretical and empirical research that is useful to develop a plausible account of the representation of tense-aspect knowledge among adult L2 learners.[6] The various theoretical proposals presented so far have been very fruitful to advance a sizeable research agenda represented in this large body of empirical evidence. Indeed, there is an 'embarrassment of riches' as Slabakova (2002) defined it. This large body of empirical findings does not seem to be so large, however, when we consider the very large questions being addressed by the studies that analyse tense-aspect phenomena. Furthermore, one could argue that there is little cross-fertilization across theoretical paradigms, even though, as some have proposed (e.g., Shirai, 2007), there is much to be gained from such endeavour.

In the present chapter, I have outlined the main challenge faced by L2 learners for the development and acquisition of the representational knowledge of tense-aspect meanings in Spanish. Furthermore, I have stated that the analysis of the theoretical construct of tense-aspect meanings will lead us to conclude that there is a continuum of representational levels of tense-aspect meanings. Previous studies assume a division of aspectual meanings according to two main levels of representation of aspectual meanings. These two levels have been variously described as a contrast between situation aspect and viewpoint aspect (e.g., Smith, 1997), lexical aspect and grammatical aspect (e.g., Andersen, 1991), and lately conceptualized as core and peripheral grammar (e.g., Slabakova and Montrul, 2002b).

In contrast with previous studies, however, I propose that the two levels of representation of aspectual meanings can be reconceptualized as a contrast instantiated by invariant and contextualized meanings (cf. Binnick, 1991; Doiz-Bienzobas, 1995, 2002). I also argue that English native speakers are able to learn the meaning of the Spanish Preterite–Imperfect contrast in the context of discourse broader than the sentence, but they are unable to attain a representation of the conceptual (invariant) meaning of the Preterite–Imperfect morphology (e.g., boundedness, iterativity).

In the subsequent chapters of this book, I survey the various definitions of tense-aspectual knowledge (instantiated in the Preterite–Imperfect contrast) and I evaluate the empirical plausibility of various well-known hypotheses on the acquisition of tense-aspect contrasts. Ultimately, the goal is to present a theoretical framework that can be useful to analyse the acquisition and development of the representational knowledge and use of the meanings conveyed by Spanish past tense inflectional morphology. In turn, the basic structure of such an account may be useful to analyse similar semantic-discursive components of the grammatical system developed by L2 learners.

Chapter 2

Delimiting Lexical and Grammatical Aspect

1. Introduction

Despite the apparent plethora of publications addressing aspect (both in terms of theoretical descriptions and acquisitional processes), Binnick (1991: 213) contends that 'no complete aspectual description of any language exists. Nor does current aspectological theory provide an adequate theoretical base for such description'. In turn, limitations in our theoretical knowledge of aspect constrain any proposed argument about the acquisition and development of temporality among second language (L2) learners.

In this chapter, I review some important concepts on aspect that can shed light on the interpretation of empirical data on L2 acquisition studies of past temporality (Sections 2–4). I subsequently focus the discussion on the ongoing debate of the possible dissociation between lexical, syntactic and discursive-pragmatic components of the overall concept of aspect (Section 5). One of the main concepts I discuss in detail in this chapter is the notion of a continuum of representational levels of tense-aspect meanings that can be used to argue for the definition of aspect as both invariant and contextualized. This continuum of invariant-contextualized meanings is applied to the classification of lexical aspectual classes (Section 6) and the classification of grammatical aspect (Section 7). Finally, in Section 8, I briefly outline two seemingly orthogonal linguistic theories (i.e., Minimalism and Cognitive Linguistics) that can be useful to frame a definition of tense-aspect meanings.

2. Definitions of Aspect

According to Binnick, the term 'aspect' is the product of a French translation of the Russian word *vid*, which is a cognate of *vision* or *view*. Indeed, Comrie's (1976: 3) definition of aspect as the 'way of viewing the internal temporal constituency of a situation' (i.e., beginning, middle and end) reflects the etymological sense of the word. More specifically, Comrie points out that there are two options to relate a situation to a timeline. First, when we 'view' (focus) the location of a situation as a specific point or segment, we are making reference to a tense concept. Conversely, when the internal temporal contour of that situation – visualized as a point or stretch on the timeline – is in focus, we are referring to the concept of aspect. Comrie later clarified that a temporal aspectual perspective presents that situation on the timeline as a 'blob', the latter being defined as a 'three dimensional object, . . . [with] internal complexity, although it is nonetheless a single object with clearly circumscribed limits' (p. 18). The representation of conceptual knowledge as visual perception is further formalized in the theory of Cognitive Grammar (e.g., Doiz-Bienzobas, 1995, 2002; Langacker, 1982, 1897, 1999). Thus, Doiz-Bienzobas (1995: 259) argues that the 'understanding of grammar and meaning rely on viewing, where the latter represents a conceptualization of perception'. More specifically, Doiz-Bienzobas posits that 'Spanish aspect reflects one of the decisions that the speaker takes depending on the particular understanding and conceptualization of the situation to be presented' (p. 50).

General definitions of aspect, however, have offered a conceptualization that goes beyond the notion of viewing. The following definitions (presented in chronological order) provide an overview of some of the basic components of a description of aspectual representation.

- Aspect represents 'a way of viewing the *internal temporal constituency* of a situation'. (Comrie, 1976: 3)
- 'Aspect *characterizes the dynamicity or closure of an event* with respect to a point or interval in time (the event frame)'. (Chung and Timberlake, 1985: 256)
- 'Sentences present aspectual information about situation type and viewpoint. Although they co-occur, the *two types of information are independent*'. (Smith, 1997: 5)
- Aspect 'concerns the *different perspectives* which a speaker can take and express with regard to the temporal course of some event, action, process, etc.'. (Klein, 1994: 16)
- '[A]spectual categorization . . . [represents] the *manner in which people, as producers and processors of texts, construe scenes*, rather than as a reflection of the properties which situations have "in the world"'. (Michaelis, 1998: 5)

Each definition of aspect focuses on specific features of aspectual phenomena. For instance, whereas Comrie's definition emphasizes features of the situation itself, Klein highlights the speaker's perspective, as opposed to the situation in reality. Despite some differences, however, the aforementioned definitions share some features in common. By and large, most definitions of aspect postulate a division of aspectual phenomena into two levels, which we can define as (inherent) lexical aspect (ontological distinctions or situation types) and grammatical aspect (viewpoint or speaker's perspective). For instance, Smith (1997: 2) explains that '[s]ituation type is conveyed by the verb constellation, which I define as a main verb and its arguments, including subject. Viewpoint is conveyed by a grammatical morpheme, usually verbal. Adverbials may give relevant information . . .'. In the remainder of this section, I focus my attention on two thorny theoretical issues that I need to address to provide an overview of two important challenges faced by any definition of tense-aspect knowledge: (1) Is aspect subjective? And (2) Is aspect deictic? Although it is not my intention to provide definitive answers to these questions, the description of the problem is necessary to provide some background information to frame the main topic of this chapter.

2.1 Is aspectual representation subjective?

Klein's and Michaelis' definitions of aspect specifically highlight the speaker's (subjective) perspective (as opposed to the situation in reality). Comrie (1976: 133) agrees with Klein and Michaelis, arguing that 'aspectual oppositions are often subjective rather than objective, i.e., do not necessarily lead to differences in truth-value, unless the speaker's view of the situation described is also included in the semantic representation'. In fact, there is a general agreement that reality and the linguistic expression of that reality do not necessarily coincide or correlate. For instance, the description of a situation with a clear outcome may include reference to its final endpoint or the latter may be left unspecified. Thus, Krifka (1998: 207) points out that 'the distinction between telicity and atelicity should not be one in the nature of the object described, but in the description applied to the object'. For instance, in the following two depictions of the same event (mentioned by Smith, 1997), one description signals a telic event (1), whereas the other one refers to an atelic event (2).

1. Susan is painting a picture.
2. Susan is painting.

Similarly, Binnick (1991: 184) argues that reality is non-discrete but 'it is language which represents the world as consisting of discrete blobs called situations, and these are arbitrary in the sense that subsituations may be situations, too'. Along the same lines, Rothstein (2004) claims that aspectual properties are properties of linguistic expressions, not properties of events. Finally, Depraetre (1995: 4) points out that the speaker is free to select what will be included in a description of a particular situation.

The subjective representation of aspectual meanings is most clearly marked through grammatical means. Thus, Comrie (1976: 4) argues that 'it is quite possible for the same speaker to refer to the same situation once with a perfective form, then with an imperfective, without in any way being self-contradictory' as in examples (3) and (4):

3. John read that book yesterday; while he was reading it, the postman came.
4. I can't wait to see what he's been doing, when he's done it.

In example (3) from Comrie, the eventuality of *reading a book* is first presented as a bounded event, then, as an unbounded event that serves as background information to frame another event. Example (4), obtained from a live TV broadcast, is from Mourelatos (1981: 195), who points out that the same event is first described as an activity (*what he's been doing*) and the second time, it is described as an accomplishment (*he's done it*).

On the other hand, Smith (1997) proposes that situation aspect is *objective* in the sense that it reflects the classification of eventualities according to their inherent semantic features, whereas viewpoint aspect is *subjective* in the sense that it represents how speakers view the same eventualities.[1] More specifically, Smith states that '[s]tandard choices focus on aspectual properties that are salient at the basic level; non-standard choices focus on other properties' (p. 7). For instance, sentences (5) and (6) are two linguistic depictions of the same event in reality (both examples are from Smith).

5. The ship moved.
6. The ship was in motion.

Smith argues that sentence (5) is the conventional one 'according to the properties that are salient perceptually and functionally'. Sentence (6) is the unconventional one: by presenting it as a state, it freezes the motion of the ship. Smith points out, however, that '. . . receivers will not be misled by unconventional choice. Knowing a language includes the standard, basic associations of verb constellation with verb type' (p. 7). Bache (1982: 65), in contrast, points out (1) that the determination of lexical aspectual classes (he uses the term Aktionsart instead) is not necessarily objective since the classification of verb categories includes the speaker's assessment of the eventuality, and vice versa, (2) that the selection of grammatical aspect is not necessarily subjective as it is, in part, constrained by the inherent semantic features of lexical aspectual classes. Along the same lines, Depraetre (1995: 4) argues that 'it is a situation as it is represented in a sentence rather than the clause or the situation as such that is telic or atelic, i.e., the speaker is free to decide how he will refer to a particular situation he observes'. Depraetre adds that '[t]he same comment applies to boundedness; it is a matter of choice on the part of the hearer how he will represent a particular situation'.

I believe that Bache and Depraetre are correct in their assessment (i.e., Aktionsart is not necessarily objective, nor is viewpoint aspect necessarily subjective). First, let us analyse the supposedly subjective nature of the selection of grammatical markers that signal viewpoint aspect.

7a. Julián sabía (IMP) la verdad.
    Julián knew the truth.
7b. Julián supo (PRET) la verdad.
    Julián knew the truth.

To determine the specific grammatical marker to be used – *sabía* versus *supo* – we need access to contextual information that will help us decide whether we want to express whether *Julián knew the truth* (i.e., *sabía*-imperfective), or, alternatively, *Julián discovered the truth* (i.e., *supo*-perfective). That is, contextual information will lead us to focus on the state itself or on the inception point of that state.[2] Thus, we conclude that use of a broad or narrow range of contextual information leads to the *subjective* interpretation of the situation in reality. Once the context has been *subjectively* determined, however, the selection of the specific marker to be used to express that particular selective description is *objective* to the extent that a focus on the inception point of the state will require the use of the Preterite, whereas the focus on the state itself will entail the use of the Imperfect (see discussion on grammatical aspect).

On the other hand, the classification of the lexical aspectual category of the verb may be regarded as subjective. In this case, we analyse the same sentence with the verb in the infinitive form to avoid the bias introduced by the inflectional markers.

8. Julián [saber] la verdad.
   Julián [to know] the truth.

In principle, we could argue that *saber* is prototypically a state in all cases, thus avoiding the consideration of any potential alternative classification. This move curtails the consideration of any possible (subjective) discrepancies about which category to assign to the given verb. Unfortunately, this is not possible given that the linguistic interpretation referenced by the verb *saber* is based on the inherently subjective assessment of whether the speaker is referring to the state or the inception of the state. In sum, both situation aspect and grammatical aspect should be regarded as 'subjective' to the extent that in both cases it is the speaker (or hearer) who selectively focuses on specific 'aspects' or features of the situation in reality. In other words, situation aspect is no more objective than grammatical aspect even though the latter is specifically labelled as viewpoint aspect. Furthermore, by making both lexical and grammatical aspect equally subjective (or objective), we develop an integrated 'view' of aspectual knowledge in which constructions (e.g., verb plus internal argument) seem to be the common thread that spans various layers of linguistic information. The argument presented thus far is supportive of a representational continuum of tense-aspect meanings, as I argue for in this book.

2.2 Is aspect deictic or non-deictic?

As discussed earlier, one immediate corollary of Comrie's conceptualization of the notions of tense and aspect is that aspect is concerned with situation-internal time (focus on internal temporal constituency), whereas tense is relative to situation-external time (focus on point on the timeline). From this perspective, aspect – unlike tense – is not a deictic category because it is not relative to the time of the utterance. Some theorists, however, define both tense and aspect in deictic terms (e.g., Klein, 1994; Doiz-Bienzobas, 1995). Let us briefly review the position advocated by Klein and Doiz-Bienzobas. First, Klein argues that any given utterance is composed of a non-finite component and a finite component. The former represents a selective description of a situation generally associated with a predicate and its arguments and even adverbials (i.e., lexical content). On the other hand, the finite component refers to the time for which the claim about the situation has been made. This time is labelled Topic Time and is explicitly defined by Klein in the following manner:

> Although a situation that is partly described by the lexical content of an utterance has a time – the time of situation (TSit) – it is not TSit, which is directly linked to the time of utterance (TU). There is an intervening link – the time for which the particular utterance makes an assertion (p. 37).

Klein argues that aspect is defined by the relationship between Topic Time and Time of the Situation: it depicts the way the situation is 'hooked up to some Topic Time'(p. 44). In contrast, tense is defined by the relationship between Topic Time and Time of the Utterance. Klein contextualizes the aforementioned contrast with a scenario in which a judge asks a witness the following question: 'What did you notice when you entered the room?' The witness responds, 'A man was lying on the floor' (p. 40). In this case, Time of the Utterance is obviously the time at which the question and answer exchange occurs, whereas Topic Time is represented by the time at which the witness entered the room. On the other hand, Time of the Situation refers to the information portrayed by the verbal predicate and associated arguments and adjuncts. That is to say, in this case, the relationship between Topic Time and Time of the Utterance (tense) represents past tense, whereas the relationship between Topic Time and Time of the Situation (aspect) represents imperfective aspect. In essence, by stating that a situation is 'hooked up to some Topic Time' we are effectively stating that the speaker (or hearer in some cases) has to define the Topic Time, given Klein's explanation that the situation is 'hooked up to some Topic Time'. For instance, is the Topic Time going to comprise the whole event, thus making it bounded? or, will the selected Topic Time be defined by an unbounded description of the same event?

On the other hand, Doiz-Bienzobas focuses explicitly on the analysis of the perfective-imperfective aspectual contrast in Spanish. Although her argument does not necessarily build on the one advanced by Klein, there is an interesting parallelism in the proposals of both researchers. Doiz-Bienzobas claims that several depictions of the perfective-imperfective meaning contrast brought about by past tense markers seem to indicate that the perfective acts as a straight tense marker, whereas the imperfective functions as a true aspectual marker. For instance, Doiz-Bienzobas proposes that the 'Imperfect does not interact with the boundedness of the situations' (p. 32).[3] In the following sentence, for example, Doiz-Bienzobas argues that the contrast in meaning between the Preterite and the Imperfect is related to a view of the given situation from a past viewpoint (9a) marked with the Imperfect, or alternatively from speech time (9b), the latter marked with the Preterite.

9a. El sermón me parecía (IMP) eterno.
    The sermon seemed interminable.
9b. El sermón me pareció (PRET) eterno.
    The sermon seemed interminable.

Doiz-Bienzobas proposes that the Preterite makes reference to a situation at a past time that is relative to *a reference point most likely equivalent to speech time.* In contrast, the Imperfect makes reference to a situation at a past time from the perspective of *a past viewpoint* relative to the speaker's position at speech time or a reference point. Thus, Doiz-Bienzobas argues that the function of the perfective is purely temporal because the perfective serves to convey the concept that the situation it modifies takes place at a past time in relation to a reference point. In contrast, the imperfective form serves to convey the concept that the situation it modifies is conceptualized in the past (i.e., the deictic reference to speech time is being downplayed). As a consequence, when the imperfective form is used, the situation is not necessarily temporally specified. That is, the 'presence of a past viewpoint away from the speaker's position and absence of temporal specification of the situation may be used for expression of notions other than the purely temporal; the exact interpretation or use of the sentences with the imperfect is determined by the context' (p. 29).

Doiz-Bienzobas' past viewpoint and reference point evoke Klein's notions of Topic Time and Time of the Utterance, respectively. Within Klein's framework, however, the relationship between Topic Time and Speech Time represents the concept of tense, whereas the relationship between Topic Time and Time of the Situation represents aspect. Thus, from the perspective of Klein's framework, Doiz-Bienzobas equates the Preterite with a straight tense marker, whereas the Imperfect would be the marker that adds the more specific nuances of aspectual meanings. As we will see, other researchers have also described the perfective marker as a tense marker, in contrast with a definition of the imperfective marker as a true aspectual marker. Giorgi and Pianesi (1997: 174), for instance, propose that – embedded in a past tense – the imperfect expresses simultaneity, thus acting as a 'present-in-the-past'. Thus, in the following sentence, Giorgi and Pianesi argue that the use of the Imperfect focuses the speaker's attention on the moment when Mario was watching Juan eat an apple.

10. Mario me dijo que Juan comía (IMP)/comió (PRET) una manzana.
    Mario told me that Juan ate/was eating an apple.

In contrast, the Preterite moves our 'viewpoint' to the moment the speaker utters the sentence. In conclusion, it appears that there is a significant level of agreement on the deictic characterization of the tense-aspectual contrasts conveyed by the perfective-imperfective markers across research paradigms. More importantly, Doiz-Bienzobas' proposed theoretical contrast accounting for the meanings of the perfective and imperfective markers in Spanish (e.g., Preterite and Imperfect) will be important to framing the hypothesis about a default past tense marker in L2 acquisition (e.g., Lubbers-Quesada, 2007; Salaberry, 1999, 2002, 2003, 2005; Wiberg, 1996).

3. Lexical Aspect

3.1 Lexical aspectual classes

The concept of lexical aspect has been labelled in multiple ways in the extant literature: actionality (Tatevosov, 2002), Aktionsart (Klein, 1994), aspectual character (Lyons, 1968), situation type (Smith, 1997), eventuality type (Filip, 1999), event (Bhatt, 1999) and of course, lexical aspect (Vendler, 1967) just to name a few. Each researcher has settled on specific terms mostly for clarity of exposition. For instance, Filip (1999: 15) prefers the term 'eventuality type instead of aspect, aspectual class or inherent lexical aspect to minimize confusion with the other category'. Despite the obvious benefits of the use of a single term, however, the reality is that there has not been any concrete attempt to settle on a single term to refer to lexical aspectual categories. In this volume, I use several of these terms interchangeably as synonymous expressions. The important distinctions among concepts, categories and classes of aspect are discussed in specific sections of this chapter.

According to Binnick (1991), the notion that verbs can be classified according to inherent semantic differences comes from Aristotle who classified verbs into two main types: verbs of *energiai (to be, to think, to know)* and verbs of *kinesis (to sing, to build)*. Eventually, however, Aristotle would reclassify verbs of *energiai* into two different subtypes: verbs of *ékhein* (equivalent to Vendler's states) and verbs of *energein* (equivalent to Vendler's activities). Verbs of *kinesis* became equivalent to Vendler's classes of accomplishments and achievements combined. Table 2.1 presents contrasts in Aristotle's and Vendler's categories of lexical aspect.

Table 2.1   Classification of verb types according to Aristotle and Vendler

Aristotle's categories			Vendler's categories
Energiai [–dynamic]	ékhein	[–dynamic]	states
	energein	[+dynamic/–telic]	atelic events
kinesis [+dynamic]		[+dynamic/–telic]	telic events

Essentially, Aristotle adopted a classification that was based on the semantic features of telicity (telic versus atelic verbs) and dynamicity (states versus events: see following discussion). Kenny (1963) maintained the unitary classification of accomplishments and achievements, which he labelled performances and distinguished these from states and processes. Vendler (1967) expanded the tripartite classification by Aristotle and Kenny into four types of verbal predicates according to their inherent semantic meanings: states (durative, non-dynamic, atelic), activities (durative, dynamic, atelic), accomplishments (durative, dynamic, telic) and achievements (non-durative, dynamic, telic). The following examples from Vendler are representative of the four classes of verbal predicates:

STATE: have, possess, know, love, hate
ACTIVITY: walk, swim, push, pull
ACCOMPLISHMENT: paint a picture, build a house
ACHIEVEMENT: recognize, stop, start

In sum, the inherent semantic meanings associated with the four lexical aspectual classes are based on a straightforward branching classification of situations (or eventualities) according to three semantic features: dynamicity, telicity and durativity. Figure 2.1 shows the division of lexical aspectual classes and semantic features in a graphical format for better visualization of the classification:

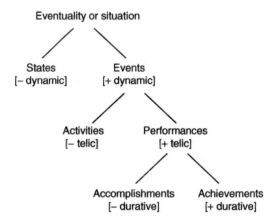

FIGURE 2.1 Lexical aspectual classes according to semantic features (based on Vendler, 1967; Mourelatos, 1981).

Figure 2.1 shows that situations are subclassified into states and dynamic events. That is, states are non-dynamic, homogeneous predicates, whereas activities, accomplishments and achievements, requiring the input of energy, are dynamic. Within the dynamic classes, accomplishment and achievements are *telic* (i.e., events with inherent endpoints), whereas activities are *atelic* (i.e., events with no inherent endpoint). Finally, telic events differ from each other with respect to durativity: Achievements are assumed to be instantaneous, such as '*John realized he made a mistake*', whereas accomplishments are assumed to include the process that leads up to the culmination of the event '*John read the novel*'. English and Spanish are both alike with respect to the existence of lexical aspectual classes. The following sentences are prototypical examples of each one of Vendler's categories:

11. Julián knew Spanish.   [state]
12. Julián walked in the park.   [activity]
13. Julián built a house.   [accomplishment]
14. Julián noticed a stain in his shirt.   [achievement]

Sentence (11) refers to a situation that is homogeneous: knowing Spanish is the same at any moment during the period described. The other three sentences make reference to some type of change over time (i.e., they are dynamic situations). For instance, walking in the park from point A to point B (even if aimlessly) implies a change in position. Sentence (12), on the other hand, is more similar to sentence (11) rather than sentences (13) and (14) because the latter two depict a resultant state: *the house was built, the stain was noticed.* That is, sentences (13) and (14) are telic. In contrast, sentences (11) and (12) are atelic because they have no resultant state associated with them: *knowing Spanish, walking in the park.* Finally, the telic sentences (i.e., (13) and (14)) can be distinguished with respect to the existence, or not, of a process that leads to the resultant state (i.e., durativity).

Another type of graphical representation of the lexical aspectual classes is the one provided by Smith's schemata (Smith, 1997: 22ff.) in Table 2.2. In this table, a straight line represents undifferentiated period of states (i.e., homogeneous), whereas the series of dots represent successive stages of events (i.e., heterogeneous).

Smith (1997: 22) claims that 'the feature [Static] denotes an undifferentiated period; [Dynamic] denotes successive stages'. Activities are dynamic situations that involve change over time, but lack a specific endpoint (e.g., *to sing*). Smith (1997: 23) points out that '[a]ctivities terminate or stop,

Table 2.2 Lexical aspectual classes according to semantic features

Statives	[+Static]	(I) _____(F)
Activities	[+Dynamic]	I ......F$_{arb}$ (Initial and arbitrary endpoints)
Accomplishments	[+Telic, +Durative]	I ......F$_{NatR}$ (Initial and natural endpoints)
Achievements	[+Telic, +Punctual]	E$_R$

Based on Smith (1997) E = Event, I = Initial, F = Final.

but they do not finish: the notion of completion is irrelevant to a process event'. Accomplishments are dynamic situations that have duration and involve an end result (e.g., *to fix the car*). Achievements refer to dynamic situations that involve an instantaneous change (e.g., *to recognize something*).[4]

3.1.1 Dynamicity and telicity

Do we need four lexical aspectual classes to account for the specific semantic nuances of lexical aspectual meanings? In other words, are the three proposed semantic features (i.e., dynamicity, telicity and durativity) that determine the four-way classificatory system equally relevant or necessary? As it turns out, some scholars propose that some semantic features are more basic than others.

At a minimum, it is generally agreed that the two most important semantic contrasts to determine lexical aspect are dynamicity and telicity. Langacker (1987: 258), for instance, contends that the state–event distinction (i.e., dynamicity) has a 'primal character', because it is linked to a basic cognitive capacity: the ability to perceive change (or stasis) over time. According to the original classification by Vendler, statives differ from dynamic events according to the notion of phase: states involve no change (e.g., *to know*), whereas dynamic situations do involve change (e.g., *to run*). More recent definitions of lexical aspect uphold the distinction between dynamic and non-dynamic verbs according to phase. Michaelis (2004: 15), for instance, asserts that 'states are internally homogeneous situations, which include no transitions (i.e., temporal boundaries). . . . Transitions are state-change events, and as such are isomorphic to achievements'. Although typical stative-dynamic pairs of verbs can be classified according to the notion of change or phase, such a categorization is only a first approximation. As Comrie points out, there are cases that are not accounted for by the previous dichotomy. For instance, Comrie argues that the state of standing may involve change, and conversely, a dynamic situation such as an oscilloscope emitting tone may not show any apparent change. Thus, Comrie proposes that an important feature that distinguishes statives from dynamic situations is input of energy. A dynamic situation 'will only continue if it is continually subject to a new input of energy . . . whether from inside (in which case we have an agentive interpretation, e.g. *John is running*), or from outside (in which case we have a non-agentive interpretation, e.g. the oscilloscope is emitting a pure tone)'. (p. 49)

The state class tends to be the one more difficult to define of the two determined by the non-dynamic-dynamic contrast. Chung and Timberlake (1985: 215) show that examples of typical stative verbs describe properties (e.g., *be tall*, *be rich*) and represent cognition/perception (*to know, to see, to understand*). On the other hand, the reference to 'typical' stative brings up the notion of a graded hierarchy of statehood. As Bertinetto (1994: 410) observes, *permanent statives* are infelicitous with temporal adverbs (15a), whereas *contingent statives* are compatible with temporal adverbs (15b).[5]

15a. *This morning, for a couple of hours, I was very tall.
15b. This morning, for a couple of hours, I was very angry with John.

Notice also that the same verb can be either stative or dynamic (cf. Mourelatos' semantic multivalence of verbs). Chung and Timberlake (1985: 215), for instance, note the contrast between *smell* as a state and *smell* as a process in sentences (16) and (17):

16. The food smells good to me.
17. I smelled the food.

Binnick (1991) asserts that the prototypical state is non-volitional, persistent and has no gaps. In terms of volition, for instance, one cannot choose to be tall. Hence, the tests of pseudo-cleft constructions (*What he did was be tall*) and imperatives (*Be tall*) effectively exclude statives. Unlike states, dynamic situations tend to stop unless actively continued. Furthermore, states like the state of being ill from Monday to Wednesday is continuous (has no gaps) throughout the given period of time, whereas dynamic verbs like 'worked for two hours' may include periods in which no working was done. As a consequence, states have no natural boundaries, no inherent structure and no onset or culmination. Hence, Binnick states that the test with aspectualizers rules out states:

18a. *John started being ill.
18b. *John finished being tall.
18c. ?John continued being patriotic.

Finally, it is important to point out that the use of perfective–imperfective morphology on states and events brings about distinct aspectual meanings. That is, whereas the perfective form used with dynamic verbs implies closure or cessation of the event (e.g., *construyó, pintó,* built, painted etc.), when the perfective is used with states, it instead conveys the concept of inception (e.g., *miró, supo;* looked, found out) (Chung and Timberlake, 1985: 217).

A major point of discrepancy in previous empirical studies has been the classification of beginning and end of states (e.g., Bybee, 1995a; Comrie, 1976; Dowty, 1986; Guitart, 1978; Klein, 1994; Smith, 1983; Studerus, 1989). For example, Hasbún (1995) does not distinguish between inception or end of a state and the state itself, whereas Robison (1990, 1995) classifies the beginning of a state as a 'punctual stative'.[6] There are also cross-linguistic differences in how the inception of a state is marked grammatically. For instance, in Spanish, the so-called 'meaning-changing Preterites' signal the inception of states: *conocer, tener, saber* and *querer* (e.g., Studerus, 1989). The following examples show that whereas Spanish uses a verbal procedure to convey the meaning associated with a state (19a) or the inception of a state (19b), English uses a lexical procedure to convey a similar contrast.

19a. Conocía (IMP) a su padre.
I knew his father.
19b. Conocí (PRET) a su padre el año pasado.
I met his father last year.

As Bybee (1995a) points out, what is significant about the uses of the Preterite with statives is that the grammatical marker brings about an inchoative meaning (the beginning of the state), even though the perfective tends to be associated with the completion of an eventuality. Note, however, that the key words here are 'tends to be associated'. In fact, Bybee points out that inchoativity is not a basic meaning of Preterites with states, but rather a meaning inferred from context. For instance, the following use of the Preterite with a stative verb (*estar*) conveys a non-inchoative meaning:

20. Estuvimos (PRET) allí tres horas y después fuimos (PRET) al cine.
We were there for three hours and then we went to the movie theater.

In line with the claim advanced by Doiz-Bienzobas (1995, 2002), the use of the Preterite in (20) does not necessarily change the status of *estar* as a stative verb, but rather it locates it in time. That is, the Preterite acts a tense marker only, thus it does not bring up the notion of inchoativity. I return to the analysis of non-inchoative meanings of the uses of the Preterite with states in Chapter 4.

Apart from dynamicity, telicity has also been regarded as essential to identify a situation. Wagner (2001: 662), for instance, argues that '[t]he primary distinction within the linguistic category of lexical aspect is between predicates describing bounded and non-bounded events (i.e., telic and atelic predicates . . .)'. Similarly, Smith (1997: 19) claims that the reason that 'telicity is generally not open to aspectual choice is that humans see it as an essential property. Telicity is not, therefore, a property that can be shifted for purposes of emphasis and point of view'. For example, if we interchange the prepositional phrase (PP) in sentence (21a), a locative PP, with the one of sentence (21b), a directional PP, the aspectual nature of the verb constellation will be fundamentally changed in terms of the telic nature of the verb: from an activity to an accomplishment (see also Maingueneau, 1994: 63).

21a. Mary walked [in the park]. (locative: atelic)
21b. Mary walked [to the park]. (directional: telic)

3.1.2 *Durativity*

In contrast to dynamicity and telicity, durativity has been considered non-essential for the classification of verbs into semantic aspectual classes by many researchers (e.g., Chung and Timberlake, 1985; de Swart, 1998; Dowty, 1986; Filip, 1999; Klein, 1994; Mourelatos, 1981; Verkuyl, 1993). Durativity, as mentioned earlier, is the only feature that distinguishes accomplishments (durative) from achievements (non-durative, punctual). Thus, while some researchers continue to uphold Vendler's four classes of states, activities, accomplishments and achievements (e.g., Michaelis, 2004; Rothstein, 2004), many have reduced Vendler's four-way classification into a tripartite distinction by collapsing accomplishments and achievements into a single category of telic events. Tenny (1994: 5), thus claims that the accomplishment-achievement distinction 'is of secondary importance'. Filip (1999: 16) more forcefully contends that '[m]any language phenomena clearly indicate that not only accomplishments and achievements form a natural class (events), but also states and processes, in some respects at least, exhibit significant semantic and syntactic similarities in their behavior'. In fact, even empirical data from L2 acquisition studies show that durativity is not a relevant semantic factor (e.g., Bardovi-Harlig and Bergström, 1996; Collins, 2002). Collins, in particular, reports that her L2 English data (gathered among L1 French speakers) did not reveal any 'significant differences between accomplishments and achievements in the use of simple past' (p. 82).

On the other hand, there may be language-specific differences that may warrant the inclusion of durativity as a relevant semantic feature as is the case in Japanese as described, among others, by Shirai and Kurono (1998). Finally, we should note that there is some variation in the labels assigned to the remaining three classes after durativity is abandoned. While Verkuyl (1993) describes the three categories as states, activities and accomplishments, both de Swart (1998) and Filip (1999) classify them into states, processes and events. By and large, however, these labels are used interchangeably.

3.1.3 Expanding the list of aspectual classes

In contrast to researchers who seek to reduce the number of aspectual classes, others distinguish more than the classic Vendlerian four lexical aspectual classes. For instance, Smith (1997) considers further combinations of semantic features to include semelfactives and a more fine-grained subclassification of activities. According to Smith, semelfactives are dynamic, atelic and instantaneous events: 'they have a set of grammatical features which contrast with those associated with duration'. Some typical semelfactives are *blink, cough, tap, peck, scratch, kick*. Smith notes that '[t]hese events often occur in repetitive sequences, rather than as single-stage events. Such sequences are multiple-event Activities. The multiple-event reading is triggered by an adverbial or other information, as in *Mary knocked for five minutes.* ... The derived interpretation is triggered by the clashing temporal features of the verb constellation and other forms'. In fact, as Smith (1997: 37) points out, both Vendler (1957) and Dowty (1979) defined semelfactives as a special atelic subclass of achievements.

Along the same lines, Barner *et al.* (2008: 4) point out that a semelfactive verb such as *jump* cannot name a single event that extends over the course of a day, but must name a plurality of individual events (22a). In contrast, a non-punctual verb such as *sleep* can name a single protracted process that extends over a day without iteration (22b). The important point is that certain verbs can encode reference to individuals, which requires an iterative interpretation when they are used in expressions that distribute phenomena over time.

22a. Jim jumped all day. (Jim performed multiple jumps)
22b. Jim slept all day. (Jim slept continuously)

If the conceptual features of iterative verbs such as *jump* are inherited by mass nouns, then these derived nouns (e.g., *some jumping*) should denote individuals. Furthermore, these mass nouns should contrast with mass nouns derived from non-iterative verbs such as *dance* (i.e., *some dancing*), which should quantify by some other dimension (e.g., time spent performing the action). The proposed association between iterativity and semelfactives will be important for the analysis of the acquisition of iterativity to be presented in Chapters 3 and 4.

Michaelis (2004) also considers more than the four traditional lexical aspectual classes. To do it, she first divides situations according to dynamicity into *events* (those that take place over time), and *states* (those that hold at a given point in time). Events are further subdivided into *directed events* (events that culminate in a specific resultant state and *episodic events* (events that *do not* culminate in a specific resultant state). Directed events are further divided into *accomplishments* (they are brought about) and *achievements* (they come about). It is in the classification of activities and states that Michaelis' categorization departs from traditional Vendlerian classifications. Thus, she subclassifies state verb types into states and state phases. Furthermore, she subclassifies activities as homogeneous activities and heterogeneous activities. Table 2.3 presents the overall classification of the six types of verbs proposed by Michaelis.

Episodic events are divided into *activities* (they occur over a period of time but they do not culminate) and *phases* (non-dynamic situations that have duration). Activities are further divided into homogeneous activities (they lack subevents) and heterogeneous activities (iterated type-identical subevents). Essentially, heterogeneous activities correspond to Smith's semelfactives: they can be parsed into small subintervals as iterated subevents (e.g., to skip, to jump). On the other hand, the state phase is predicated on the various phases of an eventuality (beginning, middle portion, end, ensuing result or state). The phase category has the single member of state phases that, like states, is a non-dynamic verb that does not require any

Table 2.3   Classification of lexical aspectual classes according to Michaelis (2004)

Situations	Events	Directed events	*Accomplishment*
			Achievement
		Episodic events	*Homogeneous activity*
			Heterogeneous activity
			Phase
	States	States	*States*

input of energy. Unlike states, however, a phase state can be assigned a specific duration and it has perfective properties. For instance, *to be sick* and *to be depressed* are state phases.

23. She was sick for three days.
24. I was depressed when I lived there.

The idea that states may be represented as the beginning phase of the state or its resultant state is not new as presented in the previous discussion about inchoative meanings of verbs in Spanish. In fact, early on Vendler noted that in some circumstances statives are felicitous with dynamic meanings (25a, b):

25a. Now I know it.
25b. And then, suddenly I knew.

Vendler points out that *to know* is similar to *to get married* (an achievement) rather than *to be married* (a state). In essence, the inceptive point of a state is determined by adverbial phrases (adjuncts). Michaelis also presents several examples of the effect of adjuncts. An important question to consider is, however, whether a state phase should be regarded as an achievement verb (as opposed to a type of stative: see also Dowty, 1986; Dry, 1983; Guitart, 1978; Smith, 1983).

Finally, Smith (1997) also expanded the classification of verbal predicates with the inclusion of three distinct types of activities: processes that are virtually unlimited (*sleep, laugh,* etc.), activities with internal stages typically triggered by mass nouns (e.g., *eat cherries*), and derived, shifted activities (e.g., The child *began* to build a castle). The first two types of activities (unlimited processes and activities with internal stages) are equivalent to homogeneous and heterogeneous activities in Michaelis' scheme (see next paragraph for details). The third type of derived and shifted activities is discussed in detail in Section 5.

3.2 Compositionality of lexical aspect

The classification of lexical aspectual classes based on the inherent semantic meaning of the verbal predicate alone is an oversimplification. There are other components associated with the verbal predicate that contribute to the aspectual interpretation of verb classes. Although the effect of components other than the verb itself had been recognized ever since Vendler proposed his four-way classification, Verkuyl (1989: 100–103) was the first to explicitly state that verb complements had an effect on the characterization of verb classes, and that aspect is compositional. Verkuyl (1993) argues that semantic features of verbs can be computed as a type of feature algebra to obtain the lexical aspect of a verb phrase: [+/–ADD TO] represents the dynamic-stative distinction, whereas [+/–SQA] (or specified quantity) represents the mass–count nature of the arguments of the verb. As noted earlier, durativity is not a semantic feature that is regarded as important in Verkuyl's feature algebra. In sum, at a minimum, most researchers agree on the important effect of internal arguments (objects), many also agree on the role played by external arguments (subjects), and some even consider the role of adjuncts (adverbials) (e.g., Mourelatos, 1981; Olsen, 1997) as relevant for the determination of lexical aspectual classes. I turn to the discussion of these various components in this section.

3.2.1 Internal arguments

One of the clearest examples of the compositionality of aspect is repre-sented in the behaviour of certain verbs that, when their internal arguments are made explicit, may refer to telic instead of atelic events. That is, the inherent end point of the direct object is transferred to the verbal predi-cate: if the direct object does not provide an inherent end point, the verb does not become telic. For example, the verb *to run* is typically an activity (atelic) when it is used intransitively:

26a. Lucas corrió (PRET).   [atelic]
         Lucas ran.

However, if the object of the verb is explicitly indicated (i.e., the distance that Lucas ran), as shown in (26b), then *run* is an accomplishment. That is, the grammatical object of the verb establishes an endpoint to the activity, thereby making the event telic (cf. Smith, 1997).

26b. Lucas corrió (PRET) cuatro kilómetros.   [telic]
         Lucas ran four kilometers.

Similarly, the mass/count distinction or the specific/non-specific features of the internal argument of a given verb will also affect the basic semantic nature of the predicate in essential ways. Essentially, mass nouns and bare plurals do not determine an inherent end point for the verbal predicate, whereas count nouns quantify specific amounts, thus providing verbal predicates with a terminus that serves to measure out the event (e.g., de Swart, 1998; Filip, 1999; Tenny, 1994; Verkuyl, 1993). Bare plurals and mass nouns share the property of cumulativity and distributivity (divisive reference). For instance, coffee plus coffee is coffee (cumulative) and parts of coffee are coffee (divisible). States and processes (both atelic) pattern with bare plurals and mass nouns insofar they have the properties of cumulativity and divisibility as well. For instance, if a state or process holds at some interval of time, it will also hold at any subinterval of the larger interval: parts of being sick mean being sick (divisibility). Furthermore, the truth of the state or process at some interval does not exclude the possibility that it will also be true at a larger interval: writing plus writing is writing (cumulativity). Most notably, telic events do not have the subinterval property, thus distinguishing atelic from telic eventualities.

As exemplified in sentences (27a) and (27b), in the absence of other adverbials, the cardinality of the object (whether count or mass noun as in *un artículo*, 'an article' and *artículos*, 'articles', respectively) can determine whether the activity is interpreted as having an inherent endpoint or not:

27a. Lucas leía (IMP) un artículo. [telic]
     Lucas was reading an article.
27b. Lucas leía (IMP) artículos. [atelic]
     Lucas would read/used to read/was reading articles.

Along the same lines, Nishida (1994) discusses another subclassification of statives that is brought up by the use of the aspectual particle *se*: delimited versus non-delimited. The distinction is argued to be similar to the telic–atelic distinction prevalent among [+dynamic] verbs. For instance, Nishida shows that although both *saber* and *querer* are prototypical state verbs, only *saber* is compatible with *se* as shown in the following examples:

28. Juan se supo (PRET) la lección.
    Juan knew the lesson.
29. *Juan se quiso (PRET) a Elena.
    Juan loved Elena.

Nishida explains that in *saberse la lección*, there is a homomorphic relation between the state verb and the object affected by the state, making the latter a quantized state. In contrast, 'the state of "loving Elena" cannot be broken into parts in such a way that each part would correspond to some proper part of "Elena"' (p. 439). This contrast between quantifiable versus non-quantifiable states is analogous to the contrast between telic and atelic events within the dynamic class of verbs.

3.2.2 External arguments

In addition to internal arguments, the nature of the subject of the utterance (the external argument) may also affect the inherent semantic aspectual value of the verb as well (e.g., Depraetre, 1995; Langacker, 1982; Maingueneau, 1994; Smith, 1997; Verkuyl, 1999). As we mentioned earlier, Smith (1997: 2) argues that situation aspect is composed of 'a main verb and its arguments, including subject'. For instance, when the external argument is a count noun or a mass noun, there will be a concomitant effect on the semantic nature of the verbal predicate. This effect is similar to the one presented earlier for the effect of internal arguments on the lexical semantics of the verb phrase. In the following examples, the use of the mass noun brings about an atelic meaning of the verb *to flow*, whereas the same verb in association with a count noun becomes a telic one (examples from Smith, 1997):

30. Oil flowed through the pipes. [mass noun = atelic]
31. 3000 litres of oil flowed through the pipes. [count noun = telic]

The effect of the external argument may also have an effect on aspectual concepts such as iterativity and habituality. For instance, in the following two sentences, the use of the perfective form focuses on the final stage of the event of crossing the bridge (these examples are based on paraphrases of sentences used by Maingueneau, 1994: 71).

32a. El ejército cruzó (PRET) el puente. [focus on final stage]
     The army crossed the bridge.
33a. Lucas cruzó (PRET) el puente. [focus on final stage]
     Lucas crossed the bridge.

Note that the external arguments in these sentences (i.e., Lucas, the army) differ in terms of the singular/plural dimension. The addition of the adverbial phrase in the following sentences, however, triggers a different semantic aspectual meaning in each sentence.

32b. El ejército cruzó (PRET) el puente durante toda la mañana. [focus on final stage]
     The army crossed the bridge all morning long.
33b. Lucas cruzó (PRET) el puente durante toda la mañana. [iterative]
     Lucas crossed the bridge all morning long.

More specifically, the construction that combines the adverbial with the singular subject brings about an iterative meaning (Lucas traversed the bridge several times during the morning), whereas the construction that combines the adverbial with the plural subject does not lead to the notion of iterativity. Given that the army is a 'singularity of many', it is reasonable to assume that it took a whole morning for the army to cross the same bridge (or, at least this is the default interpretation of the sentence). In other words, it is the combinatorial meaning of adverbial and external argument (the construction in Filip's or Michaelis' terms) what triggers the distinct aspectual meaning in each sentence.

Langacker (1982) also argues that 'a perfective predicate describes the change of a configuration through time', whereas 'an imperfective predicate describes the constancy of configuration through time'. Thus, the verb *go* in sentences (34) and (35) is presented as perfective or imperfective according to the characteristics of the *subject* of the sentence:

34. Sally went from Phoenix to Tucson.
35. This road goes from Phoenix to Tucson.

Referencing these examples, Langacker argues that

> Sally is small relative to the distance between Phoenix and Tucson; the only way this trajector can occupy all the points on the trajectory is by occupying them successively through time. . . . In [35], on the other hand, the subject *road* is such that it can occupy all of the points of the path simultaneously. . . . But this makes [35] imperfective by definition, since it describes a configuration constant through time and fully instantiated at every point in time (pp. 274–75).

In fact, the meaning contrast described by Langacker can be tested more precisely with the selections of past tense in Spanish, which reflect the perfective–imperfective meaning contrast through morphosyntax. Example (36) shows that both options (Preterite and Imperfect) are available for the sentence in which *Sally* is the subject. When the subject of the sentence is *the road*, however, only the imperfective option is acceptable:[7]

36a. Sally iba de Phoenix a Tucson.
36b. Sally fue de Phoenix a Tucson.
37a. Esta ruta iba de Phoenix a Tucson.
37b. *Esta ruta fue de Phoenix a Tucson.

In line with the explanation about the contrast between the property of an event and its actual occurrence (cf. Doiz-Bienzobas, 1995; Langacker, 1999), the judgements of acceptability presented in sentences (37a) and (37b) reflect the fact that the Imperfect conveys the notion of property whereas the Preterite conveys the notion of actual occurrence. Thus, (37b) is unacceptable because the road does not traverse the distance from Phoenix to Tucson as an actual occurrence. Rather, that covered trajectory is a property of the road.

3.2.3 Adjuncts

Adjuncts (e.g., adverbial phrases) constitute another basic element in the composition of the aspectual value of a predicate. Consider, for instance, how the adverbials in sentences (38b) and (38c) trigger the use of the Preterite, whereas sentence (38a) without any adjuncts uses the Imperfect, the latter being the prototypical marker of states (these sentences were introduced in Chapter 1).

38a. SABÍA (IMP) la verdad.
  (S/he) knew the truth.
38b. En ese momento, SUPO (PRET) la verdad.
  At that moment, (s/he) discovered the truth.
38c. Siempre SUPO (PRET) la verdad.
  (S/he) always knew the truth.

Note also that in (38b), the adverbial is punctual and in (38c), it is durative. In both cases, however, the verb is marked with the Preterite. This outcome contradicts one of the typical rules of thumb provided to L2 learners (i.e., a durative meaning triggers the use of the imperfective form). I revisit this example later in this chapter and then again in Chapter 4.

Similarly, expanding on the role of the subject of a sentence, Smith (1997: 4) argues that the following examples (originally from Verkuyl) 'show very clearly that situation type meaning is compositional: it is built up with the verb, arguments and adverbs of a sentence'.

39a. Famous movie stars discovered that little spa for years.   [atelic]
39b. A famous movie star discovered that little spa.   [telic]

Despite Smith's position as stated earlier, she makes a distinction between 'basic-level verb constellations' and 'derived-level verb constellations' (1997: 54–56).

The former are determined by compositional rules that include the effect of the main verb and its arguments (both internal and external), whereas the latter include also the effect of adverbials (e.g., *for an hour*), superlexical morphemes (e.g., *to begin, to finish*) and verbal morphology (e.g., progressive). I return to the analysis of these distinctions in Sections 5.3 and 5.4.

Interestingly, some generative proposals incorporate the role of adjuncts to their theoretical analysis. Tenny's (1994) Aspectual Interface Hypothesis (AIH), for instance, considers the effect of adjuncts (e.g., duration adverbials) on the classification of verbal predicates. The AIH is based on the aspectual notion of delimitedness: 'the property of an event's having a distinct, definite and inherent endpoint in time' (p. 4). Tenny argues that to determine whether a verbal predicate is delimited or not, it is necessary to analyse the subcategorization frame of the predicate. Each verb is associated with a specific argument structure: internal argument, indirect internal arguments (i.e., adjuncts) and external arguments. Direct and indirect internal arguments are subject to aspectual semantic constraints: the measuring-out constraint and the terminus constraint, respectively. Internal arguments 'measure out' the verb (quantification, definiteness, etc.); adjuncts specify the terminal point of an event (terminus).

3.2.4 Aspectual particles

Finally, another component that enters into the classification of lexical aspectual classes is represented by secondary modifications of basic verb meanings (Klein, 1994: 17) usually by the use of affixes. For instance, in English, verbs may be qualified in terms of aspect by means of adding prepositions, which do not alter the verb form and which are not obligatory: *eat up, read through,* and so forth. Klein mentions similar examples from German: *erblühen* (to start flowering: inchoative aspect), *blühen* (flowering) and *verblühen* (to wither: resultative aspect). Spanish also has a similar mechanism to further qualify the lexical aspect of a verbal predicate through the use of the aspectual particle *se*.[8] For instance, in the following pair of sentences, the Spanish particle *se* conveys the same type of aspectual nuance of meaning exemplified in the Germanic languages (examples are from Nishida, 1994).

40a. Juan *se tomó* (PRET) una copa de vino antes de acostarse.
     Juan *drank up* a glass of wine before going to bed.
40b. Juan *tomó* (PRET) una copa de vino antes de acostarse.
     Juan *drank* a glass of wine before going to bed.

As is the case with equivalent aspectual particles in English (e.g., up in *read up* or *eat up*), the use of the aspectual marker *se* in Spanish is optional as shown in sentences (41) and (42).

41. Juan tomó (PRET) una copa de vino.
    Juan *drank* a glass of wine.
42. Comí (PRET) diez manzanas.
    I *ate* ten apples.

Zagona (1994: 482) argues that the Spanish aspectual particle *se* is a second-ary marker of the culmination of an event, analogous to emphatic reflexives such as *herself* in *Mary did it herself*. Interestingly, however, Nishida reports that some native speakers sometimes reject the sentences without the aspectual marker *se*:

43a. *? Mi abuelito fumó (PRET) todo el puro.
     My granpa smoked the cigar.
43b. Mi abuelito se fumó (PRET) todo el puro.
     My granpa smoked up the cigar.
44a. *? Los invitados tomaron (PRET) todo el vino.
     The guests drank the wine.
44b. Los invitados se tomaron (PRET) todo el vino.
     The guests drank up the wine.

Furthermore, when the aspectual particle *se* is used with mass nouns instead of count nouns, the resulting sentences are ungrammatical:

45a. *Juan se tomó (PRET) *vino* antes de acostarse.
     *Juan *drank up* wine before going to bed.
45b. Juan se tomó (PRET) una copa de vino.
     Juan *drank up* a glass of wine before going to bed.

In other words, the Spanish aspectual particle *se* is an overt marker of quan-titatively delimited situations that is only compatible with quantitatively delimited objects.

4. Grammatical Aspect

Whereas lexical aspect makes reference to ontological distinctions expressed by verbal predicates, grammatical aspect makes reference to speakers' (and hearers') perspectives on the aspectual nature of situations conveyed with the use of inflectional morphology and related grammatical means. Dahl (1985) states that the most common tense-aspect system in his sample of sixty-four languages is a tripartite system representing the contrasts of a present, a past imperfective and a past perfective. Spanish, along with the related Romance languages, is an example of such a basic system. Furthermore, both Dahl (1985) and Bybee (1995a) argue that aspectual distinctions in Spanish (Preterite and Imperfect) are superordinate categories to tense distinctions (present and past). Aspect-prominent languages obligatorily mark aspectual distinctions grammatically, whereas tense contrasts are only marked when their meaning cannot be extracted from context.

4.1 Perfective and imperfective

Following up on the work of previous authors, Binnick (1991: 155) proposes that the contrasts in the meanings of the imperfective and perfective aspect can be made according to the following criteria:

Perfective is [9]
- Definite ('a specific episode is viewed strictly as an occurrence'). Example: He repeated his question to me.
- Iterative ('repetitive episodes rather closely spaced in time and viewed as a unit'). Example: He repeated his question several times.

Imperfective is
- Durative and continuative ('a single specific episode viewed in its extension'). Example: The young woman was sitting by the window of the railroad car and was reading.
- Habitual ('repetitive episodes somewhat distantly spaced in time are viewed as a unit'). Example: Sometimes I would reread writers whom I especially liked.
- Indefinite ('a non-specific episode'). Example: Have you read this story?

In sum, Binnick's list conforms to the traditional distinction associated with the Preterite and Imperfect in Spanish: the Preterite refers to a one-time event (with a focus on the beginning and/or resultant state) or iterated events, whereas the Imperfect refers to continuous (and progressive) events, habituals and genericity.

The perfective–imperfective contrast is expressed with inflectional morphemes (e.g., Spanish Preterite and Imperfect or French *Passé Composé/Passé Simple* and *Imparfait*) or periphrastic expressions (e.g., English Past Progressive, French periphrasis *être en train de* + verb, Spanish *soler* + verb). Caudal and Roussarie (2005: 267–268) – while discussing the functions of

French *Passé Composé–Imparfait* – assert that, by and large, the perfective form focuses on changes of state, whereas the imperfective form focuses on the permanence of the state in the world. Thus, the basic meaning of the perfective is associated with boundedness and may refer to the beginning and/or end of a situation, thus it may be inceptive, punctual or completive. In example (46a), the verb *to run* is associated with a sense of termination of the activity (i.e., the arrival).

46a. Lucas ran the Houston marathon.
46b. Lucas was running the Houston marathon.

In contrast, imperfective aspect, being 'unbounded', focuses on the internal structure of the situation, viewing it as ongoing, with no specific endpoint (imperfective aspect can be durative or habitual), as in (46b).

4.2 Spanish Preterite and Imperfect

4.2.1 Boundedness

In Spanish, the perfective–imperfective aspectual opposition is obligatorily grammaticalized in past tense only. Thus, past tense inflectional morphology indicates both tense (past) and aspect (perfective or imperfective): The Preterite (PRET) encodes perfective aspect and past tense and the Imperfect (IMP) encodes imperfective aspect and past tense, as examples (47a, b) show.

47a. Julián comió (PRET) una manzana.
     Julián ate an apple.
47b. Julián comía (IMP) una manzana.
     Julián ate/was eating an apple.

In its most prototypical use, the Preterite encodes boundedness and the Imperfect encodes unboundedness (cf. Depraetre, 1995). The aspectual distinction of boundedness marked with Preterite and Imperfect in Spanish may possibly be conveyed with the contrast of the Simple Past and the Past Progressive in English.

48. Julián comía (IMP) una manzana, cuando llegó (PRET) Lucas.
    Julián was eating an apple, when Lucas arrived.

This association between English Past Progressive and the Spanish Progressive is, however, misleading. First, the Spanish Imperfect covers a broader range of aspectual notions than the Progressive in English. Note that the previous example is only useful to translate cases in which the Imperfect describes an action in progress that is being contrasted with another event. As a consequence, to convey the meaning of habituality that the Spanish expresses with the use of the Imperfect, English lexicalizes habitual aspect in the past with the use of verbs such as *would* or *used to*, as sentence (49) shows:

49a.   Cuando era (IMP) niño, Julián comía (IMP) manzanas todos los días.
        When Julián was a child, he would eat/used to eat/ate apples every day.

In fact, Spanish also has a periphrastic option equivalent to English *used to* that is used to convey habituality: the so-called defective verb *soler*:

49b.   Cuando era (IMP) niño, Julián solía (IMP) comer manzanas todos los días.
        When Julián was a child, he would eat/used to eat/ate apples every day.

Second, the Imperfect can be freely used with any lexical aspectual class, whereas the Past Progressive in English is not prototypically used with stative verbs. Notice that in the following example, the meaning contrast conveyed by the Preterite–Imperfect with the stative verb *estar* (to be) is not as easy to translate to English:

50.   Ayer estuve (PRET)/estaba (IMP) deprimida.
       Yesterday I was depressed.

In general, the Simple Past in English corresponds to the Spanish Preterite when the verbs are eventive (non-stative):

51.   Lucas completó (PRET) el manuscrito.
       Lucas finished the manuscript.
52.   Julián construyó (PRET) un barco.
       Julián built a boat.

The aspectual meaning of the use of the English Simple Past with statives is equivalent to the use of Spanish Imperfect with statives. That is, in both cases the state may or may not have reached an end.

53a. Lucas estaba (IMP) enfermo y todavía lo está.
     Lucas was sick and he still is (sick).
53b. Lucas estaba (IMP) enfermo, pero ya no lo está más.
     Lucas was sick, but not anymore.

On the other hand, because the English Simple Past is not regarded as an aspectual marker but a tense marker, it conveys the meaning of perfectivity (i.e., boundedness) in a pragmatically 'cancellable way' (e.g., Ziegeler, 2007). Thus, the English translation of sentence (54a) shows that the state of being sick may still be going on at speech time. In Spanish, in contrast, the aspectual perfective meaning is not pragmatic but rather grammatical, thus it cannot be pragmatically cancelled (based on examples from Montrul and Salaberry, 2003).

54a. *Lucas estuvo (PRET) enfermo y todavía lo está.
     Lucas was sick, and he still is sick.
54b. Lucas estuvo (PRET) enfermo, pero ya no lo está más.
     Lucas was sick, but he is no longer sick.

In English, the 'discontinuity of the past state is only pragmatically implied, which can be cancelled by an added qualification' (Ziegeler, 2007: 1021). With eventive verbs in English (sentence (55)), however, such cancellation cannot occur because the reference to the completed event is grammatically encoded. Thus, the cancellation of an already completed telic event is ungrammatical in both English and Spanish.

55. *Lucas completó el manuscrito y todavía lo está completando.
    *Lucas finished the manuscript and he is still finishing it.

The analysis of the previous examples highlights the fact that English does not have an inflectional morphological means to convey aspectual meanings as Spanish does. As also noted by Ziegeler (2007: 1023), English does not have two representational meanings associated with the Simple Past (i.e., aspectual and tense meanings), but rather 'one prototypical use that is likely to have related to its historical development (perfectivity), and . . . any non-prototypical uses are extensions via pragmatic inferencing (past temporality)'.

4.2.2 More than boundedness

The range of meanings conveyed by the contrastive use of the Preterite–Imperfect in Spanish is broader than the simple distinction according to boundedness presented earlier. The Preterite and Imperfect may also convey more specific aspectual contrasts such as habituality versus iterativity, genericity versus specificity and property versus actual occurrence (e.g., Doiz-Bienzobas, 1995; Montrul and Salaberry, 2003; Slabakova and Montrul, 2003; Pérez-Léroux et al., 2007).

We have already discussed the meaning of habituality conveyed with the use of Imperfect, but Spanish also conveys the notion of iterativity with the use of the Preterite. As mentioned before, habituality may be formally conveyed in English with periphrases such as *used to* and *would*, but it can also be represented with the Simple Past (56). Iterativity, on the other hand, is normally only represented in English with the Simple Past Tense as shown in sentence (57).

56. Cuando era (IMP) niño, jugaba al fútbol.   [habitual]
    When I was a child, I played/used to play soccer.
57. Por años, jugué (PRET) al fútbol.   [iterative]
    For years, I played soccer.

Genericity in Spanish is always conveyed with the use of the Imperfect, whereas the reference to the actual instance(s) of an event (specific) with the Preterite has no formal equivalent in English.

58a. Los niños de mi barrio jugaban (IMP) al fútbol.   [generic]
     The children in my neighbourhood played soccer.
58b. Los niños de mi barrio jugaron (PRET) al fútbol.   [specific]
     The children in my neighbourhood played soccer.

The contrastive use of Spanish Preterite–Imperfect also allows speakers to distinguish property versus actual occurrence of an event as shown in the following sentences:

59a. El auto costaba (IMP) dos millones. (property of subject independent of time)
     The car cost two millions.
59b. El auto costó (PRET) dos millones. (someone bought the car for 2 million)
     The car cost two millions.

In some cases, this specific meaning contrast (i.e., property versus actual occurrence) conveyed by the Preterite–Imperfect distinguishes acceptable from unacceptable sentences. In particular, the Imperfect, but not the

Preterite, can be used with low-transitivity (agentless) predicates as shown in examples (60) and (61) both from Doiz-Binezobas (2005).

60. La carta decía (IMP)/*dijo (PRET) hola.
    The letter said hello.
61. El vestido llevaba (IMP)/*llevó (PRET) perlas.
    The dress had pearls.

In sum, although both Spanish and English mark aspectual distinctions, the acquisition of Spanish past tense marking among English speakers is challenging because (1) aspectual contrasts in English are not systematically marked on verb endings as is the case in Spanish Preterite–Imperfect (e.g., boundedness), (2) English aspectual markers do not exhibit a direct correspondence with equivalent markers in Spanish (e.g., Simple Past in English can convey the meanings of boundedness, habituality and iterativity) and (3) the range of aspectual concepts conveyed by specific markers in Spanish is wider and more fine-grained than equivalent expressions in English (e.g., low-transitivity, actual occurrence versus property).

5. The Interface of Lexical Aspect and Grammatical Aspect

While the majority of definitions of aspect seem to agree on the existence of two distinct levels of aspectual information, some theorists further postulate that these levels are also independent from each other (e.g. Smith, 1997). Smith explicitly stated that in her two-component theory of aspect '[t]he aspectual meaning of a sentence results from interaction between *two independent aspectual components*, situation type and viewpoint' (p. 2). The situation type represents the way humans perceive and categorize situations (verb + arguments). It constitutes a covert category of grammar instantiated in all languages (cf., cognitive concepts such as telicity). On the other hand, viewpoint aspect refers to the partial or full view of a particular situation type as marked by an overt grammatical morpheme. In this section, I review the possible interface between lexical and grammatical aspect focusing on the proposed 'shifting' of lexical aspectual values.

5.1 Operational tests of inherent lexical semantics

Among the earliest operational tests to distinguish the temporal specification of various verbs (i.e., lexical aspectual classes), were those developed by Vendler (1967) for English. Vendler described tests to distinguish statives from activities, activities from accomplishments, accomplishments from achievements and statives from achievements. For example, to distinguish between activities and accomplishments, Vendler uses a test of telicity: *drawing a circle* is an accomplishment, but *pushing a cart* is an activity based on the use of questions that focus (or not) on the endpoint of an event (pp. 100–101):

62a. For how long did you push the cart? (natural)
62b. How long did it take to push the cart? (odd)
63a. For how long did you draw a circle? (odd)
63b. How long did it take to draw a circle? (natural)

Similarly, Vendler argues that states and achievements can be distinguished through the use of questions that focus on the punctuality of the eventuality (pp. 102–103):

64. At what time did you reach the top? At noon sharp./?*For three years.
65. For how long did you love her? ?*At noon sharp./For three years.

Subsequent researchers have continued to refine these operational tests and have introduced more formal tests. For instance, Dowty (1979) distinguished statives from activities and accomplishments with the following six tests:

1. Only non-statives accept the progressive:
   *John is knowing the answer.
   John is running.
   John is building a house.
2. Only non-statives are felicitous with complements of *force, persuade*:
   *John forced Harry to know the answer.
   John forced Harry to run.
   John forced Harry to build a house.
3. Only non-statives accept the imperative:
   *Know the answer!
   Run!
   Build a house!
4. Only non-statives accept adverbs such as *deliberately, carefully*:
   *John deliberately knew the answer.
   John ran carefully.
   John carefully built a house.
5. Only non-statives appear in pseudo-cleft constructions:
   * What John did was know the answer.

What John did was run.

What John did was build a house.

6. Only non-statives have a habitual interpretation:

John knows the answer.

John runs (frequentative meaning possible).

John recites a poem (frequentative meaning possible).

As pointed out by Olsen (1997: 36–38), however, archetypal state verbs such as *know* and *love* fail to qualify as states according to some of the aforementioned semantic tests as shown in (66a–d):

66a. I'm just loving it.

66b. The recent assault forced Ted to know where Jae was at all times.

66c. Know about the movie rating system.

66d. What Ted did was always know where Jae was.

The lack of reliability of operational tests has led some researchers to review the conceptual basis on which these tests are founded. Overall, according to Klein (1994), there are two major types of evidence that determine the inherent lexical semantics of predicates and associated internal and external arguments (and possibly adjuncts): (1) the nature of the situation we are describing (the case in reality) and (2) combinatorial linguistic restrictions (operational tests of lexical content). Klein contends that the first line of evidence is inconclusive because it is 'methodologically difficult to separate what is the case in reality from what is the case in the lexicon' (p. 32), given that lexical contents refer to selective descriptions of reality. Klein concludes that in order to obtain reliable and consistent classifications of verbal predicates, it is important to classify lexical contents according to 'inner-linguistic restrictions'. Klein lists three major criteria to classify lexical contents: (1) adverb modification, (2) aspect modification and (3) presuppositions and implications.

Adverb modification is the prevalent procedure used to classify lexical aspectual classes ever since Vendler first proposed it. For instance, telic and atelic eventualities may be discriminated by adding two different adverbial phrases: *in x time (e.g., minutes)* versus *for x time (e.g., minutes)* (Dowty, 1979: 56; Vendler, 1967: 100). According to this view, telic events (i.e., accomplishments and achievements) are considered grammatical with the first adverbial phrase (*in x time*), but ungrammatical with the second phrase (*for x time*). The opposite case obtains with atelic verbs (i.e., states and processes including semelfactives). For example, let us take a look at the following sentences that serve to exemplify how the adverbial test works:

67a. Peter drew a circle in two minutes. [accomplishment felicitous]
67b. *Peter drew a circle for two minutes. [accomplishment non-felicitous]
68a. *She was in Austin in five days. [stative non-felicitous]
68b. She was in Austin for five days. [stative felicitous]

This adverbial test is supposed to work by tapping into the feature of telicity that distinguishes atelic versus telic eventualities. Thus, because states and processes do not have an inherent endpoint, they combine felicitously with for-adverbials, but not with in-adverbials. Conversely, because events do have an inherent endpoint, they combine felicitously with in-adverbials, but not with for-adverbials.

Klein (1994), Tenny (1994) and others, however, claim that the constraints exploited by tests based on adverb modification are inadequate. For example, if we follow the rationale that underlies the use of this test, the lexical content of *to open a window* would, in principle, be classified as a telic event (i.e., accomplishment or achievement):

69a. He opened the window in five seconds.
69b. *He opened the window for five seconds.

But, as Klein points out, the second statement may also be considered grammatical under a different interpretation. That is to say, *to open the window* is a combination of two different states: window not open – window open (source state and target state). It is only when we refer to both source and target state at the same time that we obtain an ungrammatical reading. If we focus our attention on the resulting state only, we obtain a possible reading:[10]

69c. He opened the window for five minutes.

In this case, the use of the adverbial phrase *for five minutes* instead of *for five seconds* shifts the focus of attention from the change from source to target state, to focus only on the target state. In other words, sentence (69c) implies that the window was closed, then opened and then closed again after five minutes. Similarly, Tenny (1994: 6) argues that sentence (70) shows that 'delimited events can be compatible with *for an hour* adverbials if they are understood in an iterative sense. This does not make them non-delimited'.

70. John broke the window (every day) for a year.

Summarizing a fairly common view on the use of tests that distinguish dynamicity, Olsen (1997: 28) concludes that these tests 'are notoriously difficult to apply' because 'context and other constituents often affect precisely the feature to be teased out'.

The second set of criteria, aspect modification, is generally used to discriminate between stative and non-stative verbs. For instance, Vendler differentiated between verbs that 'possess continuous tense and verbs that do not'. Stative verbs are not expected to accept the *-ing* morphological marker of progressive aspect in English (Vendler, 1967). Against this prediction, however, we find locative predicates (inherently statives) that normally accept the progressive even in languages like English (e.g., *I am standing on the floor*) and even non-locative predicates (e.g., *I am liking that*). Thus, Klein (1994: 34) comments that the test of aspect modification is open to the criticism of circularity if statives are defined as the verbs corresponding to the aspectual class that does not tolerate the progressive marker, or simply false, according to the aforementioned examples.

Finally, entailments are the most consistent of the available operational tests (e.g., Dowty, 1979; Hasbún, 1995; Shirai, 1991). The test of telicity distinguishes telic from atelic verbs by questioning the predicate in the following way: 'If you stop in the middle of V-ing, have you done the act of V?' If the answer is affirmative, the verbal predicate is atelic; if the answer is negative, the verbal predicate is telic. For instance, let us compare the verb phrases *to paint* versus *to paint a house*. If you stop in the middle of painting, then you have completed the act of painting. Therefore, *to paint* is an atelic predicate (activity). On the other hand, if you stop in the middle of painting the house, then you have not completed the act of painting the house. Thus, *to paint the house* is a telic predicate (accomplishment). Despite their consistency, however, entailment tests can only distinguish telic from atelic events because they are predicated on the notion of an endpoint (telicity).

5.2 Semantic multivalence of verbs

The lack of a categorical, foolproof test to distinguish lexical aspectual classes has led to acknowledging the variable semantic nature of verbal predicates. For instance, Mourelatos (1981: 196) refers to what he calls the 'semantic multivalence of state verbs' to describe how states such as *to understand* can be transformed into performances (telic events) as in the following examples (taken from Mourelatos):

71. Once Lisa understood (grasped) what Henry's intentions were, she lost all interest in him.
72. Please understand (get the point) that I am only trying to help you!

Mourelatos points out that there is 'no aberrance of English idiom in either case'. In fact, he argues that the same verb can be used as an activity as well:

73. I'm understanding more about quantum mechanics as each day goes by (Comrie, 1976: 36).

Mourelatos' position has been reaffirmed by most other researchers. Thus, Filip (1999: 17) points out that most stative predicates can be used with special interpretations in the progressive as in: *I'm not believing you, I'm understanding you, I'm really loving the play.* Along the same lines, Olsen (1999) notes that verbs unmarked for dynamicity can easily take on a dynamic interpretation, as shown by examples (74a–f):

74a. I'm liking this less and less.
74b. It looks like he's doubting it a little bit.
74c. He was hoping to see some sign.
74d. It was being a good evening.
74e. That was when Kirsten was having mice (i.e., possessing mice).
74f. Georgetown [is] needing to score on this trip.

In fact, these examples are not unusual. Following Chung and Timberlake (1985), in order to convert a stative verb into a process, one must add a sense of actual or possible change by expressing degrees of manifestation of change as it is done with *understanding* as follows:

75a. I understand my problems.
75b. I am understanding my problems more clearly every day.

or present the subject of the sentence as an agent:

76a. You are obnoxious.
76b. You are being obnoxious.

or by modalizing the concept of change by making it temporary or not as is the case with *living.*

77a. John lives with his parents.
77b. John is living/*lives with his parents until he finds a place of his own.

Similarly, de Swart (1998: 357) argues that in sentence (77c) '[t]he application of the BOUND-operator to the state variable results in a bounded, quantized portion of the state, . . . which counts as an event because it is quantized'.

77c. Susan lived in Paris for two years.

In sum, examples such as the ones reviewed in this section convinced Mourelatos, for one, that 'semantic multivalence is the rule rather than the exception'. This conclusion is important considering that in most cases the change in classification of lexical aspectual classes is related to a more expansive contextual framework of reference. On this point, Doiz-Bienzobas (1995: 49) states that Vendler's categories are based on 'conclusions reached from what we consider prototypical instances of these verbs/predicates'. As she points out, however, 'a situation may be conceived of as part of a non-prototypical setting'. Thus, 'it acquires properties which differ from the ones it would normally have and consequently the predicate may be described best as belonging to another verb type category'. How to distinguish prototypical from non-prototypical instances may not be easy, as the discussion in the following sections will show.

5.3 Lexical aspectual shifts

The theoretical analysis of the semantic multivalence of predicates is important because it has direct consequences on the conceptualization of tense-aspect meanings. In turn, an adequate definition of tense-aspect meanings is crucial to properly identify the dependent variable of L2 acquisition studies of past temporality. More specifically, the principled delimitation of situation type (i.e., lexical aspect) and viewpoint aspect can help us determine what is or is not an essential component of a definition of tense-aspect knowledge. Thus, in the following section, I present a detailed analysis of two of the most well-known perspectives on the notion of semantic multivalence of verbs: Smith's (1997) distinction between basic and derived situation types and de Swart's (1998) distinction between grammatical aspectual operators and contextual operators (coercion). The analysis will lead me to conclude that neither proposal (i.e., Smith's and de Swart's) is theoretically tenable or empirically viable for studies of L2 development.

5.3.1 Smith: Basic and derived situation types

To clearly demarcate the distinct categorization of situation aspect and viewpoint aspect, Smith (1997: 17) proposes that '[t]he situation type of a sentence is conveyed by the verb and its arguments, the verb constellation'. She adds, however, that 'the aspectual value of the basic-level verb constellation is overridden by that of an adverbial or other relevant form' (p. 55). Smith explains further that situation type-shifts may be brought about by the effect of adverbials (e.g., *for an hour*), superlexical morphemes (e.g., *to begin, to finish*), and verbal morphology (e.g., progressive) (pp. 52ff.). The following are examples of each one of the type-shifters mentioned by Smith:[11]

78a. The child *began* building a castle.   [superlexical morpheme]
78b. Guy *repeatedly* knocked at the door.   [adverbial]
78c. I am *hating* zoology class.   [dynamic verb morphology]

The three categories of type-shifters bring about a 'clash' of temporal values with the particular situation type they modify. The first example shows that if we take the accomplishment *to build a castle* and modify it with a superlexical morpheme (e.g., *began building a castle*) we focus on the inception state of the accomplishment.[12] Thus, the resultant derived basic situation type is an achievement. The shift in aspectual values triggered by the superlexical morphemes (e.g., begin, start, continue) is significant when applied to stative verbs because it changes a [–dynamic] verb to a [+dynamic] one. For instance, in the following sentence, the use of the superlexical morpheme *began* focuses on the initial stage of *understanding* and not necessarily on the protracted state of *understanding.*

79. Lucas began to understand.

The effect of adverbials is also relevant to bring about a shift in lexical aspectual value. In sentence (78b), the adverbial (*repeatedly*) 'overrides' the basic verb constellation temporal value, thus shifting the interpretation from a semelfactive to an activity (i.e., from instantaneous to durative).

Similarly, the addition of the adjunct *suddenly* to sentence (80) triggers an inchoative reading of a stative verb, effectively focusing on the beginning of the state (as opposed to the state itself).

80. Suddenly, Lucas knew the truth.

Smith also discusses the type of shift triggered by durative adverbials from a basic-level category to a multiple-event activity (p. 50). For instance, Smith points out that the basic situation type represented in the following sentences are a semelfactive (81), an achievement (82) and an accomplishment (83). As represented in the context of each sentence, however, we obtain a derived reading of an accomplishment (81), a semelfactive (82) and an activity (83). These examples are taken from Smith (1991: 86). Note that each sentence includes the addition of an adverbial that triggers the derived reading of the situation type (i.e., *for 5 minutes, for 5 days* and *for hours*).

81. Al knocked at the door for 5 minutes.
82. Al found his watch for 5 days.
83. The ferry went back and forth for hours.

Finally, Smith considers shifted situation types brought about by the dynamicity feature contributed by the addition of specific morphological markers such as the progressive marker (the so-called 'marked cases'). Smith argues that the progressive viewpoint is associated with dynamism, thus they serve to change a state (*to hate*) to a process (*I am hating zoology*), or in example (84), it endows the state 'with dynamism, a property associated with events, and focus on that property' (pp. 52).[13]

84. The river is smelling particularly bad these days. (example 42c in Smith)

To summarize thus far, Smith argues that the lexical value of aspect is composed of the inherent semantic value of the interaction between the verb (temporal) and its arguments (atemporal). Other elements that are not arguments of the verb proper, such as adverbials, phasal verbs and verbal morphology also play a role in determining categories of lexical aspect. These factors, however, give rise to derived verb classes or shifted lexical aspectual classes.

   Although Smith states that shifted situation types are defined through strictly lexical and grammatical means, she specifies that narrative and discourse principles may also have an effect on the categorization of lexical aspectual classes. For instance, in sentence (85), the second clause (i.e., *Mary threw the glass*) leads us to focus on the inception point of the state of *John being dumbfounded*. Smith concludes that '[t]he situation type of the verb constellation is indeterminate ... since both basic-level and shifted interpretations can arise' (p. 49).

85. John was dumbfounded when Mary threw the glass.

In other cases, the effect of the discursive context and world knowledge in general (including pragmatics) can be noted within the confines of a sentence-level analysis of verbal predicates. Smith (1997: 51) thus notes that in sentences (86) and (87), there is a time discrepancy in the temporal information conveyed by the verbal predicate (*riding a bicycle* and *feeding the cat*) and the adverbial (*last year*).

86. Susan rode a bicycle last year.
87. Marcia fed the cat last year.

In both sentences, the clash of temporal features between adverbial and verb type is resolved by means of a repetitive interpretation of the basic verb type. Thus, both sentences are normally and correctly interpreted as conveying a habitual meaning, on the iterativity of the respective situations. The iterative meaning, however, is not part of the verb itself or the adverbial. Rather, it is contributed by the hearer 'triggered by information in the context'. Similarly, Filip (1999) argues that '[m]any shifts require us to draw on our general knowledge. In [88] and [89], such knowledge contributes to our selecting the iterative interpretation . . .'

88. Max won for a year.
89. John rode the bus to work for three years.

The type of contextual knowledge necessary to correctly interpret the temporal meaning of a sentence can be quite sophisticated. For instance, in contrast with (88) and (89), Smith notes that sentence (90) 'is unlikely to be regarded as a habitual'.

90. John moved to a new apartment last year.

More than contextual knowledge, Smith notes that 'pragmatic knowledge is essential to the habitual stative interpretation'. Finally, Smith points out that the effect of contextual and pragmatic knowledge is even more crucial in cases in which the interpretation of verb constellations is vague and gives rise to alternative aspectual classes. For instance, the predicates in sentences (91) and (92) can be classified as either activities or accomplishments.

91. Mary combed her hair.
92. John mowed the lawn.

The addition of either the *in-adverbial* or the *for-adverbial* would be felicitous with both sentences, thus confirming that their lexical aspectual status is ambiguous in the absence of specific contextual knowledge. Smith concludes that 'vagueness is due to lexical factors of the verb constellations and pragmatic knowledge about the events'.

5.3.2 Shifts as viewpoint aspect

Smith's position on the categorical changes prompted by shifts is ambivalent. In particular, there is a significant change in her position expressed in the first and second edition of her book. In the 1991 edition, Smith distinguished derived situation types from shifted situation types. She claimed that the former do not represent cases of a shift in focus from the basic-level category. In contrast, the 1997 edition classifies all shifts as derived situation types. In essence, 'a derived situation type is formed by a situation type shift' (1997: 48). More importantly, the newly defined derived situation types are a systematic phenomenon to the extent that Smith claims that '. . . situation type meaning is compositional: it is built up with the verb, arguments and *adverbs of a sentence*' (1997: 4). Hence, we are faced with the possibility that what is described at first as an exception to the rule (category shifts) may, in fact, be part of the rule (this is reminiscent of Mourelatos' quote in Section 5.2). Ultimately, Smith argues that there is no essential 'shift' of lexical aspectual class. Smith argues that the types of mechanisms that supposedly 'shift' a lexical aspectual class present 'a situation from an unusual perspective' (p. 52). For instance, she discusses in detail the types of shifts that happen with state verbs such as perception verbs and personal property verbs as shown in (93) and (94) as follows:

93a. I saw a star.
93b. Suddenly, I saw a star. (p. 56)

94a. Joe was a hero.
94b. Joe was being a hero. (p. 58)

Smith argues that 'adverbials or other contextual support is often needed for the non-stative readings, indicating that they are derived rather than basic' (p. 57). This is similar to Klein's argument (1994: 74) that adverbials do not change type of situation; they only make the description more explicit (because lexical content says nothing about boundaries, duration, etc.). In other words, they are stative at the basic-level of categorization. Moreover, Smith proposes that 'the basic-level verb constellation is always recognizable to the receiver of the sentence' (p. 52). For instance, the lexical morphemes 'modulate the focus of a situation rather than determining the situation itself' (p. 48).

To make matters more confusing, it appears that Smith's description of shifted/derived situation types is akin to the description of viewpoint aspect. On the one hand, Smith posits that '[a]spectual viewpoints present situations with a particular perspective or focus, rather like the focus of a camera lens. *Viewpoint gives a full or partial view of the situation talked about*' (p. 2, stress added). On the other hand, while delimiting the definition of shifted/derived situation types, Smith explains that '[s]peakers may present a situation as a whole, with a broad view. Or they may take a narrower view, focusing on one endpoint or the middle of a situation' (p. 48).[14] In fact, Smith specifically points out that '[v]iewpoint aspect gives temporal perspective to a sentence. More subtly, *situation aspect also involves point of view*' (p. 1, stress added). In essence, both lexical and grammatical aspect (i.e., situation and viewpoint aspect) appear to be determined by the viewpoint of the speaker (or hearer), thus blurring the theoretical distinction between them. Furthermore, even the procedure used to convey the specific viewpoint is – in some cases at least – the same (i.e., verbal morphology).

One possible solution to the problem of accounting for the apparent shifts in meaning of lexical aspectual classes is to consider a composite definition of aspect in which there is no categorical distinction between situation type and viewpoint aspect. That position has been advanced by Lunn (1985). Making reference to Spanish in particular, Lunn claims that '(the Spanish) Preterite/Imperfect distinction is defined not in terms of categories of verbs or of time spans, but by the point of view which a speaker adopts with respect to a verbal situation' (p. 51). Lunn claims further, in contraposition to Smith, that the second component of aspect (i.e., viewpoint aspect) subsumes the first one (i.e., situation aspect). I return to the discussion of this possibility in Section 6.

5.3.3 de Swart: coercion

de Swart (1998) makes a distinction between aspectual operators such as the Perfect or the Progressive versus non-aspectual operators such as the perfective–imperfective markers: French *Passé Composé* and *Imparfait* are aspectually sensitive tenses. de Swart explains that '. . . the simple past in English is *aspectually neutral* and the aspectual nature of the eventuality is inherited from the aspectual class of the sentence' (p. 368). In contrast, the '. . . French past tenses are similar to the determiners *much/many* and *little/few*, in that they do not convert the description into an aspectually different one, but that they select for a homogeneous or a quantized eventuality description' (p. 369). In essence, the French past tenses are *aspectually sensitive* past tense operators. de Swart effectively reverses the direction of the coercion effect brought about by grammatical aspect (as proposed by Smith's viewpoint aspect). That is, instead of the *Imparfait/Passé Simple* coercing, for instance, a state into an event, de Swart argues that the French past tenses simply select for a particular eventuality and, if the eventuality is not matched (e.g., an event with *Imparfait*), the eventuality is coerced in order to match the past tense form, not unlike the process that sanctions the use of determiners *much/ many* and *little/few* in non-prototypical ways (e.g., *He drank many coffees*).

Thus, to account for the shift in meaning of basic lexical aspectual classes, de Swart proposes that there are both explicit and implicit mechanisms. More specifically, she argues for the existence of explicit aspectual operators that serve to '. . . map sets of eventualities of a certain type onto sets of eventualities of some (possibly other) type'. (p. 359). The explicit aspectual operators recognized by de Swart are: (1) duration adverbials, (2) the Progressive and (3) the Perfect. de Swart also proposes the existence of a contextual reinterpretation process called coercion. Coercion has three main characteristics: (1) it '. . . is of the same semantic type as an aspectual operator such as Perfect, the Progressive or a duration adverbial', (2) it 'is syntactically and morphologically invisible: it is governed by implicit contextual reinterpretation mechanisms triggered by the need to resolve aspectual conflicts' and (3) it 'is triggered if there is a conflict between the aspectual character of the eventuality description and the aspectual constraints of some other element in the context. The felicity of an aspectual reinterpretation is strongly dependent on linguistic context and knowledge of the world'.

For instance, de Swart claims that we can coerce a state into an event by emphasizing the starting point of the state (95a), a telic event into a process (95b), and a telic event into a state by providing an iterative meaning (95c) or a habitual meaning (95d) (all the examples are from de Swart).[15]

95a. Suddenly, I knew the answer.

95b. I read a book for a few minutes.

95c. John played the sonata for about eight hours.

95d. For months, the train arrived late.

de Swart's examples of pragmatic coercion are problematic for two reasons. First, it is not entirely clear why sentences (95a–95d) should exemplify coercion instead of the application of an explicit aspectual operator. In other words, should adjuncts (adverbials) be regarded as explicit aspectual operators? Or, alternatively, should they be regarded as implicit contextual aspectual operators, thus giving rise to coercion effects? In effect, the meaning shifts in (95a–95d) are brought about by duration adverbials (*for a few minutes, for about eight hours* and *for months*, respectively), which are defined by de Swart as explicit operators (as described earlier).[16]

Second, it is difficult to see how the coercion effect of non-durative adverbials on the classification of lexical aspectual classes should be regarded as 'syntactically invisible' (the second characteristic of coercion). For instance, in *Suddenly, I knew the answer*, we have an explicit (non-invisible) adverbial that triggers inchoativity. In this respect, it appears that the adverbial provides for an *explicit* contextual reinterpretation trigger. In other words, unless we rely on a very restrictive interpretation of what may be part of syntactic information, the adverbial *suddenly* should be regarded as an explicit component of a syntactic structure with obvious effects on the structural template of which it forms a part. I discuss a possible solution to this dilemma in Section 6.

5.3.4 The timing of the coercion mechanism

Caudal and Roussarie (2005: 265) claim that the difference in Smith's and de Swart's models can be significant, given that the primary function of Smith's viewpoints 'is not to shift an eventuality type into another, but to add information of a new kind to it'. The distinct view of coercion represented by Smith and de Swart is also distinguished by the sequential application of coercion mechanisms. In Smith's case, it is the selection of the grammatical marker of past tense (through viewpoint aspect) that determines any shift in lexical aspectual interpretation (although not necessarily the lexical aspectual classification). In de Swart's case, coercion is effected before the grammatical aspect is marked on the verb. She explains that the analysis of the following sentences leads Smith to propose that they 'present states as dynamic situations, because they use the viewpoint of the

Progressive, which in English normally only occurs with non-statives' (1998: 362).

96a. Susan is liking this play a great deal.
96b. Peter is believing in ghosts these days.

de Swart claims instead that 'the state has been coerced into a dynamic eventuality by Csd (Coercion of state into a dynamic process) before the Progressive applies, in order to satisfy the input conditions on the aspectual operator'. In other words, there is a sequential application of the coercion mechanism that is reflected in the representation of sentence (96a).

97. Susan is liking this play.
     [PRES [PROG [Csd [Susan like this play]]]]

In order to argue for a shift from one lexical aspectual class to another, we must conclude that there exist two different lexical aspectual classes: one before coercion is applied and another one brought about by coercion. The important question is whether the interpretation of the verb *to like* in sentences (96a, 97) should be classified as a shifted verb (as proposed by de Swart), or whether it should be considered as the same verb but viewed from the perspective of the grammatical marker (i.e., the Progressive), as Smith proposes.

In principle, de Swart and Smith agree on the shifted interpretation of the stative verb into a dynamic one. The main theoretical difference between these two positions is that in Smith's proposal, the Progressive is the operator that brings about a different interpretation of the verbs *to like/to believe* (effectively destativizing them; although, in principle, the verb's lexical aspectual class would remain the same). In contrast, in de Swart's model, the verb has been coerced into a different lexical aspectual class *before* the Progressive is applied. Interestingly, de Swart (1998: 351, stress added) explains that 'aspectual operators *impose a certain viewpoint on the eventuality* introduced by the eventuality description'. This is reminiscent of Smith's conceptualization of viewpoint aspect.[17]

5.4 Two categories or one? Lexical versus grammatical aspect

5.4.1 No shifts of lexical aspectual class

Contrary to Smith and de Swart, others have explicitly argued against the notion that the boundaries between grammatical and lexical aspects can be blurred (e.g., Arche, 2006; Depraetre, 1995; Filip, 1999; Ziegeler, 2007).

Depraetre (1995) argues that '[t]he (a)telic character of a sentence, unlike (un)boundedness, is not affected by the progressive', as shown in the following examples (pp. 4–5):

98. John opened the parcel.   [telic bounded]
99. John was opening the parcel.   [telic unbounded]

Depraetre further argues that Smith, among others, mistakenly assumes that the Perfect could have an effect on situation aspect: 'Although the use of the perfect affects (un)boundedness, it does not affect a sentence's aspect or Aktionsart' (p. 12). In sum, Depraetre makes a strong case to argue for the distinct meaning of telicity (associated with inherent lexical aspectual meanings) used to indicate potential endpoints of an eventuality as opposed to boundedness (associated with viewpoint or grammatical aspectual meanings), which is used to indicate actual temporal boundaries. Boundedness is determined through grammatical markings (either inflectional or periphrastic).[18] Overall, grammatical aspect, like lexical aspect, makes reference to complete versus ongoing situations. However, while telicity is used to describe the aspectual nature of events at the lexical level, the notion of 'boundedness' – which is also related to endpoints as stated by Depraetre – is relevant to describe the properties of grammatical aspect.

For instance, Güell (1998: 102) proposes that Preterite and Imperfect are defined not so much by the semantic features of punctuality or durativity, as by whether they are temporally delimited or not as shown in the following examples:

100a. Lo supo (PRET)/*sabía (IMP) durante mucho tiempo.
      (temporally delimited)
      (S/he) knew it for a long time.
100b. Lo *supo (PRET)/sabía (IMP) desde hacía mucho tiempo.
      (temporally non-delimited)
      (S/he) knew it from a long time ago.

Along the same lines, Filip (1999: 72) asks: 'Do shifts force us to abandon the assumption that individual verbs are classified into eventuality types on the basis of their inherent lexical semantic properties?' Filip answers categorically: 'Certainly not'. Filip explains that the classification of lexical aspectual classes is analogous to the mass and count nouns classification. That is, in both classification systems, there are different degrees of countability or individuation that are in agreement with a prototype theory

(Rosch and Mervis, 1975). Furthermore, from a practical point of view, by abandoning the classification of verbs into lexical aspectual classes, 'we would miss the observation that such shifts are to a large extent systematic and predictable on the basis of the inherent lexical meaning of verbs, on the one hand, and the meaning of contextual factors that induce the shift, on the other hand'.

Similarly, Arche (2006: 173) explicitly argues 'against the perspective that viewpoint values (perfective, "imperfect") are aspectual operators that can modify the inner aspect properties of eventualities'. To substantiate her point, Arche notes that 'the imperfect-habitual viewpoint is compatible with telic predicates' as shown by the following example, in which notwithstanding the use of the imperfective past tense form, every instance in which the writing of the report occurred represented a heterogeneous event.

101. Normalmente Juan redactaba (IMP) el informe en quince minutos.
     Juan used to write the report in 15 minutes.

Thus, Arche concludes that 'the viewpoint does not affect in any sense the nature of the predicate' (p. 174). She claims instead that the perfective form does not shift an atelic verb into a telic one. For instance, the use of the Preterite with atelic verbs such as *to swim* and *to walk* (i.e., *nadar* and *caminar*) does not necessarily make these verbs telic.

102. Pablo nadó (PRET).
     Pablo swam.
103. Juan caminó (PRET).
     Juan walked.

In sum, Arche explicitly argues against de Swart's claim 'that the perfective is an "event type coercer", in the sense that it has the power to turn homogeneous predicates into telic ones'. In contrast, Arche asserts that 'the perfective does not play any role in the inner-aspect properties of a predicate' (pp. 176–77). In other words, aspectual viewpoints expressed through the selection of either Preterite or Imperfect does not have 'any impact on the inner-aspect properties of predicates' (p. 178).

Finally, Ziegeler (2007: 1020) argues that the cases of aspectual conflict, discussed by de Swart (1998), 'can be viewed in different ways by investigating their relation with grammaticalisation and historical change'. For instance, Ziegeler argues that the generalization of the use of the progressive with dynamic verb types (e.g., *she was winning, he was dying*) can be regarded 'as part of the shift towards the verb end of the noun-to-verb continuum' in the transition of English. She adds that

> Coercion in such cases need not be invoked as an independent explanation for aspectual shift, when aspectual shift is part of the grammaticalisation of morphemes initially associated with lexical forms most semantically relevant to their source meanings. . . . Rather than a coercion account, it would be preferable to suggest that such shifts are evidence of prototype extensions of lexico-grammatical, aspectual source correlations over a prolonged time-period.

In other words, Ziegeler's argument substantiates the notion of a continuum of aspectual meanings. In sum, there are cogent reasons to reject the notion of shifts of lexical aspectual classes and to argue instead for a context-based continuum of aspectual meanings.

5.4.2 Privative semantic features

One theoretical approach to substantiating the notion that lexical aspectual classes do not actually shift categories is provided by Olsen's (1997) classification of lexical aspectual classes according to privative features. Olsen argues that semantic meanings may not be cancelled without contradiction or reinforced without redundancy, whereas pragmatic implicatures may be cancelled or reinforced without either. For instance, in sentences (104a, b), *slowly* is part of the semantic meaning of *plodding*, thus it cannot be cancelled. In contrast, in sentences (105a, b), *being tired* is the result of conversational implicature; hence, the sentence in which *tiredness* is associated with *plod* is acceptable.

104a. E. plodded along, #but not slowly.
104b. E. plodded along, #slowly.
105a. M. plodded along, although she wasn't tired.
105b. M. plodded along; she was very tired.

In parallel with the contrast between semantic meanings and pragmatic implicatures, Olsen contends that positive lexical aspectual features (e.g., [+telic]) belong to semantics and, in contrast, negative features (e.g., [−telic]) are associated with conversational implicatures. Moreover, she proposes that lexical aspect and grammatical aspect can be conceptualized

Table 2.4 Privative semantic features
of lexical aspectual classes

Aspectual class	Telic	Dynamic	Durative
State			+
Activity		+	+
Accomplishment	+	+	+
Achievement	+	+	
Semelfactive		+	
Stage-level state	+		+

Adapted from Olsen (1997, p. 26).

as a set of universal semantic privative features that allows for unmarked features to be marked positively, but it does not allow positively marked features to be unmarked. Crucially, she claims that '[m]arked semantic features LIMIT rather than DETERMINE lexical aspect interpretation, because some factors may be left unspecified; full interpretation is determined by pragmatic principles operating on the semantic representation within the larger discourse context' (pp. 25–26). Table 2.4 shows the representation of lexical aspectual classes according to privative features.

Olsen argues that the privative features [+durative], [+dynamic] and [+telic] 'represent the consistent semantic meanings of lexical aspect' (p. 51) denoting a temporal interval, change and an end, respectively. For instance, let us review the following two sentences in which the same verb (i.e., to run) is atelic or telic depending on the complement that accompanies it.

106a. Carl Lewis ran.   [+dynamic, +durative]
106b. Carl Lewis ran a mile.   [+dynamic, +telic]

As Olsen explains, in sentence (106a), the verb *run* is represented as [+durative] and [+dynamic]. Crucially, within a privative analysis, it does not have the semantic feature [+telic], thus, we infer that it is atelic (i.e., an activity). Furthermore, given that the feature of atelicity is unmarked, we have a pragmatic implicature and thus it may be cancelled. In effect, the addition of the durative adverbial *a mile* cancels atelicity, thus shifting the verb *run* from the category of activity to the category of accomplishment. Now, let us consider the opposite situation in which we change the telic verb to an atelic one with the addition of an adverbial of frequency as in the following sentence:

107. Carl Lewis ran a mile for years.   [+dynamic, +telic, +durative]

As previously stated, *run a mile* has the features [+dynamic] and [+telic]. Thus, neither feature is semantically cancellable. The previous sentence, however, is acceptable and, more importantly, it does have an atelic reading. In this case, the semantic meaning of telicity has not really been cancelled, but rather it has been iterated with the adverbial (see also Dowty, 1972, 1986 with regard to the blurred line between atelic and telic events).

The same argument would be applicable for the modification of an achievement verb with the only difference that the feature [+durative] is absent. For instance, an achievement verb such as *win* will be represented with the features [+dynamic] and [+telic] only.

108a. Carl Lewis won the race.   [+dynamic, +telic]

As it was the case for the verb phrase *run a mile*, the positively marked feature [+telic] is not cancellable. As shown in sentence (108b), however, the telicity of the verb *to win* can be iterated. Through iteration, we avoid the outright cancellation of the feature of telicity. I discuss the concept of iterativity in more detail in Section 7.

108b. Carl Lewis won the race for years.   [+dynamic, +telic, +durative]

Olsen makes a similar point about the asymmetry in distinction between states and dynamic events: activities, accomplishments and achievements have the semantic feature [+dynamic], whereas states do not. More specifically, Olsen argues that 'the frequent interpretation of states as dynamic is not semantic but a result of conversational pragmatic implicatures associated with unmarked lexical aspectual features. . . . As predicted by the privative analysis of the lexical aspectual features, verbs unmarked for dynamicity do not behave as a class' (p. 70). Olsen further substantiates her argument by pointing out that the operational tests typically used to distinguish dynamic versus non-dynamic verbs are used to identify dynamic verbs (e.g., imperatives, complements of persuade verbs). Thus, they are asymmetrical tests: they identify dynamic events, or alternatively, they identify when states fail to occur (p. 36).

Let us now review Olsen's claim in the context of the proposed shifting of lexical aspectual classes. Whether conceptualized as derived situation types (cf. Smith), or as coerced lexical aspectual classes (cf. de Swart), the shift of lexical aspectual classes presents us with an obvious dilemma regarding the principled distinction between the levels of lexical and viewpoint aspects. On the one hand, verbs seem to be associated with some basic aspectual meanings (e.g., Arche, 2006; Depraetre, 1995; Filip, 1999). On the other hand, there seem to be clear effects of interaction between those basic meanings and the meaning contributed by the larger contextual framework in which those verbs are embedded. One solution, proposed in different guises by Smith and de Swart, is to think of these changes in meaning as category shifts of lexical aspectual classes. Another possibility is implicitly described in Olsen's proposal about the use of privative semantic features to classify lexical aspectual classes. Olsen's framework entails that there may be some default meanings that are further specified in the context of a larger piece of discourse.

6. Aspect as a Contextual Phenomenon

In a two-component theory of tense-aspect meanings as proposed by Smith (1997), there are two theoretical constructs (i.e., situation and viewpoint aspects). In contrast, the proposal that tense-aspect meanings are defined on a continuum spanning a range of options from general, invariant to highly contextualized meanings represents a single-construct theory of aspect (cf. Lunn, 1985). In this section, I describe a single construct definition of tense-aspect meanings and in so doing I define the main dependent variable of studies on the L2 acquisition of tense-aspect.

6.1 Scope of analysis of tense-aspectual knowledge

The discussion of Smith's derived situation types and de Swart's distinction between grammatical and pragmatic operators leads us to conclude that the representation of tense-aspectual knowledge may vary significantly depending on the scope of information regarded as necessary towards a definition of aspect. Klein (1994), for instance, recognizes three different levels for the selective description of a situation: (1) the lexical content (predicates and associated arguments and adjuncts), (2) the proposition level (structure-based contextual information) and (3) the utterance interpretation through inferred contextual information. Chung and Timberlake (1985), for their part, propose the existence of four levels of semantic structure for the representation of the properties of aspect: (1) the verbal predicate alone, (2) the verbal predicate and its syntactic arguments (internal and external), (3) the verbal predicate plus the predicate frame (the proposition) and (4) the proposition in the context of connected sentences (text). The distinction is illustrated with the following examples for each level:

Lexical verb: to get angry
Verb phrase: John got angry at a stranger.
Proposition: John got angry at a stranger on the bus today.
Narrative: John got angry at a stranger on the bus today and then apologized.

Chung and Timberlake claim that 'languages that encode aspect by obligatory choices of verbal morphology make reference to aspect parameters at the level of the proposition' (p. 216). Their position broadly coincides with the position advocated by Smith reviewed earlier (cf. derived situation types), and, by extension, by the majority of L2 researchers who agree with Smith on the categorization of lexical and grammatical aspect as two independent components of aspectual knowledge. In contrast, de Swart's argument limits the definition of aspect to the verb-phrase level, given that most adverbials bring about coercion, which is defined as a pragmatic mechanism separate from grammatically defined processes. In this section, I summarize some proposals that have argued for a representation of tense-aspectual meanings above the verb-phrase level.

6.2 Syntactic constructions

As correctly pointed out by Smith and de Swart, the most prototypical lexical aspectual class assigned to a verb may sometimes conflict with the eventuality type expressed by the overall temporal meaning of the verb in the context in which it is embedded. Michaelis (2004: 25) shows how the conflict is resolved with example (109):

109. It worked, sir! We **bored** them right out of the game.
    (Marcie, *Peanuts* 10/97)

In its prototypical representation, the verb *bore* licenses two thematic roles: theme and experiencer. In the shifted interpretation of the same verb, as presented in the example selected by Michaelis, *bore* licenses three thematic roles: an agent, a theme and a goal. 'Accordingly, the sentence has a construal in which boring is a means of propulsion' (p. 26). Michaelis, following Filip and others, proposes that verbs are embedded in constructions, which generate aspectual interpretations that convey meanings that represent more than just the sum of the parts that constitute any particular construction. Michaelis thus argues that 'constructions can alter what words (and their syntactic projections) designate' (p. 30). For example, when a stative verb receives an inchoative construal (e.g., the onset of boredom in *They were bored in a minute*), the situation described 'counts as an achievement'. On the other hand, state verbs receive episodic readings when they are associated with frequency adverbial constructions, because the latter 'denotes a more general situation type, the event type' (p. 35). For instance, in the sentence *I'm liking your explanation*, the 'activity feature "wins out" over the stative feature of the input lexical item'. As a consequence, the temporary states expressed in similar sentences 'are not in fact states but homogeneous activities'. Similarly, Michaelis points out that '[a]n achievement predication, which entails the occurrence of a preparatory activity is for all intents and purposes an accomplishment', as can be seen in the identical lexical aspectual nature of the sentences *She was winning the race* and *She was fixing the fence* (p. 39).

Along the same lines, Filip proposes that 'verbs (along with their arguments) and adjuncts are mutually constraining . . . this is in essence the strategy I propose here for the treatment of adjuncts that function as aspectual operators' (p. 132). For instance, the analysis of the following pair of sentences leads Filip to conclude that 'it is not an adjunct on its own that determines the telicity of a given sentence'.

110a. The conductor DANCED into the orchestra pit. (telic)
110b. ?The conductor SMILED into the orchestra pit. (atelic)

In essence, both verbs in sentences (110a) and (110b) are atelic verbs (activities), but only the first one becomes a telic event after the addition of the same adverbial clause. In other words, each verb seems to be associated with specific nuances of meaning that make each one viable (or not) for specific changes in aspectual interpretations. In sum, Filip concludes that '[g]rammatical constructions have meanings that do not arise compositionally from the meaning of their constituents' (p. 133). Filip specifies further that 'there is no "shift" or "overriding" of the verb's meaning. The inherent meanings of verbs are part of the meaning of a construction, but the construction as a whole in addition contributes its own meaning' (p. 142).

6.3 Discourse

Looking beyond the level of syntactic constructions, several researchers have argued that aspectual contrasts should be defined as discourse-level rather than as sentence-level phenomena (e.g., Dowty, 1986; Dry, 1983; Hopper, 1979, 1982; Kamp and Rohrer, 1983; Silva-Corvalán, 1983, 1986;

Smith, 1997; Vet and Vetters, 1994; Waugh, 1990). Doiz-Bienzobas (1995: 20–27) claims that discourse-based approaches to the analysis of aspectual contrasts can be classified into three main strands defined by grounding (e.g., Hopper, 1979, 1982), text-structure (e.g., Silva-Corvalán, 1983, 1986) and temporal relationships between sentences (e.g., Dowty, 1986; Kamp and Rohrer, 1983).

6.3.1 Grounding

Hopper (1979, 1982) proposes that narrative grounding (i.e., foreground and background) is correlated with the use of the perfective–imperfective aspectual markers. Hopper (1982: 6, stress added) argues that 'the encoding of percepts in the world takes place within a discourse rather than a sentence framework, and that the *potential or real bounding of events* in this discourse is a significant parameter in the strategies for formulating an utterance'. For instance, given that the perfective form conveys boundedness and that foregrounded events in a narrative are bounded, we conclude that the perfective form is mostly used in the foreground of a narrative. Conversely, the imperfective is mostly restricted to the marking of eventualities in the background of a story. With regard to Spanish in particular, the Imperfect is associated with backgrounded situations of a narrative, while the Preterite is associated with the foregrounded eventualities.

Along the same lines, Dowty (1986: 48) proposes that the sequence or overlap of events and states in a narrative is determined by 'the times at which we assume that states or events actually obtain or transpire in the real world, intervals of time which may in some cases be greater than the intervals for which they are simply asserted'. For instance, for non-dynamic predicates one normally makes the assumption that the stative was true in advance of the beginning point asserted by the narrative, as well as after that time. In the following example from Dowty, however, the adverb *suddenly* cancels the assumption that the state obtained before a specific inception point (reference time).

111. John went over the day's perplexing events once more in his mind.
     Suddenly, he was fast asleep.

In this case, the stative (i.e., *to be fast asleep*) moves narrative time forward because the state of sleeping is not interpreted to overlap with previous events (see also Klein, 1994: 74). Thus, by placing the stative in the foreground of the narrative, we obtain a non-prototypical reading of the stative verb. Finally, the argument about grounding is also supported by Binnick's (1991: 372) list of functional uses of the perfective–imperfective contrast: narration versus description, principal action versus secondary circumstances and sequenced versus non-sequenced action.

6.3.2 Text structure

For her part, Silva-Corvalán (1983, 1986) argues that the use of the perfective–imperfective contrast in Spanish is correlated with specific sections (text-structure) of a narrative. Taking Labov's framework of narrative structure as a point of departure, she states that a fully developed narrative contains the following sections: abstract, orientation, complicating action, evaluation, result or resolution and coda. On the basis of data from oral narratives produced by thirty native speakers, she observed that the uses of the Imperfect and the Preterite in the narrative were unequally distributed among the different sections.[19] More specifically, the Imperfect was mostly restricted to the orientation and evaluation: 48 per cent in the orientation, 38 per cent in evaluation and 13 per cent in the complicating action. In contrast, the Preterite was mostly used in the sections of the complicating action, the resolution and coda.[20] Moreover, in terms of proportional use within each section, the contrasts were even more pronounced. In the orientation section, the proportional use of the Imperfect reached 70 per cent, whereas the Preterite was used only with 4 per cent of verbs. This is not surprising given that the function of both the orientation and the Imperfect coincide to the extent that they provide a background for the narrative. Indeed, in the orientation section, there is information about the time, place and participants in the event. In contrast, within the resolution-coda sections, there was, on average, a 76 per cent of use of the Preterite.

Silva-Corvalán concluded that, while the Imperfect may have the meaning of habituality or continuousness, deciding which one of these two meanings is conveyed by the Imperfect is partly determined by the narrative context. She points out that sentences marked with the Imperfect *in the orientation section* of a narrative may convey either habituality or continuousness. In the sections on *complicating action* of a narrative, however, the habitual meaning of the Imperfect is disallowed. Let us see how this works with an excerpt from a narrative analysed by Silva-Corvalán.

112.   g. Entonces botó (PRET) el, el el cuaderno de sociales al suelo
       h. *y con el pie lo daba (IMP) vuelta, la hoja,*
       i. *y miraba (IMP) de arriba p'abajo así*
       j. *y estaba copiando (PROGR) lo más feliz y contento.*

k. *Ya iba (IMP) en la sexta ya.*
l. El professor estaba (IMP) en la otra esquina.
m. Y a esto que el professor le, le hace así (gesture),

g. Then he dropped the, the, the social sciences notebook on the floor
h. and with the foot he'd turn it over, the page,
i. and he'd look from top to bottom like this
j. and he was copying so happily.
k. He was in the sixth one already.
l. The teacher was in the other corner.
m. And suddenly the teacher goes, goes like this (gesture),

In the aforementioned extract, all lines, but for line *l*, are part of the complicating action; line *l*, the only outlier, is part of the orientation section. Focusing thus on the lines that comprise the complicating action, we notice that only lines *g* and *m* are part of the narrative plot. In contrast, lines *h* through *k* (highlighted in italics in the excerpt) are restricted clauses that are not temporally ordered; that is, they can be reshuffled without altering the temporal sequence. Interestingly, lines *h* through *k* are marked with the Imperfect. The meaning of the Imperfect in these sentences, however, cannot be habituality but continuousness. Effectively, Silva-Corvalán argues 'the narrative context cancels out the meaning of repetition or habitualness' (1986: 240).

On the other hand, the use of the Preterite does not guarantee that its use with the description of events will necessarily entail temporal juncture. In the following example from Silva-Corvalán, for instance, the series of events that occurred at the party did not necessarily occur in sequential order (in fact, it is quite likely that they all overlapped or they occurred repeatedly in turns):

113. A: ¿Y cómo lo pasaste (PRET) en la fiesta?
        So how was the party?
     B: Estupendo. Bailé (PRET), canté (PRET) y comí (PRET) montones.
        Great. I danced, sang and ate a lot.

Notice that if we try to replace the Preterite with the Imperfect, the result is ungrammatical. This is true in spite of the fact that the notion of coexistence has been postulated as one of the defining features of the Imperfect (e.g., Guitart, 1978).

114. A: ¿Y cómo lo pasaste en la fiesta?
     B: *Estupendo. Bailaba (IMP), cantaba (IMP) y comía (IMP) montones.

Because of this contrast in the use of the Preterite and Imperfect, Silva-Corvalán concludes that 'the identification of coexistence and recurrence may also be the function of the Preterite in certain contexts. This lends support to my hypothesis that the general referential meaning of a verbal form may in part overlap with the meaning of another and that form-specific meanings must be identified in contexts of use' (p. 244). She argues that verbal forms in isolation (cf., aspectual morphology) do not have specific meanings, but rather general referential meaning that becomes specific in accordance with the type of speech event in which they are embedded. In agreement with this position, Binnick (1991: 155) argues that 'there are a number of different *contextual* meanings which the aspects seem to bear in particular contexts, though they may not bear each of these meanings in *all* contexts'.

6.3.3 Sentence sequencing

Finally, Kamp and Rohrer (1983) proposed a formal approach to account for the choice of grammatical aspect within the context of discourse representation structure (DRS). The main argument behind DRS is that certain temporal phenomena can only be analysed according to how interlocutors or discourse participants in general process information within the confines of the discourse being constructed. For this reason, the meaning of the perfective–imperfective distinction instantiated in the Romance languages cannot be understood from the analysis of sentences in isolation (see, for instance, Birdsong's 1992 critique of Coppieters' 1987 study). DRS entails the application of construction rules to each adjacent pair of sentences (e.g., precedence relation, overlap relation and interpretation relation). In a normal narrative text, there exists a partial correspondence between the temporal order of the reported events and the order of presentation of those events. That is to say, the sequence of events of the narrative mirrors the sequence of events in reality: there is temporal juncture. Moreover, each event provides the reference point for the next event in the sequence.

Dowty (1986) argued that the discourse semantics advocated by Kamp and Rohrer could be more adequately explained by taking into account the contribution of both semantic and pragmatic principles.

More specifically, Dowty proposes that the temporal relationships between sentences in discourse are represented by (1) semantic aspectual classes, (2) a single temporal discourse interpretation principle: the reference time of each sentence in a discourse is interpreted to be a time consistent with the time adverbials of the sentence, or otherwise immediately following the reference time of the previous sentence (see Reinhart, 1984; von Stutterheim and Klein, 1987) and (3) 'a large dose of Gricean conversational implicature and "common sense" reasoning based on the hearer's knowledge of real world communication' (p. 41). In fact, Dowty argues further that these pragmatic presuppositions obtain for sentences separated from their reference by other sentences, and that presuppositions are not independent of the type of state involved. For instance, sentence (115) generates an abnormal discourse under the common sense (pragmatic) assumption that inanimate objects do not move on their own (unless otherwise specified by the narrator).

115. The book$_i$ was on the table at t_0 . . . Mary put the book$_i$ on the table at t_n.

On the other hand, the pragmatic interpretation of the previous situation does not entail that the hearer will assume the same for all types of statives. In the following sentence, John will not necessarily remain at the finish line after the specific time when the narrator specifies that the state obtains:

116. The runner$_i$ was at the finish line at t_0 . . . the runner$_i$ returned to the finish line at t_n.

Of course, there is a graded hierarchy of likelihood that one situation will obtain before or after a reference time, and not everyone will necessarily agree that sentence (116) obtains any more than sentence (115). This is explained by the fact that there is a prototypical meaning associated with statives. But, it is the pragmatic conditions that determine the overriding effect of those underlying default interpretations what makes the value of the pragmatic principles more attractive if we are to provide a comprehensive account of aspect marking phenomena. Because of this, Dowty claims that 'an enormous amount of real-world knowledge and expectation must be built into any system which mimics the understanding that humans bring to the temporal interpretations of statives in discourse, so no simple, nonpragmatic theory of discourse interpretation is going to handle them effectively' (p. 52).

6.4 Default lexical aspectual classes

I introduced Section 6 with the claim that the representation of tense-aspect is predicated on a continuum spanning a range of meanings, from invariant to highly contextualized. The discussion thus far has substantiated the claim that aspectual contrasts should be defined as discourse-level rather than as sentence-level phenomena. The outstanding question, however, is how to relate this discourse-level representation of tense-aspect meanings with the apparent existence of distinct aspectual meanings represented at the verb-phrase level (discussed at length in Section 5). One possible solution is to consider that lexical aspectual classes should be more precisely defined as default classes (i.e., prototypes) that are further specified in context. The basic rationale for this claim is based on Binnick's (1991) distinction between contextually determined uses and invariant meanings of the perfective–imperfective distinction, an argument that was applied to the analysis of Spanish in particular by Doiz-Bienzobas (1995, 2002). I will also analyse the claim that prototypes or default classes provide for a different way to account for shifts in lexical aspectual categories.

As I discussed in Section 2, an utterance is a partial description of a situation (both at the level of situation aspect and viewpoint aspect). Thus, it is necessary to distinguish between a situation with its associated properties and the linguistic expression that may or may not make those properties explicit. For instance, as pointed out by Klein (1994), if we compare a typical activity verb (a process) such as *to sleep* and a telic event such as *to leave the room*, we readily think of the notion of boundary (telicity) as the discriminating semantic feature that distinguishes these two predicates. There is no reason, however, to believe that sleeping has no boundaries, nor that the process of sleeping is more homogeneous (a defining feature of activity verbs) than leaving a room. In this respect, Klein (1994: 75) proposes two maxims to account for the amount of information conveyed by lexical means (e.g., lexical aspect): *maxim of minimality* (put as little as possible into the lexical content) and *maxim of contrast* (add some feature to the lexical content if otherwise the expression cannot be distinguished in lexical content from some other expression).

In other words, most temporal information will not be part of lexical content, but will be part of world knowledge (unless the maxim of contrast forces us to be more specific). The question, thus, is: how much lexical information do speakers need to explicitly mention in each particular case? In many cases, the answer would be: Not much. For instance, the native speakers of Coppieter's (1987) study were able to reach high levels of agreement about the 'appropriate' past tense marker in French even though they were tested with decontextualized sentences. As noted, however, near-native speakers were apparently unable to rely on these default values of the verbs used in the test sentences. I return to the analysis of findings like the ones from Coppieters in subsequent chapters.

Thus, as a corollary of the application of Klein's maxim of minimality, verbs are typically perceived as belonging to a specific aspectual class by default (unmarked or prototypical reading). For instance, *to breathe* is naturally perceived as an atelic event or activity, whereas *to build* is naturally perceived as a telic event (or, alternatively, as an accomplishment within a classification system that considers the feature of durativity). The difference in lexical aspectual interpretation between these verbs appears to be related to the association with an internal argument that, although not explicitly stated, serves to measure out the event (Tenny, 1994). That is, each verb tends to be associated with a particular type of internal argument that could be a mass or a count noun (for *breathe*), or alternatively, a singular or a plural one (for *build*). By way of illustration, let us analyse the following two combinatorial possibilities for each verb:

117a. (To breathe) air [default]
117b. (To breathe) a poisonous substance
118a. (To build) houses
118b. (To build) a house [default]

The default (unmarked) reading assigned to the verb *to breathe* is associated with the internal argument *air* as a mass noun (117), whereas the default (unmarked) reading assigned to the verb *to build* is associated with the internal argument *a house* as a count noun (118). In contrast, on the basis of Klein's maxim of contrast, the explicit reference to internal arguments that do not act as defaults (*a poisonous substance* and *houses*) renders a non-prototypical reading of *to breathe* and *to build*. The same can be said about all the examples of lexical aspectual classes presented in Section 2 and reproduced again here for the reader's convenience:

States (e.g., *to be, to have, to want*)
Activities (e.g., *to run, to walk, to breathe*)
Accomplishments (e.g., *to write a novel, to build a house, to make a chair*)
Achievements (e.g., *to notice something/someone, to realize something, to reach the peak*)

Notice, for instance, that the examples of accomplishments are all presented in association with a *singular* count noun. More importantly, should these verbs be associated with a *plural* count noun, their classification would change to the category of activity (e.g., *to write novels, to make chairs*). On the other hand, none of the aforementioned activity verbs is associated with any specific internal argument (an unmarked or default interpretation), but should they be associated with a count noun, they would be reclassified as telic events (or accomplishments) (e.g., *to run a mile, to walk 100 meters*).

Let us recapitulate the argument thus far. On the one hand, verbs seem to have some basic aspectual meanings associated with them (e.g., Arche, 2006; Depraetre, 1995; Filip, 1999). On the other hand, there seem to be clear effects of interaction between those basic meanings and the meaning contributed by the larger contextual framework in which those verbs are embedded (e.g., Dowty, 1986; Dry, 1983; Hopper, 1979, 1982; Kamp and Rohrer, 1983; Silva-Corvalán, 1983, 1986; Smith, 1997; Vet and Vetters, 1994; Waugh, 1990). Hence, lexical aspectual categories can be defined as prototypical classes whose meaning can be further specified in the context of a larger piece of discourse. Thus, we can posit the existence of default lexical aspectual classes that are further defined in the context of a larger piece of discourse. The continuum of default to contextualized meanings of lexical aspect underscores the existence of a core meaning that, rather than shifted, is further complexified. The concept of an invariant-contextualized dichotomy within the realm of lexical aspect can also be applied to grammatical aspect. In fact, Doiz-Bienzobas' (1995: 29) claim that the 'contextual uses of the Imperfect and the Preterite are instantiations of their general meanings'. Thus, although the selection of the Preterite–Imperfect is based on the effect of the context in which a verbal predicate is embedded, there are, nevertheless, some invariant aspectual meanings associated with the Preterite and Imperfect that convey some specific nuances of meaning in association with those markers (e.g., iterativity, habituality, genericity).

7. Invariant and Contextualized Meanings

In this section, I discuss in detail one of the invariant meanings conveyed through the use of past tense markers: iterativity. In Chapter 3, I expand the analysis of iterativity to include the notions of boundedness and genericity.

7.1 Iterativity and habituality

Non-native speakers seem to have difficulty incorporating the contrastive meanings of iterativity and habituality to their L2 grammar. For instance, Pérez-Leroux *et al.* (2007: 434) point out that iterativity (episodic repetition) is prototypically marked with the Preterite; whereas habituality is prototypically marked with the Imperfect as exemplified in sentences (119) and (120) (examples are from Pérez-Leroux *et al.*).[21]

119. Jugaban (IMP) en el parque.   [habitual]
     The children (habitually) played in the park.
120a. Los niños se cambiaron (PRET)
      de asiento(una vez).   [punctual event]
      The children changed seats (once).
120b. Los niños se cambiaron (PRET)
      de asiento repetidamente.   [iterative]
      The children changed seats repeatedly.
120c. Los niños se cambiaron (PRET)
      de asiento por horas.   [iterative]
      The children changed seats for hours.

Pérez-Leroux *et al.* explain that in sentence (119), the past habitual sense is *normally* expressed with the Imperfect; whereas in sentence (120a), a single telic event is *prototypically* expressed with the perfective form. Notice, though, that the iterative meaning of a punctual event, as shown in sentences (120b) and (120c), is also *prototypically* expressed with the Preterite.[22] The point made by Pérez-Leroux et al. is noteworthy: That is, iterativity and habituality are not the same.

7.2 Iterativity as opposed to habituality

The principled distinction between iterativity and habituality in the previous literature has been, however, vague. For instance, de Swart (1998: 359) points out that, 'events can be coerced into states by giving the sentence an iterative (121a) or a habitual reading (121b)':

121a. John played the sonata for about eight hours.
121b. For months, the train arrived late.

de Swart, however, does not explicitly specify why playing the sonata would be iterative and the train arrival habitual. Notice that both sentences contain a telic event and a durative adverbial. Perhaps, the only noticeable difference would be the magnitude of the time interval denoted by each adverbial. Indeed, Michaelis (2004: 20) points out that

> [t]he generic–episodic distinction is a contextual one in part because it hinges on inferences about the size of the relevant time scales. If the intervals separating the events are judged to be small, as in the case of *The light flashed,* the predication will be judged as episodic; if the relevant events are judged to be widely dispersed through time, as in *The Romans laid siege to Gallic cities,* the predication will be judged generic.

Note, however, that the argument about time magnitude to distinguish habituals from iterated events does not represent an adequate criterion to explain their differences. Michaelis, for one, points out that any reference to time-magnitudes would have to be based on pragmatic inferences. Thus, she argues that 'habitual-event radicals and iterated-event radicals are indistinguishable at the level of Aktionsart structure: both qualify as heterogeneous activities' (p. 21).

On the other hand, Comrie (1976: 27) warns us that equating habituality with iterativity is misleading for two reasons. First, the repetition of an event is not enough to make it a habitual because all of the repeated instances of the event 'can be viewed as a single situation, albeit with internal structure, and referred to by a perfective form'. Second, 'a situation can be referred to by a habitual form without there being any iterativity at all' as is the case for *The temple of Diana used to stand at Ephesus,* or *Jones used to live in Patagonia* (both examples from Comrie).[23] Chung and Timberlake (1985: 221) argue that iteratives mostly refer to events that are 'composed of a multiple number of essentially equivalent subevents that are iterated over time'.[24]

Comrie proposes that there are two features that define a habitual. The first feature common to all habituals (whether iterated or not) is that of 'an extended period of time, so extended in fact that the situation referred to is viewed not as an incidental property of the moment but, precisely, as a characteristic feature of the whole period' (p. 28). Comrie points out, however, that what defines an extended period of time is conceptual rather than linguistic. The second feature that defines a habitual is that the situation described no longer holds, although this stipulation is represented by an implicature and not an implication in the strict sense. For instance, the habitual sentence *Bill used to belong to a subversive organization* can be cancelled without contradiction if someone were to say: *yes, he used to be a member and he still is.* Suppose, however, Comrie says that someone questioned whether Bill belonged to a subversive organization, and assume further that the respondent knows that Bill still belongs to it. If the respondent were to answer *yes, he used to be*, we have to conclude that the response would be misleading or that it would be an outright lie. Thus, Comrie argues that habituals no longer hold only as a result of an implicature, which is weaker than an implication: if denied, the situation no longer holds, 'but if not denied, or suspended by an explicit remark from the speaker to the effect that he does not know whether or not it holds, then it will be taken to hold' (p. 29).

Binnick (1991: 155) also makes a distinction between iterativity and habituality while also arguing for a close correlation between iterativity and habituality and perfective and imperfective meanings, respectively. That is, Binnick proposes that the imperfective may convey habituality ('repetitive episodes somewhat distantly spaced in time are viewed as a unit') whereas the perfective conveys iterativity ('repetitive episodes rather closely spaced in time and viewed as a unit'). As we can see, both habitual and iterated events have one important feature in common: they are viewed as a unit. On the other hand, they also differ in one important way: they are either distantly or closely spaced in time. As discussed by Comrie and Michaelis, however, time magnitude is a relative criterion. Binnick specifies further that a series of iterated events 'may be viewed as constituting phases of one act' (p. 182). This stipulation has one important consequence pertaining to the frequency and regularity of the event. For instance, in the following example (borrowed from Binnick), we notice that the phases of the iterated-event are frequent and regular whereas the habitual does not necessarily imply such meaning:

122a. (When John came in) they wagged their tails.   [Iterative]
122b. (Every now and then) they would wag their tails.   [Habitual]

Obviously, making reference to iteratives as a series of events constituting phases of one act conjures up the image of semelfactives. And indeed, Klein (1994: 47–48) equates iteratives with semelfactives. Within the scope of his conceptualization of aspect as Time of the Situation (Tsit) related to Topic Times (TT), habituals are represented by a series of topic times, whereas iteratives refer to one single TT. Iteratives are represented by situations in which a 'single but complex lexical content is linked to one TT, whereas in habituals, the same lexical content is linked to several Ts'.

Finally, Bhatt (1999: 53) states that 'habitual differs from iterative and frequentative crucially by the fact that the former is inductive whereas the latter are deductive'. That is, inductive refers to the fact that an event is habitual upon the observation of only one occurrence of the event; whereas for iteratives, we need to observe several occurrences of the event. For instance, frequency adverbials such as *once, twice, ten times* are relevant for iteratives but not for habituals. Bhatt, however, clarifies that habituals do 'involve quantification over a set of occasions in the sense that the event is predicted (inductively) to be occurring on a majority of such occasions' (p. 53). Although interesting on their own, the arguments proposed to distinguish iterativity from habituality discussed thus far are not very convincing because they are very sensitive to contextualization effects (e.g., time magnitude), or not comprehensive enough (e.g., implication and implicatures).

7.3 Principled distinction

Langacker (1987, 1999) makes the most promising proposal on how to distinguish iteratives from habituals. His rationale can theoretically account for the preferential use of the Spanish Preterite to express iterativity, and vice versa, the preferential use of the Imperfect to express habituality.[25] Langacker (1999: 251–3) makes a distinction between what he refers to as repetitive (iterative) sentences on the one hand, and habitual and generic sentences on the other hand. The distinction, Langacker argues, hinges on the existence of two types of knowledge that he labels as the actual plane and the structural plane (based on Goldsmith and Woisetschlaeger's (1982) distinction between phenomenal and structural knowledge). Langacker argues that the actual plane (that corresponds to iterative sentences) 'comprises event instances that are conceived as actually occurring', whereas the structural plane (that corresponds to habitual sentences) 'comprises event instances with no status in actuality' (p. 251). Thus, iterated-event predications express actual events like other kinds of episodic predications. In contrast, habitual sentences express structural events similar to the meanings expressed by generic sentences. Langacker offers the following examples to substantiate his argument:

123a. My cat repeatedly stalked that bird.   [Repetitive]
123b. My cat stalks that bird every morning.   [Habitual]
123c. Cats stalk birds.   [Generic]

Langacker argues that the repetitive in sentence (123a) shows the component events of individual instances of cats and dogs anchored to particular points in time (expressing actual, episodic events). In contrast, in a habitual sentence as in (123b), the component events are not anchored to any particular points in time (thus conveying a habitual meaning). The difference between a habitual and a generic sentence is that in the latter, there is no reference to any particular instance of individuals, but rather there is reference to the type *cat* and *bird* (see also Depraetre, 1995).

Following up on the proposal made by Langacker, Doiz-Bienzobas (1995) describes the distinction between iterative and habitual meanings expressed through Spanish Preterite–Imperfect verbal morphology. Doiz-Bienzobas distinguishes two cases in which multiple instances of the same event are described as exemplified in the following sentences (p. 107):

124a. El año pasado iba (IMP) a nadar todos los días.
     Last year I used to go swimming every day.
124b. El año pasado fui (PRET) a nadar todos los días.
     Last year I went swimming every day.

The event of swimming is presented as habitual with the Imperfect (124a) and as iterative with the Preterite (124b). Doiz-Bienzobas argues that the aforementioned contrast is substantiated by two facts. First, as argued by Comrie, whereas the implicature of swimming in (124a) is that the habit does not continue into the present, there is no such implicature from sentence (124b). Second, in line with Langacker's proposal, only the habitual allows for the failure of the event to take place at one particular time during last year. Thus, sentence (124b) implies that the speaker went to swim every day last year. The latter conclusion is accounted for by the fact that all of the instances of the event of swimming depicted in (124b), in association with the use of the Preterite, are anchored to particular points in time. In contrast, the instances of the event of swimming depicted with the use of the Imperfect (124a) are not anchored to particular points in time; thus, any one of them may fail to be present without necessarily affecting the interpretation of the habitual meaning of the sentence.

The proposed theoretical description of iterativity versus habituality will become important in the context of the discussion of studies on L2 acquisition to be reviewed in Chapter 3. More specifically, I argue that L2 learners may have difficulty learning the invariant meaning of iterativity conveyed through past tense morphology in L2 Spanish.

8. Theoretical Frameworks of Reference

Most studies on the L2 acquisition of temporality marking during the 1980s and 1990s were not explicitly linked to any specific linguistic theory. For instance, the LAH was based on the concept of a semantic division of verbal predicates, a classification that, despite some discrepancies, is generally accepted across linguistic theories. More recently, however, studies of the L2 development of tense-aspect have been unambiguously carried out as part of the research agenda of a linguistic theory. This is the case of the studies conducted by Montrul and Slabakova, which are couched within the theory of Minimalism. Some of their studies are reviewed in more detail in the following chapter. There are, however, competing linguistic theories that, even though they have not been used as the guiding framework of analysis of previous L2 acquisition studies, they seem to provide a good theoretical framework for the analysis of phenomena that span syntactic, semantic and pragmatic dimensions. Cognitive Linguistics, in particular, seems to be a good theory of language to assess those meanings of past tense-aspect in Spanish, when those meanings are defined according to the proposed definition of aspect described in the previous sections (i.e., invariant-contextualized continuum). In this section, I conclude this chapter with a brief review of the main tenets of both Minimalism and Cognitive Grammar with regard to the concepts of tense and aspect. This section will serve to frame the analysis of the empirical data on the development of knowledge and use of the L2 Spanish Preterite and Imperfect to be presented in the following chapter.

8.1 Minimalism

Within the generative framework of analysis, aspectual phenomena are ana-lysed within a strictly morpho-syntactic framework. Slabakova (1997: 77), for instance, argues that 'subtle differences in aspectual interpretation . . . are due to the different structural positions of aspectual morphemes in the two languages'. Similarly, Giorgi and Pianesi (1997: 6) argue that '. . . the differences across languages in the temporal and aspectual information are due to, and can be explained by, differences in the morphological system, which is employed to express them'. More specifically, grammatical aspect is represented as a functional category AspP (Aspectual Phrase) that varies cross-linguistically (Giorgi and Pianesi, 1997; Schmitt, 2001; Slabakova, 2001; Tenny, 1994; Travis, 1994; Zagona, 1994). In turn, information about lexical aspect is located in a different position in the sentence structure (hierarchically lower than grammatical aspect). The lower functional cate-gory AspP [± telic] is located close to the lexical verb and carries information about lexical aspect. In contrast, the higher functional category AspP [± perfective] conveys information about grammatical aspect.

The contrastive analysis of the representation of tense-aspect meanings in English and Spanish gives rise to specific hypotheses about L2 acquisition. In English, Giorgi and Pianesi propose that verbs are always perfective (denote bounded events) because 'this is the only way for them to get the correct categorical features and for allowing the derivation to converge' (p. 164). More specifically, given the fact that in English, verbs are not associated with visible markers of inflectional morphology, the way verbs [+V; −N] are disambiguated from nouns [−V; +N] is through the association with aspectual features. That is, English associates the feature value [+perfective] to all eventive predicates [+perfective; +V; −N]. In contrast, in Romance languages (Italian is the example mentioned by Giorgi and Pianesi), the verb does not need to recourse to the aspectual feature of the verb ([+perfective]) because of Italian's rich inflectional morphology (unambiguous association with relevant categorial features).

As an evidence for their proposal, Giorgi and Pianesi point out that in contrast with Romance languages, the English present tense does not have a continuous (imperfective) interpretation. For instance, *John runs* cannot refer to the action of John running at this very moment, whereas the equivalent sentence in Spanish (*Juan corre*) readily admits both a continuous and non-continuous interpretation. To obtain a continuous reading of that sentence in English, the progressive is necessary: *John is running*. The only exception to this generalization in English would be cases of reportive reading (as in recounting a movie or broadcasting a sports game) that allow the interpretation of a continuous reading of the simple present tense in English in the same way that Romance languages do. Giorgi and Pianesi support their claim with additional evidence from perceptual reports. The authors argue that in English (125a) entails a telic interpretation, in contrast with (125b) that entails an atelic interpretation (the *telos* or inherent end point of the activity has not yet been reached). Giorgi and Pianesi adduce that the contrast in interpretation between the (a) and (b) sentences is because English eventive verbs are [+perfective].

125a. John saw Mary eat an apple.
125b. John saw Mary eating an apple.

In contrast, in Romance languages, the *telos* of the event is not clear (it is ambiguous) because eventive verbs in Romance languages are not [+perfective].

126. Ho visto Gianni mangiare una mela.
     Vi (PRET) a Juan comer una manzana.
     I saw Juan eat an apple.

With respect to the nature of states, Giorgi and Pianesi claim that both habituals and states are not associated with the feature [+perfective], but rather with a quantificational feature associated in turn with a generic operator (Gen) through which they can be marked for tense (based on Chierchia, 1995). Chierchia asserts that all languages have a distinct habitual morpheme (Hab), which can take different overt realizations, and which heads an aspectual projection (a functional category above Verb pharse (VP)). This morpheme carries a functional feature that requires the presence of Gen in its Specifier. In Chierchia's quantificational analysis, the intrinsic ambiguity of imperfective sentence subjects is attributed to the presence versus absence of Gen.

Giorgi and Pianesi's account has not gone unchallenged. For instance, Schmitt (2001: 433) points out that 'Portuguese verbs, unlike English verbs, cannot be confused with nouns. . . . Nonetheless, the present tenses of the two languages behave alike in this respect: The present tense of eventive verbs disallows continuous readings'. Similarly, Arche (2006: 175) argues that associating habituals with states – as proposed by Chierchia (1995) – is problematic given that habituality and lexical aspect are independent. For instance, making a telic event habitual does not necessarily change the nature of the telic event.

Irrespective of theoretical debates, the representation of tense-aspect meanings in English and Spanish framed within the Minimalist framework leads to specific theoretical claims that can be empirically verified. In Spanish, the formal features [± perfective] are checked through overt tense/aspect morphology (i.e., Preterite and Imperfect in Spanish).[26] In English, in contrast, there are two possible structural representation of grammatical aspect that may help us account for specific developmental trends demonstrated in previous empirical studies of L2 Spanish. One possibility is that the postulated higher AspP (encoding the perfective/imperfective distinction) contains the feature [+ perfective] only. Thus, the lack of the [–perfective] feature value in the higher AspP in English is hypothesized to account for the difficulty in the acquisition of morphological and interpretative properties of Spanish Preterite and Imperfect. Another theoretical possibility proposed by Montrul and Slabakova (2002: 145) is that English 'lacks the functional category AspP altogether and that simple past only instantiates tense'. Thus, the challenge for

English-speaking learners is: (1) to recognize that Spanish verbs are morphologically complex not associated with the feature [+perfective] in the lexicon, (2) to learn the morphological distinction Preterite/Imperfect, (3) to map the formal features [+/−perfective] in Spanish with Preterite/Imperfect morpho-phonology, respectively and (4) to link Imperfect morphology to the empty quantifier or operator that is part of the English representation of states.

8.2 Cognitive linguistics

The basic theoretical assumption of Cognitive Linguistics is that language is both embodied in general cognition (i.e., it is non-modular) and situated in a specific functional environment (i.e., it grows out of language use, so to speak). Two important corollaries that follow from the previous assumptions are: (1) meaning is central to the definition of language and (2) language is the product of structured conceptualization and mental processing. As a consequence Cognitive Linguistics differs from the perspective advanced by Minimalism in two important respects. First, Cognitive Linguistics does not make a categorical distinction between syntactic and semantic information. Second, even though Cognitive Linguistics does not reject the possibility that humans have innate abilities that will guide the development of most cognitive abilities, it does reject the idea that language is a modular component of human cognition that is separate from the rest of cognition. In general, Cognitive Linguistics uses concepts from Gestalt psychology and visual perception (Ungerer and Schmidt, 1996). Within Cognitive Grammar, for instance, the distinct conceptualization of verbs and nouns is modelled on the nature of distinct general cognitive processes such as sequential and summary scanning (e.g., Langacker, 1982, 1987, 1999). A verb can be described as the product of a conceptualizer sequentially scanning a series of stative relations distributed throughout a given period of time. In contrast, nouns can be described as a single picture of an event that occurs as the outcome of the conceptualizer engaging in summary scanning. With respect to the conceptualization of temporality, the notions of trajectory and landmark provide an organizational structure to scenes and events and this structure is reflected in grammatical structure.

To the best of my knowledge, the only book-length monograph on the aspectual nature of Spanish past tense morphology framed within the perspective of Cognitive Linguistics is Doiz-Bienzobas' (1995) doctoral dissertation. Thus, I summarize the perspective of Cognitive Grammar on the Spanish Preterite–Imperfect with specific reference to her work.

In line with Langacker's proposal, Doiz-Bienzobas considers two dimensions for the analysis of aspectual contrasts in Spanish: position of viewpoint (speech time versus past situation time in association with the Preterite and Imperfect, respectively) and time specification (whereas the Preterite always locates the situation in time, situations in the Imperfect are not always temporally specified). Viewpoint can be described with the use of the following sentence from Lunn (1985) introduced before:

127a. El sermón me pareció (PRET) eterno.
    The sermon seemed interminable.
127b. El sermón me parecía (IMP) eterno.
    The sermon seemed interminable.

Doiz-Bienzobas (1995: 29) proposes that the Preterite (127a) states that 'the situation it modifies takes place at a past time in relation to a reference point', whereas with the use of the Imperfect (127b) 'the experience is recalled from the past situation time', thus creating a sense of immediacy to the eventuality not achieved with the use of the Preterite. The aforementioned semantic effect created by the use of the Imperfect can be analysed with telic events as well. Thus, Doiz-Bienzobas argues that the use of the Imperfect with telic events is used to (1) designate the concluding event of a series of events, (2) to express emotions and make judgements and finally (3) to create a temporal setting. First, the following example from Doiz-Bienzobas demonstrates that the use of the Imperfect serves to change the perspective on the description of one of the events that make the series of events identified in the sentence.

128. En 1978 Julián cayó (PRET) enfermo, se arruinó (PRET) en dos
    años y poco después moría/murió (IMP/PRET) alejado de sus
    familiares.
    In 1978 Julián became ill, he went bankrupt in two years and soon
    after that he died away from his family.

The first two situations depicted in sentence (128) are conceptualized from the point of view of speech time (Preterite), whereas the last one (i.e., to die) is perceived from the perspective of the situation time in the past (Imperfect). As such, the last situation stands out and helps to create 'a sense of immediacy between the situation and the narrator' (p. 94). This is representative of the so-called '*Imperfecto de ruptura*' (Imperfect of fracture).

A second aspectual nuance of meaning conveyed by the Imperfect is the expression of a judgement as portrayed in the following sentence:

129. Ayer Juan les escribía (IMP)/escribió (PRET) una carta a sus padres por primera vez en cinco años.
Yesterday Juan was writing/wrote a letter to his parents for the first time in five years.

Whereas the Preterite appears neutral, the meaning of the Imperfect can be described as a judgement: 'Juan has not written to his parents in five years!' Doiz-Bienzobas explains that 'by adopting a viewpoint that does not conceptualize the situation from speech time, the speaker gets "involved"'. That is, 'the speaker does not report what s/he saw merely, but is also passing a judgment' (p. 95). To further substantiate the previous point, notice that the contextual information provided by the complement (i.e., *por primera vez en cinco años*) is what 'opens the possibility of contrasting Juan's behavior against a scale of what is 'an acceptable behavior' in the context of letter writing'. By deleting the complement as was done in (130), the use of the Imperfect is no longer acceptable.[27]

130. Ayer Juan les *escribía (IMP)/escribió (PRET) una carta a sus padres.
Yesterday Juan *was writing/wrote a letter to his parents.

Finally, the use of the Imperfect with telic events serves to create a temporal setting as shown in (131a,b).

131a. El año pasado hacía (IMP) calor en Paris.
Last year in Paris it was hot.
131b. El año pasado me mudaba (IMP).
Last year I was moving.

The use of the Imperfect conveys the meaning that the depicted situation (i.e., to be hot, to move) lasted throughout the whole period. In contrast, when the Preterite is used, it is unlikely that the situation could be 'viewed as expanding over the whole period' (p. 97).

The second dimension regarded by Doiz-Bienzobas as essential for a definition of the Preterite–Imperfect in Spanish is time specification. With regard to time specification, situations with the Preterite are always temporally located, whereas situations marked with the Imperfect are not always temporally specified. This theoretical distinction carries important consequences. First, the lack of temporal specification entails that the Imperfect can be used to convey habituality. In contrast, time specification conveyed by the Preterite allows the latter to be used with non-habitual iterative situations (e.g., *fui a nadar todos los días*). Second, the Imperfect (but not the Preterite) can be used with low-transitivity predicates (e.g., *la carta decía/*dijo hola*). Third, difference in temporal specification with the use of Preterite–Imperfect allows to distinguish property versus actual occurrence as in (132a,b).

132a. El auto costaba (IMP) dos millones. (property of subject
　　　independent of time)
　　　The car cost two millions.
132b. El auto costó (PRET) dos millones. (someone actually bought the
　　　car for 2 million)
　　　The car cost me two millions.

In sum, Doiz-Bienzobas posits that the 'Spanish aspect reflects one of the decisions that the speaker takes depending on the particular understanding and conceptualization of the situation to be presented' (p. 50). With regard to the specific nuances of meaning conveyed by the perfective and imperfective past tense forms, she argues that the Imperfect presents a conceptualization of situations from the point of view of a past time, whereas the Preterite presents a conceptualization of situations from the point of view of speech time (p. 31, inter alia). Thus, the difference between the meanings of the Preterite and the Imperfect constitutes a difference in the conceptualization of the situation they modify.

9. Conclusion

The review of some definitions of aspect presented in this chapter confirms Binnick's claim, summarized in the chapter opening, that the study of tense-aspect meanings is an example of work in progress (Section 2). In particular, the debate on the demarcation of aspectual meanings that correspond to the categories of lexical as opposed to viewpoint or grammatical aspect is, arguably, an open discussion (Sections 3 and 4). The theoretical analysis of the semantic multivalence of predicates (blurring the demarcation line between lexical and grammatical aspect) has direct implications on the conceptualization of tense-aspect meanings. In turn, an adequate definition of tense-aspect meanings is crucial to properly identify the dependent variable of L2 acquisition studies of past temporality. More specifically, the principled delimitation of situation type (a.k.a. lexical aspect) and grammatical aspect can help us determine what is or is not an essential component of a definition of tense-aspect knowledge.

The proposed shifting of lexical aspectual classes, whether conceptualized as derived situation types (cf. Smith), or as coerced lexical aspectual classes (cf. de Swart) presents us with an obvious dilemma regarding the categorical distinction among the various lexical aspectual classes. On the one hand, verbs seem to have some basic aspectual meanings associated with them (e.g., Arche, 2006; Depraetre, 1995; Filip, 1999). On the other hand, there seem to be clear effects of interaction between those basic meanings and the meaning contributed by the larger contextual framework in which those verbs are embedded (e.g., Smith, 1997; de Swart, 1998). One solution, proposed by Smith and de Swart, is to think of these changes in meaning as category shifts of lexical aspectual classes. Another possibility implicit in Olsen's (1997) proposal about the use of privative semantic features to classify lexical aspectual classes is that there may be some default meanings (invariant, generalized, characterizing) that are further specified in the context of a larger piece of discourse (contextualized). Extending Olsen's claim about lexical aspectual classes to the perfective–imperfective distinction instantiated in grammatical aspect (representative of viewpoint aspect), Binnick (1991) also distinguished between contextually determined uses and invariant meanings. Furthermore, focusing on Spanish in particular, Doiz-Bienzobas (1995: 29) proposed that the 'contextual uses of the Imperfect and the Preterite are instantiations of their general meanings'.

Given that the previous literature on tense-aspect supports the distinct separation of two levels of representation, I have argued that one possible solution to the theoretical dilemma of shifting meanings of lexical aspectual classes is to frame the analysis of the representation of aspectual knowledge within a discourse-based approach. The use of a larger contextualization framework as the point of departure of our analysis, as opposed to considering context as a problem to be avoided, can be useful (Section 6). At a minimum, a contextually based definition of tense-aspect meanings allows us to define lexical aspectual classes as both default classes (i.e., prototypes) and as contextually specified categories. Although, in principle, this does not constitute a major departure from the conceptualization of the semantic meaning of predicates advanced by Smith and de Swart, among others, the notion of prototypes or default classes provides for a different way to account for shifts in lexical aspectual categories. The essential difference, as stated earlier, is that context is not regarded as a problem to be avoided but rather as an inherent component of the meaning of lexical aspect (Section 6) as well as grammatical aspect (Section 7). The relevance of this claim will become more evident in the analysis of L2 acquisition data.

Chapter 3

Hypotheses about the L2 Development
of Tense-Aspect Knowledge

1. Introduction

In a summative article published in 1999, Bardovi-Harlig reported on seven studies on the acquisition of tense-aspect morphological marking in Spanish as a second language. As of 2007 there are, to the best of my knowledge, 27 studies on that same topic (see Table 3.1). That is, within the span of eight years, the number of studies tracking the development of Spanish past tense morphology has increased fourfold. A quick review of the studies included in Table 3.1 shows the following generalizations: (1) most of them include subjects whose native language is English (22), (2) most of the studies (22) analyse data from adult students learning Spanish in a foreign-language environment, whereas the other five include a combination of natural and foreign-language settings or mostly the natural setting and (3) approximately half of the studies (15) are cross sectional.

It is noteworthy that the more recent studies offer an expanded view on theoretical descriptions as well as methodological approaches towards the analysis of the development of tense-aspect morphology in Spanish. For instance, up to 1999, the only theoretical hypothesis that had been empirically tested was the lexical aspect hypothesis (LAH; with the exception of one unpublished study that is, nevertheless, frequently cited: Lafford, 1996). Starting in 2000, other theoretical perspectives were considered either as part of the research design (e.g., Slabakova and Montrul, 2002a, 2002b, 2003) or in the discussion of potential alternative theoretical explanations (e.g., Liskin-Gasparro, 2000; Salaberry, 2002, 2003, 2005). Despite the previous assertion, however, the effect of the lexical aspectual value of verbal predicates remains an independent variable considered by the majority of studies. Given the recent introduction of new theoretical perspectives as well as methodological procedures to analyse the development

Table 3.1 L2 Spanish studies on tense-aspect acquisition for the period 1999–2007

Date	Authors	L1	N	Control	Predicates	Description
1986	Andersen	English	2	None	1,629	Longitudinal, 2 years, 2 conversational samples
1988	García and van Putte	Dutch	20	15	185	Rewrite story in past tense
1990	Ramsay	English	30	6	2,130	Cross-sectional, oral retell of picture book
1994	Martínez-Baztán	Dutch	15	None	662	In-class compositions
1995	Hasbún	English	80	20	3,606	Cross-sectional, written film retell
1996	Lafford	English	13	None	387	Cross-sectional, oral film retell
1999	Salaberry	English	15	4	2,054	Cross-sectional, oral film retell
1999	Lubbers-Quesada	English	32	None	589	Written narratives, Spanish-speaking setting
2000	Cadierno	Danish	10	None	656 + 1,353	One level, oral and written narratives
2000	Liskin-Gasparro	English	8	None	701	Oral film retell, retrospection
2000	López-Ortega	French/Moroccan	4	None	478	Oral interviews, Spanish-speaking setting
2000	Schell	English	5	6	165	Longitudinal, fill-in-blank tests, Spanish-speaking setting
2002	Camps	English	15	None	1,208	Five oral narratives (3 personal and 2 with pictures)

2002	Montrul	English	39	20	1,638+	Cross-sectional, 30-item fill-in-the-blanks/oral retell/42-sentence conjunction test
2002	Montrul and Slabakova	English	71	23	2,982	Cross-sectional, 30-item fill-in-the-blanks/42-item 5-point scale conjunction test
2002	Salaberry	English	49	32	2,009	Cross-sectional, 41-item fill-in-the-blanks written test
2002a	Slabakova and Montrul	English	60	27	2,520	Cross-sectional, 5-point scale judgment of states, accomp. and achievements
2002b	Slabakova and Montrul	English	60	27	2,940	Cross-sectional, 5-point scale judgment of act-acc and stative-event shifts
2003	González	Dutch	40	None	1,040	Cross-sectional, fill-in-the-blanks tests and written free compositions
2003	Montrul and Slabakova	English	64	20	4,352 + 2,688	Cross-sectional, 80-item truth-value judgment task/56-item conjunction test
2003	Salaberry	English	105	9	5,040	Cross-sectional, 46-item multiple choice tests (film/personal-based)
2003	Slabakova and Montrul	English	69	18	5,520	Cross-sectional, 80 story-based truth value judgement task
2004	Granda	English	15	10	517	Written film retell, Spanish-speaking setting
2005	Potowski	English/Spanish	52	None	1,445	Written narrative (535 tokens)/oral narratives (910 tokens)
2007	Lubbers-Quesada	English	30	10	1,602	Cross-sectional, oral narrative, Spanish-speaking setting
2007	Pérez-Leroux et al.	English	41	10	3,468	Cross-sectional, grammaticality judgement and translation tasks
Forth	Salaberry	English	286	149	11,400	Cross-sectional, two-choice written test

of aspectual knowledge in L2 acquisition, it is appropriate and timely to assess the significance of the various hypotheses and empirical studies as a whole.

Thus, in this chapter, I review the basic tenets of the important theoretical hypotheses considered so far to account for the development of Spanish past tense marking. In particular, I review the effect of lexical semantics, discursive structure, perceptual saliency of input data, L1 transfer and syntactic structures on the development of knowledge and use of past tense aspect. Some studies will be reviewed in more detail than others. I use two main criteria to decide which studies to review in depth. First, I will focus on recent studies, mostly carried out after 1999, given that the majority of studies published before that year have already been critically reviewed in previous volumes (e.g., Bardovi-Harlig, 2000; Ayoun and Salaberry, 2005; Salaberry, 2000a; Salaberry and Shirai, 2002). Second, I primarily focus on studies that provide empirical information to ascertain the relevance of a strictly syntactic-semantic, or alternatively, a syntactic-discursive definition of tense-aspect meanings. The latter are primarily represented in studies testing the LAH, the discourse hypothesis (DH) or the default past tense hypothesis (DPTH), whereas the former are mostly studies conducted within the Minimalist framework. As described in Chapter 2, the narrow or broad definition of tense-aspect meanings has become a major focus of research that should inform future empirical studies. The conclusions gathered from the analysis of the findings of selected empirical studies presented in this chapter serve as the foundation for the proposal of a theoretical framework of tense-aspect learning to be discussed in Chapter 4.

2. The Independent Variables

In this section, I present an analysis of some of the main factors that have been isolated as independent variables in previous studies of the development of tense-aspect phenomena in L2 acquisition. The discussion presents a brief review of some relevant studies in order to contextualize the claims advanced by each research strand. In Section 3, in contrast, I present an in-depth review of some recent studies that may be regarded as evidence to support a syntactic or a discursive definition of tense-aspect knowledge.

2.1 The effect of lexical aspect

No other theoretical proposal about the development of tense-aspect morphology has generated more empirical research – directly or indirectly – than the LAH. The LAH is known by a variety of other labels: the aspect hypothesis (e.g., Shirai, 2007), the primacy of aspect hypothesis (e.g., Robison, 1990) and the redundant marking hypothesis (e.g., Shirai and Kurono, 1998). To the best of my knowledge, there is no substantial difference among these various labels.[1] For the purpose of consistency I use the single label of the LAH. The basic claim of the LAH is that L2 learners start the developmental process of acquisition of tense-aspect knowledge using inflectional endings that are semantically associated with lexical aspect (i.e., prototypical choices). Furthermore, there is a process that favours the use of past tense verbal endings with the perfective marker at the beginning and a gradual spreading of its use across lexical aspectual classes throughout time. Conversely, the use of the imperfective marker is expected to be incorporated soon after the perfective marker is first used. That is, initially, verbal morphology encodes inherent aspectual distinctions (i.e., it does not encode tense or grammatical aspect).[2] Andersen and Shirai (1994: 133, stress added), for instance, argue that 'first and second language learners *will initially be influenced* by the inherent semantic aspect of verbs or predicates in the acquisition of tense and aspect markers associated with or affixed to these verbs'. The LAH also predicts that L2 learners will gradually incorporate non-prototypical choices of tense-aspect marking as their experience with the L2 increases.

The proposed correlation between tense/aspect morphemes and lexical aspectual classes is based on the *Relevance Principle* (i.e., aspect is more relevant to the meaning of the verb than tense, mood or agreement) and the *Congruence Principle* (i.e., learners choose the morpheme whose aspectual meaning is most congruent with the aspectual meaning of the verb). Both principles – discussed in detail by Andersen and Shirai (1994) – are based on arguments initially made for the evolution of linguistic systems across time and for the development of L1 acquisition. With regard to historical language changes, several researchers have observed that in emergent linguistic systems, aspect markers precede the appearance of tense markers (e.g., Bybee, 1985, 1995a; Bybee and Dahl, 1989; Frawley, 1992; Jakobson, 1957). I discuss the claim about the developmental effect of lexical semantics in L1 acquisition in more detail in this chapter, given the direct relevance of that argument to substantiate the LAH in L2 acquisition.

2.1.1 L1 acquisition studies

The argument about a developmental trend in association with specific lexical aspectual classes can be traced back to early L1 acquisition studies carried out during the 1970s and 1980s (e.g., Antinucci and Miller, 1976; Bloom, Lifter and Hafitz, 1980; Bronckart and Sinclair, 1973; Brown, 1973; Rispoli and Bloom, 1985; Smith and Weist, 1987). Among the earliest studies on the development of L1 verbal morphology, Bronckart and Sinclair (1973) noticed that three-year-old children would usually use past tense verbal morphology in association with the telicity of the eventuality described. For instance, children would use present tense with some atelic events (e.g., *Il lave la voiture* = He is washing the car), but they would use past tense when referring to telic events (e.g., *Il a poussé la balle* = He kicked the ball). Bronckart and Sinclair furnished empirical evidence to support the claim about the effect of telicity on the use of past tense markers in French (i.e., *Passé Composé–Imparfait*). Their data were collected from 74 L1 French-speaking children whose ages ranged from 2;11 to 8;7 (years; months). The analysis of the data revealed that children used present tense forms mostly with durative verbs and past tense forms with achievement and accomplishment verbs (i.e., actions with clear end results). Moreover, younger children tended to use past forms more often for events of shorter duration. This tendency diminished as the children grew older, thus approximating adult use. The results of their study, framed within a Piagetian approach to cognitive development, were attributed to a cognitive deficit: children have no concept of tense during the pre-operational stage.

Along the lines of Bronckart and Sinclair, Antinucci and Miller (1976: 182) analysed data from L1 Italian and also concluded that 'the child is able to make reference and encode past events only when their character is such that they result in a present end-state of some object'. Antinucci and Miller argued further that state and activity verbs were marked with the Imperfect at a later stage (between ages 2;0 and 2;8) in the specific context of story telling. They further pointed out that in this case 'the child is not narrating a past event, and in most cases is not even narrating a story that someone previously told him' (p. 186). In other words, the Imperfect was being used to signal something other than the traditional notion of temporality associated with past tense verbal morphology. That is, it was used to mark the distinction between pretend-world versus real-world. Antinucci and Miller surmised that this non-temporal notion accounted for the later development of the imperfective form: 'the ability to make this distinction, as Piaget shows, is more complex and later to develop than the ability to take account of a physical transformation' (pp. 186–7).

The findings from L1 acquisition have been contrasted with similar results from adult L2 acquisition. Thus, Andersen and Shirai (1994) pointed out that empirical findings from L2 adult learners show results equivalent to the ones obtained by Bronckart and Sinclair. Andersen and Shirai argued, however, that it cannot be claimed that adults are 'cognitively deficient' to express past time reference. As an alternative to the cognitive-deficit explanation, Bloom, Lifter and Hafitz (1980) had attributed the bias in the distribution of verbal morphology exhibited by children to the aspectual contour of the actions (i.e., lexical aspect) rather than the actual end state of the action. Their theoretical perspective follows the cognitive saliency rationale offered by Jakobson (1957), who claimed that aspect marking is closer to the stem than the shifting deictic forms of tense marking. Further expanding Bloom et al.'s approach, Shirai and Andersen (1995: 759) proposed that the development of verbal morphology among children is guided by prototypes (e.g., Rosch and Mervis, 1975): 'initially children restrict their use of tense/aspect inflections to the prototype of the category, then gradually extend the category boundary, and eventually acquire the adult norm'. The proposed effect of lexical aspect on the use of verbal morphology was, however, rejected by other L1 acquisition researchers. Weist (1983) and Weist et al. (1984), among others, presented a more nuanced perspective, while showing that both aspect and tense emerge simultaneously in Polish children as young as 2;6 years. In this respect, it is noteworthy that Weist and colleagues departed from the analysis of English and focused instead on Polish, a language in which both tense and aspect are grammaticalized with both prefixes and suffixes. Thus, Wagner (2001: 665) cautions that 'in order for this learning story to make sense [aspect before tense], it must be the case that children are oblivious to tense information when it is in fact present in the verbal morphology. . . . The real force of the Aspect First Hypothesis, therefore, is its claim that tense information is *not* being coded by children's early verbal morphology'. It is possible, thus, that lexical aspect is only one among several factors that may guide the development of past tense verbal endings in L1 acquisition.

Apart from the effect of lexical aspect, other factors such as the distributional characteristics of the input data available to children have also been regarded as possible independent variables that could explain specific patterns of development of past tense verbal morphology. For instance, based on the analysis of a data set of 5,106 verbs collected from conversations between L1 English children and their caretakers, Shirai (1991) concluded that the language input made available to children contained some very specific biases that could account for the development of children's verbal morphology. In particular, Shirai noticed that *motherese*[3] (i.e., language used by caretakers in general while addressing children) had the following features: (1) the Simple Past was primarily used with achievements and (2) the

Progressive was primarily used with activities. In further support of Shirai's argument but with a focus on L1 Spanish, Morales (1989) analysed data from 15 Puerto Rican children of ages 2 to 6 and concluded that children used the Preterite first with a small set of verbs. The majority of verbs (77 per cent) first marked with the Preterite (children of ages 2;0 to 2;9) were *irse, acabarse, caerse* and *romperse* (to leave, to run out of, to fall, to break). Morales pointed out, however, that the first verbs marked with past tense in L1 English are similar (Brown, 1973): *fell, dropped, slipped, crashed and broke*. Morales concluded that children start using past tense with the most frequent verbs they find in the input and they adapt those forms to fulfil the semantic functions they can handle at their age (p. 129). On the other hand, Krasinski (1995) showed that the emergence of past forms in a bilingual Spanish–English child was different in the two target languages. Verbs in English emerged in their base form, whereas verbs in Spanish were marked first with third person singular (default in Spanish), but also in the form of 'imperatives, infinitives and past forms. These forms were initially invariant' (p. 268). Krasinski argued that the Spanish verb form that emerged first 'was the most frequent in the input' (p. 269). As for English, the first instances of past marking were irregular past forms, which is consistent with the claim of input effects (item learning). Thus, the earlier appearance of past forms in Spanish when compared to English can be explained by the type of input available in each language. In Spanish, past forms are consistently used in all environments; whereas in English, the phenomenon of negatives and question formation (the auxiliary *did* with base form of the verb) create a more complicated system for the child to analyse. This is also consistent with the finding that the first verb forms in past tense in English were irregular forms.

More recent studies on the L1 acquisition of inflectional morphology have looked into additional factors. Wagner (2006), for instance, presents empirical evidence to show that children as young as 2;10 use transitivity as a cue to telicity. In contrast, five-year-olds seem to relax this constraint while they start to rely more on spatio-temporal information. In other words, children develop an understanding of the semantics of tense and aspect through the use of structural cues available from the input data (i.e., transitive sentences tend to be telic). Wagner points out that children's 'focus on transitivity as a cue to meaning that goes beyond mere linguistic analysis' may be based on a number of possible processes that underlie the powerful development of the L1: (1) statistical patterns in the input, (2) non-linguistic conceptions of events or (3) part of a universal grammar. In sum, the analysis of the L1 acquisition data shows the influence of factors other than just the lexical semantics of verbal predicates, most notably, the effect of distributional biases associated with the use of specific verbs and morphological endings (e.g., Krasinski, 1995; Shirai, 1991) as well as syntactic structures (e.g., Wagner, 2006).

2.1.2 The lexical aspect hypothesis

Andersen was the first researcher to use Vendler's classification of four lexical aspectual classes as the theoretical framework for the analysis of the development of verbal morphology among L2 learners. Andersen's claim was first published in 1986 in an article written in Spanish. In it, he analysed the use of Spanish Preterite and Imperfect in a variety of spontaneous oral tasks produced by two adolescent native English speakers learning Spanish in Puerto Rico in an untutored setting. Andersen (1991) further outlined his hypothesis about the effect of lexical aspect as an independent variable on the development of past tense verbal morphology in Spanish. Andersen argued that L2 learners follow a developmental sequence in the acquisition of aspectual markers correlated with the classification of lexical aspectual classes: no marking → punctual verbs → telic verbs → dynamic verbs → statives (1991: 318). The basic postulates of the LAH, originally described by Shirai (1991: 9–10) and later reformulated with very minor editing in Andersen and Shirai (1996: 533) and Bardovi-Harlig (2000: 227), are the following:

1. Learners first use (perfective) past marking on achievements and accomplishments, eventually extending its use to activities and statives.
2. In languages that encode the perfective/imperfective distinction, imperfective past appears later than perfective past, and imperfective past marking begins with statives, extending next to activities, then to accomplishments and finally to achievements.
3. In languages that have PROGRESSIVE aspect, PROGRESSIVE marking begins with activities, and then extends to accomplishments and achievements.
4. Progressive markings are not incorrectly overextended to statives.

The application of that developmental sequence to the acquisition of L2 Spanish renders a sequence of eight developmental stages as shown in Figure 3.1. Items in bold reflect the first appearance of the past tense marker within any given lexical aspectual class. As obvious, the sequence of emergence of the past tense markers is fairly symmetrical from both ends of the continuum, although the timing of the movement across lexical aspectual categories is delayed for the Imperfect.

	STATE	ACTIVITY	ACCOMPLISHMENT	ACHIEVEMENT
1	tiene	juega	enseña	se parte
2	tiene	juega	enseña	**se partió**
3	**tenía**	juega	enseña	*se partió*
4	*tenía*	**jugaba**	**enseñó**	*se partió*
5	*tenía*	jugaba	*enseñó*	*se partió*
			enseñaba	
6	*tenía*	jugaba	*enseñó*	*se partió*
		jugó	*enseñaba*	
7	*tenía*	jugaba	*enseñó*	*se partió*
		jugó	*enseñaba*	**se partía**
8	*tenía*	jugaba	*enseñó*	*se partió*
	tuvo	*jugó*	*enseñaba*	*se partía*

FIGURE 3.1 Sequential development of past tense morphology according to lexical aspectual classes (based on Andersen, 1986, 1991).
Note: The selected Spanish examples from Andersen may be translated in the following way: *tener:* to have; *jugar:* to play; *enseñar:* to teach; and *partir* (*se parte*): to break.

There are some important theoretical and methodological caveats that qualify the claims of the LAH. Most important among those caveats is the fact that the LAH does not offer a theoretical account for what happens after lexical aspect alone can no longer determine the choice of perfective or imperfective. That is, starting at stage 5, the use of verbal morphology cannot be determined by lexical aspectual category: accomplishments (telic events) can now be marked with Imperfect or Preterite. Similarly, the use of both Preterite and Imperfect can be used with activities at stage 6, with achievements at stage 7 and finally with states at stage 8. Thus, we must conclude that the Congruence Principle (i.e., learners choose the morpheme whose aspectual meaning is most congruent with the aspectual meaning of the verb) cannot account for the use of the Preterite and Imperfect after stage 5. Furthermore, there are methodological factors that limit the generalizability of Andersen's original findings. Indeed, Andersen cautioned other researchers that he obtained confirmatory empirical evidence for only four of his eight proposed stages of development. As a matter of fact, there were data supporting only two stages of acquisition per subject. Stages 2 and 6 were empirically substantiated with data from Anthony and stages 4 and 8 with data from Annette.[4] Finally, Andersen's original study was based on data collected among adolescent learners immersed in the L2 environment who did not have access to an academic setting of instruction. Thus, to extrapolate from Andersen's original findings to a population of adult learners with access to the L2 through formal instruction in a class-room setting requires empirical evidence representative of those learning conditions.

Despite the aforementioned caveats, the LAH is, arguably, supported by a considerable body of empirical evidence (e.g., Andersen, 1986, 1991; Bardovi-Harlig, 1992a; Bardovi-Harlig and Bergström, 1996; Bardovi-Harlig and Reynolds, 1995; Camps, 2002, 2005; Collins, 2002, 2004; Comajoan, 2006; Hasbún, 1995; Salaberry, 1998; Shirai and Kurono, 1998). Summing up the status of studies investigating the effect of lexical semantics, Shirai and Kurono (1998: 248, stress added) argue that 'studies on the acquisition of verb morphology that systematically investigated the relationship between verb morphology and inherent aspect have *consistently indicated* that children acquiring an L1 and adults acquiring an L2 are *strongly influenced by the inherent aspect of the verb to which the morphology is attached*'. Shirai and Kurono's claim – as stated – is generally accepted by the majority of research-ers (e.g., Gass and Selinker, 2001; Mitchell and Myles, 2004). As I discuss in more detail in later sections, however, there is a growing body of empirical evidence, which shows that (1) the effect of lexical aspect is associated with higher rather than lower levels of L2 proficiency and (2) the use of the Imperfect seems to be categorically associated with certain specific and frequent verbs.

2.2 The effect of discourse structure

The second most influential hypothesis about the development of tense-aspect morphology in L2 acquisition is the discourse hypothesis (DH). Although Andersen and Shirai (1994) – inter alia – include the role of dis-cursive grounding among the various factors that influence L2 development of past tense morphology, Bardovi-Harlig has empirically substantiated the DH. Bardovi-Harlig (1994: 43) explains that the basic claim of the DH is that 'learners use emerging verbal morphology to distinguish foreground from background in narratives'. Similar to the claim advanced by the LAH, the DH predicts that the effect of the independent variable (in this case, narrative grounding) on the use of verbal morphology subsides as learners become more experienced and proficient in the L2. Bardovi-Harlig (1995: 264) explicitly claims that 'advanced learners must eventually use past in both foreground and background to reach a target-like use of tense in English narratives'. The essential claim proposed by the DH is based on a substantial theoretical literature that characterizes aspectual phenomena at a level of analysis above the phrase- and the sentence-level. For instance,

Hopper (1982: 16) argues that the nature of aspectual distinctions cannot be characterized by lexical-verbal semantics in a consistent way; the adequate reference may only come from a *global discourse function*. Moreover, the correlation of aspectual differences and perceptual contrasts associated with the concept of narrative grounding (e.g., Givón, 1982; Reid, 1980; Wallace, 1982) falls within the scope of a well-developed theoretical approach such as Cognitive Grammar (Langacker, 1999).

An important question that comes up in the context of the DH is: How do we classify the eventualities that make up a narrative according to grounding? Hopper (1979: 215) explains that a narrative is comprised of two types of events. The events that move the story line forward (the main plot of the story) constitute the foreground of a narrative. In contrast, the ones that do not advance the story line but, nevertheless, introduce new information through observations, commentaries and evaluation, constitute the background of a narrative. In essence, thus, the foreground of a story is associated with the plot line, whereas the background refers to the supportive or ancillary information about the story. This functional distinction between foregrounded and backgrounded events has formal correlates. Most important, backgrounded events tend to be marked with a wide range of verbal morphology (e.g., present, future, subjunctive) because they give 'details of indirect relevance to the narrative, that may be part of the prehistory, provide a preview . . . or suggest contingent but unrealized events' (p. 239). The foreground, in contrast, tends to be less varied in choices of verbal morphology. The criteria used in L2 acquisition studies to classify foregrounded from backgrounded events follow very closely the criteria set forth by Hopper (1979) and Reinhart (1984). These criteria are mostly focused on the notions of punctuality, completeness and sequentiality. Comajoan (2001), for instance, argues that the foreground is defined by clauses that move the story forward, are chronologically ordered and that answer the question 'what happened?'

2.2.1 Narrative type

Compared to the body of empirical research testing the claim of the LAH, there have been fewer studies explicitly focused on the testing of the DH (e.g., Bardovi-Harlig, 1992b, 1995; Comajoan and Pérez Saldanya, 2005; Housen, 1994; Lafford; 1996; López-Ortega, 2000). On the other hand, the body of empirical evidence that supports the claims of the DH has pointed towards new findings. For instance, the analysis of narrative grounding – required to assess the validity of the DH – leads us to focus on particular conditions that may affect the use of past tense verbal morphology that would not have been considered by theoretical approaches restricted to the analysis of verb-phrase or sentence-level phenomena. The distribution of lexical aspectual classes in different types of narratives (e.g., personal versus fictional narratives) is a case in point. For instance, the higher proportion of achievements verbs versus other lexical aspectual classes is highly significant in most empirical studies that analyse data from fictional stories. More specifically, Bardovi-Harlig (2000) concludes that in most retell narratives such as the *Modern Times* story, achievements constitute approximately half the tokens in those narratives. Other studies have reported similar – if not higher – proportions of use of achievements (e.g., Bergström, 1995 and Salaberry, 1998 for L2 French data, Hasbún, 1995 and Salaberry, 1999 for L2 Spanish data). As it turns out, the high proportion of telic events is associated with the high use of the perfective form. In contrast with the results from fictional narratives, Noyau (1990) argues that personal retellings yield more background information, thus resulting in higher use of stative verbs and concomitantly, higher use of the Imperfect. Wiberg (1996) speculates that in narratives, economy in speech entails that the events in the foreground are narrated, whereas background information is left unspecified for the reader/listener to infer from context. In contrast, personal retellings are more likely than impersonal narratives to explicitly identify background information (e.g., make reference to the person doing the retelling and to mention where the person has been, what s/he has done, etc.).

Some studies, however, fail to show higher uses of the imperfective rather than the perfective past tense marker in personal narratives. In Wiberg (1996), for instance, the analysis of oral personal retellings among ten L1 Italian speakers revealed that the perfective form was used twice as often as the imperfective form: a combined total of 374 tokens of *Passato Prossimo* against a combined total of 179 tokens of verbs marked with *Imperfetto*. An in-depth analysis of the data, however, revealed that whereas some students remained faithful to the task and produced personal retellings, others shifted into narrating non-personal stories. Thus, Wiberg's data are representative of a mix of personal and impersonal narratives. The results from other studies are yet more nuanced. Cadierno's findings (2000), for instance, seem to contradict the assertion about the distribution of Spanish perfective–imperfective markers in personal narratives in written format, but not in the oral format. Instead of asking learners to retell a film, Cadierno asked her informants to talk about their happiest and unhappiest experience in their lives, to recount what they had done over Christmas and

Table 3.2 Distribution of tokens of perfective and imperfective markers across some studies

	Camps (2002)	Salaberry (1998)	Wiberg (1996)	Cadierno (2000) Written	Oral
Perfective	738	475	374	366	640
Imperfective	158	158	179	290	713

some exciting trip they had taken. The findings from Cadierno's study show that students produced more Preterite forms than Imperfect forms in the written narrative (366 tokens of Preterite versus 290 tokens of Imperfect). On the other hand, they marked more verbs with Imperfect than with Preterite in the oral narrative (640 tokens versus 713 tokens, respectively). That is, the proportion of Preterite–Imperfect use in the written and oral tasks based on personal narratives was 1.26 and 0.89, respectively. The almost flat 1-to-1 ratio from Cadierno's study contrasts with a typical ratio of 2 to 1 or higher for typical impersonal narratives based on film prompts. Some of the data discussed so far are presented in graphical format in Table 3.2.

In Table 3.2, typical impersonal narratives represented by the studies carried out by Camps (2002) with Spanish data and Salaberry (1998) with French data show a high proportional use of the perfective form. In contrast, the personal narratives, most clearly represented in the study of Cadierno (2000) show an almost flat proportional rate of use of perfective and imperfective markers of past tense. In sum, the effect of narrative type (e.g., personal versus impersonal) cannot be underestimated given that it may account for some contradictory findings (e.g., Salaberry, 2003).

2.2.2 Conflating the LAH and the DH?

To some extent, it can be argued that the LAH and the DH are two versions of the same hypothesis. More specifically, the criteria used to distinguish foreground versus background information overlap with some of the principled criteria that serve to classify verb phrases into different lexical aspectual classes. For instance, foregrounded events are determined by temporal criteria that include reference to punctuality and completeness. Thus, the events in the foregrounded parts of a narrative are punctual (as opposed to durative or iterated) and dynamic (as opposed to stative). The opposite is the case for backgrounded eventualities: they are non-dynamic (states) or durative (atelic events). Thus, Bardovi-Harlig (1994: 286) argues that the predictions of the LAH and the DH 'may be too fine-grained for a study of interlanguage'. In later publications, however, Bardovi-Harlig (1998, 2000) states that the predictions of the LAH and the DH can be distinguished. In particular, she points out that '... even an activity whose inherent aspectual features are [–punctual, –telic] takes on – as a foreground predicate – the features of punctuality and completeness ...' (2000: 235). In general, atelic predicates in the foreground and telic events in the background are good test cases to ascertain the predictive validity of the LAH or the DH. Indeed, some studies have empirically compared the LAH and the DH (e.g., Housen, 1994; Lafford, 1996; López-Ortega, 2000; Salaberry, forthcoming).

Housen (1994) analysed the relative weight of semantico-conceptual universals (dynamicity and punctuality as part of lexical aspect) and discourse-pragmatic universals (grounding) in the development of aspectual distinctions in past tense Dutch. Housen's study was based on two open-ended conversations with an English-speaking adolescent. The conversations were separated by a one-year time gap. A summary of the results of his analysis is presented in Table 3.3.

Data analysis presented in Table 3.3 shows two important findings: (1) irrespective of verb type (dynamic or non-dynamic), marking past tense in the background of the narrative is more challenging than in the foreground (although more so for statives) and (2) the improvement in past tense marking from time 1 to time 2 seems to be more pronounced for dynamic verbs (i.e., states are more difficult). Although based on a small data set of only one learner, Housen's findings have been replicated in subsequent empirical studies with more subjects and in different languages (e.g., for French, see Bergström, 1995; for Spanish, see Lubbers-Quesada, 1999, 2007; Salaberry, 1998, 1999, 2002, 2004).

Table 3.3 Past tense marking discriminated by grounding and dynamicity

Verb type	Grounding	Time 1	Time 2	Change
Dynamic verbs	Foreground	55%	85%	30%
	Background	30%	74%	44%
	Difference	25%	11%	
Stative verbs	Foreground	50%	73%	23%
	Background	3%	26%	23%
	Difference	47%	47%	

Based on data from Housen (1994).

Table 3.4   Distribution of morphological marking of verbs according to telicity in the foreground in percentages

	Pres (%)	Prog	Imp	Pret (%)	Inf (%)	Other (%)
Atelic-FG						
Int-Low	18	0	0	55	27	0
Int-Mid	59	0	0	23	0	18
Int-High	11	0	0	74	0	15
Telic-FG						
Int-Low	11	0	0	56	22	11
Int-Mid	44	0	0	41	7	0
Int-High	10	0	0	65	12	12

Based on data from Lafford (1996).

Among the few studies that purposefully set out to compare the predictions of the LAH and the DH on the use of Spanish Preterite and Imperfect, Lafford (1996) analysed oral recalls of a seven-minute silent video (*The Sorcerer's Apprentice* from Disney). The data were collected from thirteen L2 Spanish students from three different levels of intermediate proficiency on the basis of the ACTFL-OPI scale (Intermediate-low, Intermediate-mid- and Intermediate-high). There were no cases of telic verbs in the background of the narratives for the Intermediate-low and Intermediate-mid learners and very few tokens among the Intermediate-high learners. Thus, the analysis of findings from Lafford will be restricted to the distribution of verb tokens in the foreground.

Table 3.4 shows that among Intermediate-low or Intermediate-mid learners, the Imperfect is not used and the Preterite is the first past tense form used, irrespective of verb type. This finding is consistent with the claim that the Preterite may be used as a default marker of past tense (e.g., Kihlstedt, 2002; Salaberry, 1999, 2002, 2003; Wiberg, 1996). Second, note that in general – but especially so for the Intermediate-low learners – lexical aspect does not have an effect on the distribution of verbs: the distribution of the uses of both the Preterite and the Imperfect is approximately the same for both telic and atelic verbs. Thus, Lafford concluded that her data provides evidence in favour of the strong version of the DH: both atelic and telic verbs in the foreground are marked primarily with the Preterite. That is, grounding overrides telicity (at least in the foreground of the narrative).

Another study that specifically compared the effect of lexical aspect and grounding on the use of L2 Spanish past tense in the same data set was López-Ortega (2000). Her analysis was based on narratives collected

Table 3.5 Distribution of morphological marking of verbs according to lexical aspect and grounding in percentages

	ST (%)	ACT (%)	ACC (%)	ACH (%)
Perfective-foreground	100	97	99	100
Perfective-background	50	40	27	14
Imperfective-foreground	0	33	0	11
Imperfective-background	97	97	92	73

Based on data from Comajoan and Pérez Saldanya (2005).

through personal interviews with four Arabic/French speakers learning Spanish in Spain. López-Ortega concluded that the LAH and the DH are 'necessary and complementary frameworks of analysis'. More importantly, in apparent contrast with the findings from Lafford, López-Ortega tentatively concluded that 'lexical aspect may play a relevant role in overriding other temporal reference and discourse principles occasionally when the three (grammatical aspect, lexical aspect and grounding) do not agree with native distributions' (p. 499). In a more recent study, Comajoan and Pérez Saldanya (2005) reviewed the empirical evidence from Comajoan's (2001) dissertation to ascertain whether the LAH or the DH would be a more encompassing hypothesis. The analysis was based on L2 Catalan longitudinal data collected from six L1 English speakers who already had 'extensive knowledge of other Romance languages' (p. 47). A summary of the results across all six learners is presented in Table 3.5.

Comajoan and Pérez Saldanya stated that in the prototypical combinations, the perfective form (a periphrastic past in Catalan) in the foreground was used appropriately between 97 and 100 per cent across lexical aspectual classes. On the other hand, the Imperfect in the background was used appropriately most of the time (92 and 97 per cent), except for achievements (73 per cent). Interestingly, however, there was no clear outcome in favour of either lexical aspect or grounding. For instance, the highest level of past tense use with states occurred both in the foreground and the background, thus negating the categorical role of grounding as an explanatory factor (though not necessarily ruling it out). In contrast, states were marked with the perfective form at approximately the same level as other lexical aspectual classes, thus contradicting the claim about lexical aspectual class as a categorical determinant of past tense use. There was, however, an apparent effect associated with the Imperfect: it was used appropriately at a high level in all classes except achievements. In principle, one could argue that these learners can be placed at one of the last stages on Andersen's developmental scale (Figure 3.1).

Finally, Salaberry (forthcoming) compared the relative effect of inherent lexical aspect and discursive grounding on the use of L2 Spanish Preterite and Imperfect using the data from a written 40-item discourse-based multiple-choice task among 286 English-speaking learners of Spanish. Salaberry concluded that both lexical aspect and grounding have an increasing effect on past tense marking as experience with the target language increases. That is, instead of a decrease in the association of lexical aspect and grounding with past tense marking, the analysis of data shows that the learners constantly move towards prototypical associations as their knowledge of the language increases. Furthermore, given that only the effect of grounding was statistically significant across most levels of proficiency, it was concluded that grounding is the construct that most clearly distinguishes learners from native speakers. That is, the factor that differentiated L2 learners from native speakers was the selection of past tense markers according to grounding (i.e., background and foreground). Salaberry's findings reaffirm and expand the claim made by Lafford (1996) with the use of a larger data set of learners, the inclusion of a control group of 149 native speakers and the use of more powerful statistical tests (repeated measures analysis of variance (ANOVA)). In essence, Salaberry argued that given the fact that grounding covers a larger 'contextual space', it represents a more demanding determinant of the selection of grammatical markers of past tense. This argument is in line with previous findings from Coppieters (1987), García and van Putte (1988) and so on.

2.3 The effect of perceptual saliency

2.3.1 Rule-based versus exemplar-based approaches

Several studies have observed a primary role of the regular–irregular verb distinction in the development of past tense morphology (e.g., Ellis, 1987; Bayley, 1994; Giacalone-Ramat, 1992; Housen, 2002; Klein, Dietrich and Noyau, 1995; Lafford, 1996; Salaberry, 2000b). In many cases, the advantage is attributed to the irregular forms because they are more cognitively salient than regular verb forms due to their frequency in the input and their perceptual saliency. Klein et al. (1995: 271), for instance, point out that 'irregular verbs are typically frequent and the morphological differences are perceptually salient, compared to a regular ending such as *-ed*, which may be hard to process for many learners'. Furthermore, with regard to developmental processes, Giacalone-Ramat (1992: 304) claims that 'a production strategy at the [L2] learner's disposal is to use a sort of lexical unit with no morphological variation, gradually developing the necessary morphological devices for word class assignments'. Hence, it is possible that the use of irregular past tense morphology precedes the appearance of regularized morphology in L2 development.[5]

The possible effect of the perceptual saliency represented in irregular versus regular morphology has been elaborated as an acquisition/development hypothesis. For instance, Wolfram's (1985: 247) principle of perceptual saliency states that 'the more distant phonetically the past tense irregular form is from the non-past, the more likely it will be marked for tense'. Along the lines of Wolfram's claim, Bayley (1994: 161) proposed that 'the more salient the difference between the present and past tense forms, the more likely a past-reference verb is to be marked'. With respect to Spanish in particular, Lafford (1996: 16) proposed the saliency-foregrounding hypothesis: 'phonologically salient verb forms are used to reflect salient (foregrounded) actions in L2 narrative discourse'. In terms of phonological saliency, both Spanish past tense regular Preterites with final stress and irregular Preterites with internal vowel changes stand out phonologically in comparison with verbs that carry penultimate stress and that have only three irregular forms (i.e., the Imperfect).

The previous proposals (Wolfram's in particular) introduce a categorical distinction between two levels of information: discourse level and surface level factors. The discourse level factors are represented in tense and lexical aspect. Surface level factors are represented by (1) regular versus irregular morphology, (2) type of irregular formation (e.g., suppletive form, internal vowel changes, internal vowel changes plus suffix, final consonant replacement), (3) phonetic shape of the suffix on the regular verb (/t/, /d/ and /id/), (4) the phonological environment that follows the verb (e.g., cluster reduction – with subsequent deletion of the past tense suffix – is favoured when following vowel is preceded by a consonant) and (5) frequency of the verb (usually irregulars such as *be, have, do, come, go*). Thus, one could argue that both semantic and surface factors are complementary. In fact, as we see, researchers working within the theoretical framework of Minimalism, argue (correctly) that the appropriate use of verbal morphology (likely associated with the good use of surface level information) should not be confused with knowledge of semantic meanings of aspectual contrasts represented in, for instance, Preterite and Imperfect (see Chapter 5).

The claim about the effect of surface-level factors in the acquisition of past tense verbal morphology may have important theoretical consequences beyond the appropriate use of the forms. For instance, some empirical studies have specifically considered a possible dissociation in the acquisition of regular versus irregular past tense morphology, leading thus to the proposal of a dual-system to represent past tense verbal morphology. That is, irregular verbs are represented as formulaic exemplars or lexical items that are stored (memorized) as individual lexical entries. In contrast, regular verbs are represented as the application of a generative rule. Rohde's (1996) findings, for instance, revealed that the regular past was almost exclusively used with achievement verbs, whereas the irregular past was used with more lexical aspectual classes and in particular with statives. Similarly, Housen (2002) concluded that the irregular state verbs (*was, had*) were the first past forms to emerge in the data from his subject, thus contradicting the LAH. In contrast, the distribution of regular verbs across lexical aspectual categories in Housen's data provided empirical support for the prediction of the LAH. Along the same lines, Kihlstedt (2002) suggested that the early marking of high-frequency statives with the Imperfect was not the result of a regularization process (i.e., a rule), but rather the result of an associationistic process (lexicalized). It should be noted, however, that the majority of these studies were based on data from adolescent learners.

Salaberry (2000b) studied the relative effect of irregular and past tense morphology in English among instructed adult learners. His analysis showed that L2 learners marked past tense more frequently with irregular than regular verbs. As for lexical aspect, telic verbs were used much more than states. Approximately, 77 and 74 per cent of all verbs corresponded to telic events in the oral and written narratives, respectively. In contrast, stative verbs corresponded to approximately 12 and 15 per cent of all verbs in the oral and written narratives, respectively. Among verbs marked with past tense in both narratives, approximately twice as many were irregular verbs: 40 per cent irregulars versus 22 per cent regulars in the oral narratives and 56 per cent irregulars versus 26 per cent regulars in the written narratives. The past tense marking of the irregular and frequent verb *to be* (i.e., *was*) was probably due to its perceptual saliency rather than its lexical aspectual class. Salaberry's participants were, however, not very advanced; therefore, it is possible that the effect of lexical aspect would have occurred at more advanced stages of L2 development. Hence, it is possible that the effects of perceptual saliency and the lexical semantics of the verb on the use of past tense morphology are related to different developmental stages. In line with the studies carried out with adolescents, Salaberry concluded that adult learners master the endings associated with irregular and frequent morphology first and only then do they start to make associations with lexical aspectual classes.

Interestingly, the findings in support of a dissociation between the representation of regular and irregular morphology are contradicted by a recent study from Buck (2007, forthcoming). Given its unique findings, I review this study in more detail. Buck (forthcoming) analysed data from 27 university students enrolled in English as a foreign language course in Mexico City (i.e., classroom setting). Twenty students were enrolled in a fifth semester course (approximately 300 hours of English instruction) and seven were taking an eighth semester course (approximately 420 hours of instruction). The data collected from students were based on retell narratives of an excerpt from the silent comic film *Modern Times* with Charlie Chaplin (*Alone and Hungry*). Taking into account the appropriate use of past morphology in the narratives, the students were subsequently divided into a low-proficiency group constituted by 13 students (Group I) and a high-proficiency group represented by 14 students (Group II). The low-proficiency group obtained 50–79 per cent appropriate use of past tense and the high-proficiency group had an appropriate use of past tense in the range of 80–100 per cent. Students produced a total of 833 verb tokens comprising 710 past tense tokens and 123 non-past tokens. The proportional distribution of past tense use was correlated with level of proficiency: there was a 94 to 6 per cent past tense to non-past tense use among the higher-proficiency group compared to an equivalent 76 to 24 per cent proportional distribution among the lower-proficiency group.

With regard to the effect of lexical semantics, Buck's analysis shows that the distribution of past tense verb tokens according to lexical aspectual classes was very similar across proficiency groups. For the high-proficiency group in particular, the distribution was: 13 , 10 , 33 and 44 per cent for states, activities, accomplishments and achievements, respectively. For the low-proficiency group, the equivalent scale was 16 , 8 , 30 and 46 per cent. In other words, there does not seem to be any developmental effect of lexical aspectual classes on the selection of past tense markers. In principle, one could argue that these learners are so advanced that no developmental trends associated with the LAH will be apparent in the data. On the other hand, when we factor in the role played by irregular morphology, we note that the majority of stative verbs used were mainly irregular (see Table 3.6). In part, this is due to the fact that the use of the verb *to be* was very frequent (*was* = 50 out of 87 instances of irregular tokens).

With reference to the effect of irregular morphology, the distribution of past tense use according to irregular and regular tokens was approximately the same for both proficiency groups: 68 per cent irregulars to 32 per cent regulars versus 61 to 39 per cent for the high- and low-proficiency groups,

Table 3.6 Distribution of regular and irregular perfective past morphology by aspectual category

Group	State		Activity		Accompl.		Achievement	
	Irr/%	Reg (%)	Irr/%	Reg (%)	Irr/%	Reg (%)	Irr/%	Reg (%)
I	43/90	5/10	10/38	16/62	49/52	45/48	88/62	53/38
II	44/80	11/20	15/38	24/62	83/61	54/39	135/75	44/25

Based on data from Buck (forthcoming).

Table 3.7 Token frequency analysis by narrative structure of regular and irregular perfective past forms

Group	Grounding	Irregular past		Regular past		Total	
		Tokens	%	Tokens	%	Tokens	%
I	Foreground	150	49	106	34	256	83
	Background	40	13	13	4	53	17
II	Foreground	238	58	118	29	356	87
	Background	39	10	15	4	54	13
		467	65	252	35	719	100

Based on data from Buck (forthcoming).

respectively. When the use of non-past is also computed, the distribution of verbal morphology for the low-proficiency group is 50, 26 and 24 per cent for the sequence of irregular, regular and non-past, respectively. For the high-proficiency group, the equivalent spread is 62, 32 and 6 per cent, respectively (see Table 3.6 for the information about actual tokens). As we can see, the number of irregular verb tokens was more frequent among students from the high-proficiency group than the low-proficiency group. Finally, taking into account the combined effect of lexical semantics and irregular morphology, Table 3.6 shows that the second highest proportional use of irregulars across both groups occurred with achievements (the highest proportion is associated with states). Moreover, the more advanced students are the ones who used irregulars to signal past tense the most.

Most previous studies show that irregular morphology should have an effect during beginning stages of development of the L2. In contrast, Buck's data reveal an increasing effect of irregular and frequent verbal morphology. Buck (2007) also concluded that the difference does not seem to be associated with grounding. As Table 3.7 shows, the increasing level of past tense marking with irregulars as proficiency increases happens in both the foreground and the background of the narratives.

To further investigate these findings in terms of type frequency, Buck (2007) analysed the most frequent irregular and regular verb types across both groups of proficiency. Tables 3.8 and 3.9 show the number of tokens associated with irregular and regular verbs, respectively. The combined total of these verbs alone represents about a third of all the verb tokens produced by both groups of learners.

In sum, contrary to previous claims, the more proficient students in Buck's study relied even more on irregular verb morphology than the less proficient learners. This is even more striking given that – as Buck points out – the advanced learners had been in contact with the rules for the formation of the English Simple past with regular verbs for at least three

Table 3.8 Irregular verbs used most frequently

Verb type	No. of tokens used	
	Group I	**Group II**
Told	16	34
Went	11	19
Took	8	16
Ate	4	10
Got	3	14
Could	2	9
Came	1	6
Left	0	7
Total	**45**	**115**

Based on data from Buck (2007).

Table 3.9 Regular verbs used most frequently

Verb type	No. of tokens used	
	Group I	**Group II**
Arrested	20	24
Arrived	6	12
Wanted	2	7
Walked	1	5
Tried	4	9
Happened	2	9
Called	6	9
Decided	1	4
Total	**42**	**79**

Based on data from Buck (2007).

semesters. On the one hand, Buck's findings do confirm that irregular forms take the lead in tense marking in the earlier stages of acquisition as previous studies proposed. On the other hand, Buck's data also show that this tendency does not diminish in higher levels of proficiency. Quite the opposite, more advanced learners rely on the guidance of irregular inflectional endings even more than less proficient learners.

Buck argues that her findings offer empirical support for a single representational system as described by Bybee's (1995b) associative network model. In contrast with the claim about a two-dimensional system represented by (grammar) rules and (lexically based) associations, an associative network model makes no qualitative differences in the processing of regular and irregular forms. Bybee's lexically based continuum relies on a range of lexically based representations and processes of verbal morphology spanning from irregular items to best exemplars (pseudo-regulars). The model is comprised of two levels of analysis. First, both irregular forms as well as high-frequency regulars are stored as lexical forms on the basis of a simple associative mechanism. At this level, there is no major difference with previous claims about the role of irregular morphology. Bybee's system adds a second representational layer in which low-frequency regular forms are processed according to a schema that uses the base form as its lexical foundation. Essentially, both lexical morphemes and inflectional morphemes such as the –*ed* ending signalling regular past tense are *lexically* represented and processed on the basis of lexical schemas. As a consequence, for both representation and processing, lexical strength depends on frequency of use. Although Bybee's model may not be relevant to model the semantic aspectual meanings conveyed by the Preterite–Imperfect contrast (i.e., Bybee's model is about form, not meaning), it may be regarded as complementary to an approach that defines tense-aspect meanings at a more contextualized level of representation.

2.3.2 The distributional bias hypothesis

Another factor inherently defined by perceptual saliency of input data is the relative distribution of past tense markers across different verb types. The distributional bias hypothesis (DBH; Andersen, 1994; Andersen and Shirai, 1996), in particular, is based on the claim that L2 learners' production reflects the distributional biases of native speaker input with regard to lexical aspectual classes. For instance, Shirai (2004: 103) explains that

> . . . in cross-sectional studies involving production data, the prototypical association becomes *stronger* as the learner's proficiency increases. I suggest

that the increasing association is the result of developing form-meaning mapping based on L2 input, which is biased in the direction predicted by the . . . Distributional Bias Hypothesis . . .

In essence, the DBH represents an additional independent variable on the use of past tense markers, which accounts for some empirical studies that provide evidence that contradicts one of the main claims of the LAH. The theoretical relevance of this proposal is that it effectively raises the possibility that what guides the development of past tense marking is not necessarily lexical semantics, but simply by distributional biases in the input data.

For instance, Tracy's (2007) analysis of a corpus of written and oral data shows that many verbs are 'clearly biased toward the Preterit or Imperfect, 70% or more of the time'. Tracy provides the examples of many achievement verbs almost always marked with the Preterite (e.g., *nacer, morir, decidir, terminar, empezar and comenzar*). Conversely, many stative verbs are almost always marked with the Imperfect (e.g., *existir, necesitar, haber, saber, ser and estar*). Furthermore, the use of either Preterite or Imperfect with some verbs is determined by the association with specific grammatical structures, as shown in the following two examples:

1. . . . Sí, estaba (IMP) realmente enamorado de su hermana . . .
   . . . Yes, I was really in love with her sister . . .
2. . . . El otro día cuando estuve (PRET) con él, me dijo . . .
   . . . The other day when I was with him, he told me . . .

For instance, when the verb *estar* is used with adjectives, it is typically marked with the Imperfect. In contrast, when it is used with prepositional phrases and/or specific time references, it tends to be used with the Preterite. In sum, the argument about distributional biases raises the distinct probability that it is not lexical aspect, but rather particular frequencies and patterning of input data that guides L2 learners towards an ever-increasing native-like competence/performance.

An additional argument that supports the role played by distributional biases is represented by the range of verb types used by L2 learners. For instance, let us analyse the distribution of verb types among native and non-native speakers in the data from Salaberry (1998) presented in Table 3.10. The findings from this particular study are representative of many other studies. Three outcomes are noticeable in these data. First, native speakers use twice as many verb types as non-native speakers. Second, the proportional distribution of verb types across lexical aspectual classes is approximately the same for both natives and non-natives. Third, the total number

Table 3.10 Proportional use of verb types among native and non-native speakers according to lexical aspectual class

Lexical aspect	Native speakers		Non-native speakers	
	Verb types	Percentage	Verb types	Percentage
States	21	15	14	19
Activities	29	21	17	24
Accomplishments	14	10	6	8
Achievements	76	54	35	49
Total types	140	100	72	100
Total tokens	562	100	633	100

Adapted from Salaberry (1998).

of verb tokens is roughly similar across both groups. Thus, these data seem to indicate that learners manage fewer verb types to narrate stories that are as long as the ones produced by native speakers (while the latter group uses twice as many verb types). In essence, this scenario seems to be ideal for the association of a few verb types with specific grammatical markers. Thus, learners may be able to rely on a distributional bias in reverse (they produce the biases in their own speech), effectively creating a feedback loop.

2.4 The effect of L1 transfer

Although most hypotheses do take into account the effect of L1 transfer, the hypothesis that is clearly associated with L1 effects is the default past tense hypothesis (DPTH). The DPTH originated as an offshoot of the LAH intended to account for empirical finding (most of them based on the L1 English–L2 Spanish pairing) that conflicted with some of the main tenets of the LAH. The DPTH specifically predicts that during the first stages of L2 development, learners will mark tense rather than aspectual distinctions. This is mostly a consequence of the fact that in English the Simple past marks only tense, but not aspect, coupled with the claim that learners are relying on the use of general (non-modular) cognitive processes to learn the L2. As learners become more experienced with the L2, their use of past tense markers will likely be affected by the lexical semantics of verb phrases and other factors other than simple tense contrasts. To illustrate the claim made by the DPTH, let us analyse the following example taken from an oral interview between a native speaker (NS) and a second semester learner of Spanish reported in Salaberry (2004):

3. NS: ¿Si? ¿De dónde eran (IMP) tus profesores de la secundaria?
            Yes? Where were your high school teachers from?

   Learner: ¿De dónde eran (IMP)? . . . Fueron (PRET) de California
            y . . . Maryland.
            Where were they from? . . . They were from California and . . .
            Maryland.

Note that the learner's repetition of imperfective *'eran'* signals that she understood the form used by the interlocutor. Despite such repetition of the imperfective form, the learner insisted on using a perfective form in her answer. Notice, too, that the imperfective form of the verb *ser* (to be) is usually the most common in most input environments provided to learners.[6] We can also reasonably surmise that the learner is attempting to mark past tense on the verb, given that past tense is also marked morphologically in English, the learner's native language (i.e., L1 transfer).

2.4.1 Complementary hypotheses

The empirical evidence about the DPTH has been mostly indirect, in many cases represented as conflicting findings that are not easily accounted for by the LAH (but see Comajoan, 2005a for a substantive critique of the DPTH). In some early studies of the LAH, evidence incompatible with basic tenets of the LAH could not have been assessed as supportive of the DPTH. With regard to L2 Spanish studies, however, Salaberry (2000a) provides a reinterpretation of contradictory findings in light of the claim of the DPTH. For instance, Salaberry shows that the analysis of Ramsay's (1990) data – often counted in support of the LAH (e.g., Andersen and Shirai, 1996; Bardovi-Harlig, 2000; Shirai, 2004) – shows that all verb types (including states) used by the very lowest level of proficiency were marked for past tense given that both the Preterite and the Imperfect were used. Although specific verbs were used exclusively with only one of the two possible past tense endings, it would be inaccurate to argue that tense contrasts were not represented in Ramsay's data.

   More recent studies have explicitly argued for the role of a default past tense marker in the acquisition of L2 Spanish in particular (e.g., Lubbers-Quesada, 1999, 2007; Salaberry, 1999, 2002, 2003, 2005, 2007; Wiberg, 1996).[7] In fact, the evidence about the use of a default past tense comes from a wide spectrum of theoretical frameworks, including some of the studies conducted with natural language learners by the European Science Foundation Project (ESFP). For instance, in an overall review of findings, Dietrich, Klein and Noyau (1995) conclude that the marking of tense precedes the marking of aspect. Furthermore, the studies from the ESFP cover a wide range of languages. For instance, using data from English and German speakers learning Italian, Giacalone-Ramat (2002) shows that the perfective develops first along the lines of a prototype combining congruent features of situations with the imperfective developing later starting with the copula and spreading to stative predicates and finally to other verb classes. Giacalone-Ramat points out, however, that learners show difficulties in identifying a recognizable function for the imperfective form. More importantly, she notes that such difficulties do not show up in the use of the perfective form. Giacalone-Ramat adduces that the difficulty associated with the imperfective is most likely due to the fact that it covers a wider range of aspectual concepts. In Chapter 4, however, I describe difficulties that learners face with the use of the perfective form to convey aspectual concepts (e.g., iterativity) and even to mark tense (e.g., with state verbs).

The fact that the DPTH is not necessarily incompatible with the claims advanced by the LAH or the DH is evident considering that researchers, who support the role of lexical aspect as an early determinant of past tense use, consider the role of a default marker of past tense viable. Thus, Shirai (2004) stated that the DPTH is worthy of consideration, at least with regard to the developmental process of some learners – more specifically, adults in classroom settings. Similarly, following up on an extensive review of the findings from previous studies, Bardovi-Harlig (2005: 409) concluded that the available data on L2 tense-aspect marking requires a significant modification of the LAH to account for the fact that 'the acquisition of the Imperfect is so delayed that it begins to cross from statives to activities only after the perfective past has completed its spread across the dynamic predicates, all the way to activities'. That is, all dynamic classes are marked with the perfective form before the imperfective becomes part of the developing aspectual system.

2.4.2 *Timing*

The empirical evidence that supports some of the basic tenets of the LAH (i.e., initially the use of tense-aspectual morphology is guided by lexical aspect) and the DH (i.e., initially the use of tense-aspectual morphology is guided by narrative grounding) need to be weighed against empirical evidence that conflict with some of those basic principles. In this respect, there are empirical data that contradict the proposed timing of the effect of lexical aspect on the selection of verbal markers of past tense. For instance, among the early studies that empirically assessed the claims of the LAH, Robison (1990) analysed L2 English data gathered through interviews with an L1 Spanish speaker learning

English. Robison specifies that the Primacy of Aspect hypothesis 'holds that *in the initial stages of language acquisition*, verbal morphemes are used redundantly to encode lexical aspect – the temporal features inherent in the lexical meaning of the predicate – and not grammatical aspect or tense' (p. 316, italics added). Robison analysed two aspectual contrasts: the stative–dynamic distinction and the punctual–durative distinction. The results of the data analysis were mixed: while there was empirical support for the punctual–durative distinction, the stative–dynamic distinction did not show a correlation of lexical aspect with grammatical marking.

Among other conclusions, Robison proposed a significant change to the LAH on the basis of the empirical evidence from his study: 'the prediction supported by this study is that . . . verbal morphology correlates with lexical aspect at least *during some stage during the development of an interlanguage*' (pp. 329–330, italics added). Salaberry (2000: 80) points out that '[t]he change in Robison's perspective is substantial because the sequence and timing of appearance of morphological markers of temporality are central for the analysis of the development of aspectual distinctions in L2 acquisition' (see Bardovi-Harlig, 2000 for a similar analysis of Robison's argument). Finally, although Bardovi-Harlig (2000: 192) is correct in her conclusion that '[o]n the whole, the range of elicitation tasks serves to strengthen the support for the aspect hypothesis', I would add, however, that we also need to identify whether the association of lexical aspectual classes and verbal morphology is correlated with developmental stages as explicitly argued by the LAH.

2.4.3 Spreading

As indicated by Bardovi-Harlig, the earliest indications that the LAH was not adequate to explain some of the empirical findings on the use of past tense verbal morphology are given by studies that failed to empirically demonstrate the proposed spreading of grammatical markings according to lexical semantic features, this being a crucial tenet of the LAH. In particular, some studies revealed that, although the emergence of perfective morphology in telic classes is well supported, the proposed spreading of its use over to the atelic classes is not substantiated (tenet 1 of the LAH, see Section 2.2). Conversely, there has been little evidence, overall, of the spread of imperfective morphology from atelic to telic classes.[8] On this point, Shirai (2004: 101) argues that

[t]he development from prototype to non-prototype is not always observed in the cross-sectional and longitudinal studies that used oral or

written production data. In fact, for many cases *the prototypical association is stronger for the intermediate level than for the beginning level* (stress added).[9]

In fact, studies that have analysed data from populations of students during their first year of studies in an academic setting have failed to show the proposed signs of spreading of inflectional morphology according to lexical aspectual classes. For instance, among some of the early studies in L2 French, the findings from Bergström (1995) and Salaberry (1998) reveal that the learners' data from second semester students (the lowest level of experience with the L2 taken into account in these studies) did not show any signs of spreading of past tense endings from one dynamic class to another. In fact, both studies show that early on in the process, all dynamic lexical aspectual classes (achievements, accomplishments and activities) were marked by past tense with the perfective form (*Passé Composé*). The previous unexpected finding led Bergström to conclude that her data 'show firm use of the *Passé Composé* not only with accomplishments and achievements but with all three dynamic verbs (activities, accomplishments, achievements) regardless of level' (p. 153). In fact, it appears that even when we consider other learning settings or L1s, the lack of spreading across dynamic verbs is also substantiated with empirical data. For instance, in Harley's (1989) study, her L2 French students overused the *Passé Composé* with all dynamic verbs. Similarly, Kihlstedt's (2002) analysis of interview data from four university students of French (Swedish L1) revealed the extended use of *Passé Composé*, but not of *Imparfait*. Kihlstedt argued that learners first used the imperfective form (i.e., *Imparfait*) with frequently used stative verbs, and that they shifted its use to activities only after the latter had already been marked with the perfective form (i.e., *Passé Composé*).

The findings obtained in studies with L2 French data are also corroborated by studies of L2 Spanish (e.g., Camps, 2002; Lubbers-Quesada, 1999, 2007; Salaberry, 1999, 2002; Slabakova and Montrul, 2003), which reveal that the use of the perfective marker of past tense was evident in all dynamic classes of verbs. For instance, Camps (2002) argues that the evidence from his study shows the higher use of the Preterite with all dynamic verbs than with states. Despite Camps' argument in favour of the basic claim of the LAH, the data clearly show that the use of the Preterite was in competition with the Imperfect even within the category of statives. A summary of the data from Camps' study presented in Table 3.11 shows that the Preterite is used almost as often as the Imperfect with statives (72 versus 79 tokens, respectively).

The data from Table 3.11 is even more informative if we analyse it in terms of percentages as shown in Table 3.12. What is relevant for our analysis

Table 3.11 Distribution of verb forms across lexical aspectual class in tokens

	ACH	ACC	ACT	STA	Total
Preterite	64	154	448	72	**738**
Imperfect	6	11	62	79	**158**

Based on data from Table 1 in Camps (2002: 190).

Table 3.12 Distribution of verb forms across lexical aspectual class in percentages

	ACH (%)	ACC (%)	ACT (%)	STA (%)	Total (%)
Preterite	56	71	69	32	61
Imperfect	5	5	10	35	13
Total	**61**	**76**	**79**	**67**	**74**

Based on data from Table 1 in Camps (2002: 190).

is that the marking of past tense (irrespective of whether this is done with Imperfect or Preterite) across lexical aspectual classes is similar, ranging from a low past tense marking of 61 per cent for achievements to a high past tense marking of 79 per cent for activities. In other words, learners are marking all verb types with past tense. It is clear that the Preterite is the preferred marker across all dynamic lexical aspectual classes. For statives, however, the marking of past tense is split between Imperfect and Preterite. We need to keep in mind, however, that Camps' (2002) data were collected from 15 students from a second semester course of Spanish. In other words, there is no direct evidence of any developmental trend in Camps' data because the data came from one single group of students.[10]

2.5 The effect of syntactic structure

Recently, there has been great interest among researchers working within strictly syntactic approaches to account for the behaviour of L2 learners acquiring knowledge about temporality and tense-aspect markings. In particular, there have been several L2 empirical studies carried out along the lines of the theory of Minimalism (e.g., Ayoun, 2005; Montrul and Slabakova, 2002; Schell, 2000; Slabakova and Montrul, 2002a, 2002b, 2003). Although none of these studies has specifically labelled their guiding hypothesis, we can describe it as the syntactic structure hypothesis (SSH) given its basic premise that tense-aspectual phenomena are defined according to the syntactic structure within which these concepts are embedded.

Starting with de Miguel (1992), proposals based on the claim about an innate, modular Universal Grammar (UG) have assumed that information about lexical and grammatical aspect are located in different positions within the clause structure: inner and outer aspect (e.g., Kempchinsky, 2000; Travis, 1994). As shown in Figure 3.2, inner aspect is located at the verbal phrase level and it encodes the information about the lexical semantics of the verb (and associated arguments). Outer aspect or sentential aspect encodes a functional projection above the VP (verb phrase) that represents boundedness. It is at the level of outer aspect that the features [+/−perfective] are checked by the Preterite–Imperfect contrast in past tense Spanish.

In sum, lexical aspect is represented in a lower functional category (i.e., inner aspect) where the semantic features [± telic] are checked. Grammatical aspect, in contrast, is located at a higher level (i.e., outer aspect), above the verb phrase (VP) and below the TP (tense phrase), where the features [± perfective] are checked through overt tense/aspect morphology (i.e., Preterite and Imperfect in Spanish). In essence, within the syntactic structure proposed by Minimalism, Smith's (1997) situation type and viewpoint aspect correspond to inner and outer aspect, respectively.

2.5.1 Main theoretical concepts

Apart from the overarching claim that aspectual meanings are syntactically located in two different positions (i.e., inner and outer aspect), L2 researchers

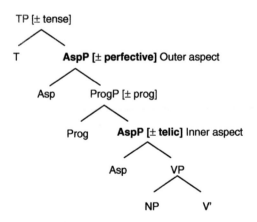

FIGURE 3.2 Syntactic representation of Inner and Outer aspect (based on Montrul & Salaberry (2003)).

assessing the extent to which the SSH can account for L2 data have relied upon two main theoretical concepts: (1) feature specification of the Aspectual Phrase (e.g., Giorgi and Pianesi, 1997) and (2) the role of pragmatic coercion as distinct from other grammatical processes (e.g., de Swart, 1998). First, in keeping with Giorgi and Pianesi's proposal, many studies carried out within the generative framework have examined the interpretations that Spanish L2 speakers assign to tense/aspect morphemes under the assumption that there is a parametric difference among speakers of Romance and Germanic languages (e.g., Montrul and Slabakova, 2002, 2003; Schell, 2000; Slabakova and Montrul, 2002). This assumption is based on the argument that in English verbs are always perfective (i.e., they denote bounded events) because 'this is the only way for [them] to get the correct categorical features and for allowing the derivation to converge' (Giorgi and Pianesi, 1997: 164). In contrast, in the Romance languages (Giorgi and Pianesi substantiate their case with examples from Italian) the verb does not need to recourse to the aspectual feature of the verb ([+perfective]) because Italian's rich inflectional morphology provides unambiguous association with relevant categorical features. Thus, Montrul (2004) claims that 'L1 English speakers learning Spanish must learn that the AspP in Spanish encodes [+/−perfective] features. Until learners are able to integrate this major difference into their evolving intergrammars, they will not acquire all the subtleties of the Imperfect marker regulated by [−perfective] feature' (p. 156).

The second important theoretical concept that has guided much of the work carried out under the guidance of the SSH is the concept of pragmatic coercion. As discussed in Chapter 2, the separation of strictly grammatical from pragmatic processes has important consequences. For instance, Slabakova (2002: 185) argues that the '. . . "prototypical" combinations are interpretable only using the syntactic module of grammatical competence but the nonprototypical combinations necessitate pragmatic competence over and above the syntactic competence, . . .' That is, by definition, the SSH can only account for the use of tense-aspectual knowledge represented in the use of the Preterite with telic events and the Imperfect with states, but not in cases in which the Preterite is used with states or the Imperfect with telic events. The latter are cases that, by and large, are regarded to be determined by pragmatic information. Although this is a plausible theoretical approach, it is a position not without challenges. In essence, by discounting the knowledge exhibited by (native or non-native) speakers for the selection of, for instance, the Preterite with states and the Imperfect with achievements, Slabakova's argument leaves a significant component of what constitutes the meaning of aspectual contrasts outside of the syntactic-semantic analysis. A potential corollary of this dissociation between grammatical and pragmatic levels is that it becomes much easier to ascertain ultimate attainment (i.e., native-like knowledge) in the domain of tense-aspect knowledge when the latter is defined as syntactic-semantic phenomena. The question, though, is whether what is being regarded to be a pragmatically determined decision should not be part of semantic information that makes up the representation of tense-aspectual meanings instantiated in the Spanish Preterite–Imperfect.

2.5.2 Distinctions among generative proposals

Despite the fact that L2 researchers working within the framework of the SSH have relied upon a similar theoretical model (i.e., Minimalism), there are some notable variations in the theoretical position advocated in various studies. There are at least three important theoretical strands that are noteworthy. The first line of research is represented by the studies conducted by Montrul and Slabakova. Their studies closely follow the main premise of both Giorgi and Pianesi's featural account of aspectual meanings and de Swart's contention about the nature of pragmatic coercion. Montrul and Slabakova's overall theoretical position on the L2 acquisition of tense-aspect is predicated on two main claims: (1) the process of L2 acquisition is modular (informationally encapsulated from other general learning processes) and (2) L2 learners can successfully acquire knowledge about tense-aspect meanings in the target language. In other words, Montrul and Slabakova (2002: 144) propose that 'the acquisition of the Preterite/Imperfect contrast falls within the range of UG phenomena and is not subject to a critical period effect . . .' Montrul and Slabakova have also included in their analyses theoretical arguments about psycholinguistic processing constraints (e.g., Piñango et al., 1999). More specifically, it is adduced that processing the semantic meanings of aspectual distinctions in a discursive context (beyond the verb phrase) is computationally more costly than the processing of semantic meanings at the level of the verb phrase. At the moment, Montrul and Slabakova's research agenda on the L2 acquisition of tense-aspect is ambitious and wide ranging to the point of leading the most prolific research project on tense-aspect development in the last seven years.

A second theoretical strand on the acquisition of tense-aspect is the one based on the notion of Constructionism advocated by Herschensohn (2000). To my knowledge, however, there is only one empirical study on the acquisition of tense-aspect knowledge following the premises of Constructionism (i.e., Schell, 2000). Constructionism represents a distinct theoretical strand mostly due to its unabashed claim about the gradual nature of acquisition. Herschensohn (2000: 109–110) argues that 'L2 parameter setting . . . is not an all-at-once phenomenon, but Progressive learning, construction by construction'. As a corollary, Schell (2000: 139–140) argues that some of the theoretical advantages of Constructionism are (1) it accounts for transfer from the L1 and (2) it accounts for variability in intermediate L2 production. More importantly, Constructionism seems to entail a first step towards the incorporation of general learning processes to the acquisition of L2 morphosyntactic knowledge. In fact, I believe that the definition of the different stages of development of L2 knowledge about the Spanish Preterite–Imperfect adduced by Schell focuses mostly on the effect of nonmodular processes: (1) initial state (transfer L1 values to L2), (2) intermediate state (lexical aspect become crucial) and finally, (3) final expert state (mastering peripheral as opposed to core aspects).

Finally, a third strand is represented by the position advocated by Pérez-Leroux et al. (2007). From a theoretical point of view, Pérez-Leroux et al. argue that the aspectual meanings correlated with [±perfective] morphology are actually dissociated from each other in the representational system of the L2 learners. Effectively, this entails that learners may acquire a representation of [+perfective] separately from the representation of [−perfective] morphology. They posit that the model adopted by Montrul and Slabakova assumes that

> acquisition depends on the activation of the [±perfective] feature, and the distinction should emerge as a coherent achievement. *Once this feature is encoded in the morphology, the full semantics of the past tense system should be available to L2 learners* and variations from the target depend solely on performance factors. (p. 443, stress added).

In essence, whereas Slabakova and Montrul (2002a, 2002b, and so on) propose that acquisition is theoretically represented as feature activation, Pérez-Leroux et al. contend that acquisition is theoretically represented as lexical development, where learners must bootstrap the selectional features of each functional head independently. Thus, Pérez-Leroux et al. argue that the selectional approach does not make any prediction about any across-the-board competence in L2 tense-aspectual knowledge. The aspectual interpretation is determined compositionally by the elements involved (the verb phrase, the aspectual operators and the tense head). In addition, the aspectual operator can be freely introduced to resolve type mismatches by type-shifting. In other words, learners may learn the semantic selectional restrictions associated with the Preterite but not the Imperfect and vice versa.

3. Review of Findings from Selected Studies

Given the importance accorded to the L2 acquisition of tense-aspect in the last two decades, several empirical studies have already been critically reviewed in previous monographs (e.g., Ayoun   and Salaberry, 2005; Bardovi-Harlig, 1999; Labeau, 2005; Salaberry, 2000a; Salaberry and Shirai, 2002). Thus, for the sake of expediency, I only review the findings from a selected number of studies on the acquisition and development of past tense verbal morphology. The selected studies will, arguably, provide evidence to substantiate two seemingly orthogonal (separate) lines of research based on distinct definitions of tense-aspect knowledge: a discursive one (from the perspective of the DPTH) and a syntactic one (from the perspective of a SSH).

The review of findings from two distinct theoretical perspectives is crucial to bridge the gap between two separate research paradigms (cf. Shirai, 2007). All too often, studies tend to restrict the analyses of their findings to the bounds of their proposed theoretical framework. In this section, I show that irrespective of research agenda, we improve our understanding of tense-aspect phenomena if we 'cast a wide net' in terms of our analysis of empirical findings. For instance, studies carried out within the Minimalist paradigm have introduced the analysis of iterativity and habituality, a topic that has hardly received much attention in lexical aspect studies. Conversely, studies focused on the analysis of discursive phenomena have brought up the notion of narrative types (e.g., personal versus impersonal), a topic that has been sidelined by syntactic approaches. At first, readers more familiar with one of the two main research paradigms that are the focus of this review may regard the findings from the other framework irrelevant. I believe, however, that the analysis of studies carried out by both research paradigms is necessary to develop an overarching model of tense-aspect development.

3.1 A default marker of past tense

The DPTH applied to the acquisition of L2 Spanish is based on the claim that the Preterite is the basic past tense marker, whereas the Imperfect is a more straightforward aspectual marker (cf. Doiz-Bienzobas, 1995, 2002). This basic claim is predicated on the more overarching argument that the perfective form is the more basic one of the perfective–imperfective contrast (e.g., Binnick, 1991; Comrie, 1985; Fleischman, 1990). Although, the DPTH was first proposed for beginning learners (e.g., Rocca, 2005; Salaberry, 1999, 2003; Wiberg, 1996), more recent studies have provided evidence to claim that its application may be extended to more advanced levels of proficiency (e.g., Antonio, 2007; Liskin-Gasparro, 2000; Lubbers-Quesada, 1999, 2007). Furthermore, the DPTH appears to be relevant for the analysis of data from natural learners (e.g., Giacalone-Ramat, 2002) and heritage learners (e.g., Silva-Corvalán, 1994) as well. In this section, I assess the claim of the DPTH with the analysis of data from L1 English speakers learning L2 Spanish primarily, but I will also make reference to other native and target languages.

3.1.1 Data from L1 English–L2 Spanish

3.1.1.1 Data from classroom learners

Salaberry (1999) made the first study to ascertain the potential role of a default past tense marker in the beginning stages of development among L2 Spanish learners. Four characteristics of the research design of this study differed from the majority of previous studies on the topic: (1) it was a quasi-longitudinal analysis (data collected from the same learners twice within a period of two months), (2) it relied on the analysis of oral data as opposed to written data, (3) the film prompts that were used to generate the narratives were shown only once to minimize the effect of planning and monitoring and (4) it incorporated a functional communicative procedure to prompt the production of participants' narratives. The participants in the study were 15 college-level students enrolled in four separate courses of instruction separated by semesters (from second to fifth semester of instruction). The narratives were based on retellings of two short excerpts from the Charlie Chaplin silent film *Modern Times* (i.e., *Alone and Hungry* and *An Accident Occurred at the Store*). The task was also further contextualized to make it more realistic through a role-play scenario. More specifically, students were asked to role-play the character of an observer who had witnessed the events depicted in the movie and who had to narrate what had happened to a detective taking notes of the story. Participants were also told that the person playing the role of detective (another student) was to rely on their narrative to recount the events to a third person, who had to verify the story. The elaborate procedure was meant to increase the functional demands of the task. A summary of the distribution of past tense markers in the oral narratives produced by all students in terms of raw tokens is presented in Table 3.13.

The findings of the data analysis of the oral narratives revealed that the learners at the lowest proficiency level, by and large, did not use the Imperfect

Table 3.13   Raw counts of morphological marking by lexical class

	Time 1			Time 2		
	Telic	**Atelic**	**Stative**	**Telic**	**Atelic**	**Stative**
Second semester (*n*=4)						
Preterite	28	12	7	61	5	9
Imperfect	0	0	1	2	0	2
Present	55	9	27	41	9	20
Third semester (*n*=4)						
Preterite	150	24	29	124	13	12
Imperfect	14	8	20	10	0	19
Present	23	5	40	33	1	34
Fourth semester (*n*=4)						
Preterite	87	7	8	94	6	5
Imperfect	4	5	38	2	3	25
Present	9	2	26	12	11	21
Fifth semester (*n*=3)						
Preterite	164	8	3	148	14	10
Imperfect	6	6	73	12	4	76
Present	59	14	39	42	7	27

Based on data from Salaberry (1999).

during the first or the second session of data collection. Note, though, that these learners had received explicit instruction and practice on the use of the Imperfect during the two weeks before the session when they produced their second oral narratives (the Preterite had been introduced before). On the other hand, the use of the Preterite and Imperfect in the data from the other learners (from third to fifth semester) was correlated with the value of lexical aspectual classes. That is, the use of the perfective form was associated with telic events and, vice versa, the use of the imperfective form was associated with states. In contrast with the claim of the LAH, the influence of lexical aspect increased constantly as a function of proficiency and experience with the L2. In sum, Salaberry proposed that during the initial stages of L2 development, L1 English speakers use the Spanish Preterite as a default marker of past tense across lexical aspectual classes. The role of lexical aspect becomes relevant as experience with the language increases (i.e., third to fifth semester). Another relevant finding of this study was that the more advanced students made selections of past tense morphology that were more radically associated with lexical aspectual classes than the options selected by the control group of native speakers.

The claim advanced by Salaberry is, however, tentative at best given some of the limitations of the study. In particular, there are some research design constraints that should be taken into account. First, the findings are restricted to the analysis of data from fictional narratives collected among adult classroom learners. Thus, it is open to question whether learners producing personal narratives will also reveal the same trends depicted in this study. Second, as pointed out by Slabakova (2002: 175) Salaberry's study did not have 'an independent measure of proficiency apart from the university placement tests'. This shortcoming mostly applies to the finding of the increasing effect of lexical aspect throughout levels of proficiency per the study's classification system. On the other hand, the lack of an independent measure of proficiency is immaterial to the fact that the beginning learners in this study were impervious to the teaching of the Imperfect and relied, instead, on the use of a single marker of past tense. In fact, if the claim was that the learners classified as beginners in Salaberry's study were actually more advanced than their classification entails, the claim about the effect of the use of a default past tense marker would be even more compelling given that it would be applicable to more proficient learners.

Despite the previous caveats, in a follow-up study, Salaberry (2002) extended the claim advanced by Salaberry (1999) with the use of a written cloze-type fill-in-the-blanks test. Even though a written cloze-type task is less spontaneous than oral narrative data, the former allows for the collection of a larger data set, and accordingly, the use of more powerful statistical procedures. Moreover, Salaberry's follow-up study introduced a new independent variable: the explicit analysis of non-prototypical selections of Preterite–Imperfect in Spanish. The main participants in this study were students from two college-level Spanish language courses: 25 students from a third semester course and 24 students from a sixth semester course. Thus, learners were classified into two proficiency levels according to the spacing of three semesters of instruction. A group of 32 monolingual native speakers of Spanish residing in their native country acted as a control group. The texts used to contextualize the choices of past tense forms made by the informants contained original selections of Preterite and Imperfect that were non-prototypical (e.g., *saber*, to know, was conjugated with the Preterite *supo*). The test comprised four different short texts. Three of the texts were original excerpts from two famous Spanish-speaking literary authors.[11] The author wrote a fourth passage to incorporate examples of non-prototypical use of non-stative verbs (e.g., Preterite with stative verbs) that were not exemplified in the chosen literary texts. The original narratives were transformed into a 41-item cloze-type task by replacing verb entries

Table 3.14 Distribution of use of Imperfect/Preterite by verb type and level in percentages

Verb type (N)	Third semester		Sixth semester		Natives	
	IMP	PRET	IMP	PRET	IMP	PRET
Stative (10)	27	73	63	23	25	75
Atelic events (14)	15	85	40	60	30	70
Telic (17)	08	92	18	82	18	82

Based on data from Salaberry (2002).

with blank spaces. The main findings from the study are presented in graphical format in Table 3.14.

The analysis of the data revealed a clear relationship between lexical aspectual classes and past tense verbal endings among the advanced students. That is, the use of Imperfect was associated with stative verbs (63 per cent) to a much higher extent than with telic events (18 per cent). Conversely, the use of Preterite with the telic event category (82 per cent) revealed a much stronger association than with states (23 per cent). In contrast, the morphological marking of verbs among the intermediate learners was not necessarily correlated with lexical aspectual types. For instance, the use of the Preterite was represented in all lexical aspectual categories: from 73 per cent with states to 92 per cent with telic events. Conversely, the use of the Imperfect was minimally used across all aspectual categories of verbs: from 27 per cent with states to 8 per cent with telic events. Thus, these data corroborate the findings from Salaberry (1999) with regard to (1) the use of default past tense marker among less proficient learners and (2) the increasing effect of the lexical aspectual semantics of verbs as learners become more proficient in the L2. That is, L2 Spanish learners start using a default marker of past tense (i.e., Preterite) and eventually take into account the effect of the distribution of lexical aspectual classes as an additional factor to decide when to use the perfective and imperfective markers. In line with the findings from Salaberry (1999), a third important finding of the present study showed that the more advanced students make selections of past tense morphology that are more radically associated with lexical aspectual classes than the options selected by the control group of native speakers. That is, it appears that as soon as learners realize that verb types are typically associated with specific markers (i.e., prototypical), they 'bet' heavily on this association.

Findings from a subsequent study conducted by Salaberry (2003), however, revealed that the default marker of past tense proposed by Salaberry

(1999, 2002) may be affected by the type of narrative (e.g., personal versus fictional). The objective pursued in this study was based on Noyau's (1990) claim that personal narratives – unlike impersonal narratives – allow for a departure from the chiefly chronological series of events typical of the movie narratives (used in most previous studies of L2 acquisition). Thus, it is possible that the use of a default past tense value may be applicable to only one type of narrative (i.e., fictional). The study was based on data collected from 105 L1 English speakers divided into three levels of proficiency according to their placement into second, fourth and sixth quarter of instruction (every three quarters of instruction corresponded to two academic semesters). The analysis used two multiple-choice tasks based on two different texts of similar lengths: one text was based on a fictional narrative and the other on a personal narrative. Both texts were originally written by students and modified according to lexical criteria (i.e., to make the text accessible to the less proficient students) and methodological criteria (i.e., to keep an adequate balance of lexical aspectual classes). The findings for both tasks are summarized in Table 3.15.

The analysis of the data based on the fictional narrative test provided confirmatory evidence for the claim of a default past tense marker. In particular,

Table 3.15 Percentage of use of verbal endings in both the personal and fictional narrative texts

Verb type	Group	Preterite		Imperfect		Present	
		Person	Fiction	Person	Fiction	Person	Fiction
States	Second quarter	**21.2**	50.3	**46.1**	30.3	10.8	14.3
	Fourth quarter	31.7	37.7	52.7	31.3	14.0	27.6
	Sixth quarter	40.3	42.3	53.3	48.0	6.4	8.0
	Near-natives	22.2	62.2	77.8	37.8	0	0
	Natives	26.0	62.0	74.0	38.0	0	0
Atelic	Second quarter	**29.1**	65.9	**46.1**	24.0	6.7	5.7
	Fourth quarter	37.8	51.4	39.3	25.7	20.7	19.4
	Sixth quarter	61.0	68.2	32.0	27.1	5.7	3.9
	Near-natives	40.0	72.3	60.0	27.8	0	0
	Natives	46.0	55.0	54.0	45.0	0	0
Telic	Second quarter	**31.4**	67.0	**41.7**	21.2	9.1	7.4
	Fourth quarter	42.6	55.3	41.7	20.4	13.4	20.6
	Sixth quarter	70.4	83.8	26.4	10.1	2.2	4.5
	Near-natives	87.5	94.7	12.5	5.9	0	0
	Natives	81.0	94.0	19.0	6.0	0	0

Based on data from Salaberry (2003).

the Preterite was used more often than the Imperfect with statives in all but the highest level of proficiency. The analysis of data across levels of proficiency also confirms the trend towards the increasing effect of lexical aspect on the selection of past tense morphology in association with increasing levels of L2 proficiency. On the other hand, analysis of data from the text based on the personal narrative revealed a dramatic contrast: among the lowest level of proficiency, the Imperfect was used more often than the Preterite with statives (46.1 per cent versus 21.2 per cent, respectively), with atelic events (46.1 per cent versus 29.1 per cent, respectively) and with telic events (41.7 per cent versus 31.4 per cent, respectively). Even though it is expected that atelic verbs can be marked with the imperfective form, it is surprising that telic verbs would be marked with the Imperfect as well. One possible explanation of this result is that all respondents (including natives and near-natives) may have reassessed the categorization of lexical aspectual classes in the context of the personal narrative in which the concept of habituality is central to the text. That is, it is possible that telic events that are represented as habitual were – correctly – marked with the Imperfect.

To substantiate this claim, we need to assess the findings from the control group. In fact, note that the control groups of natives and near-native speakers were slightly affected by the narrative type in their selection of past tense endings with telic events. That is, for near-natives, the use of Preterite with telic verbs increases from 87.5 per cent in personal narratives to 94.7 per cent in the fictional narratives. Among native speakers, the change is even more radical: from 81 per cent in personal narratives to 94 per cent in the fictional narratives. Conversely, near-natives and natives increased their use of the Imperfect in the personal narrative by 6 per cent and 13 per cent, respectively. As a matter of fact, proportionally speaking, the shift towards the use of the Imperfect with telic events in the personal narrative is more pronounced among the members of the control group.

In sum, the textual nature of the personal narrative is likely to have promoted a distinct 'visualization' of telic events as habitual events in the past that were marked with the Imperfect. Moreover, it appears that learners are aware of these distinct aspectual meanings and that they can override the use of the default past tense marker they used in the fictional narrative (i.e., the Preterite). In other words, these findings seem to indicate that discursive factors may determine the selection of the default marker of past tense. There are, however, a number of methodological constraints that should also be taken into account to properly assess the significance of these findings. First, the use of the movie excerpt to provide a visual background for the fictional narrative task may have provided the students with a level of contextualization richer than for the task associated with the personal narrative. Second, there was an unequal distribution of verb types in the fictional and personal narratives. Most notably, whereas in the fictional narrative there were 17 telic events and five statives, the proportion of telic events to states in the personal narrative was eight to nine. Finally, it is open to question whether a multiple-choice fixed text is really representative of a personal narrative that by definition would require some personal involvement from each respondent. In sum, what may have been logistical conveniences to address the research questions became methodological liabilities that should be addressed in subsequent studies.

Dinan (2007) replicated Salaberry's study to ascertain that the results of the latter were not an artefact of the unequal distribution of tokens corresponding to different lexical aspectual classes. In other words, the verbal predicates used in Dinan's study were proportionally allocated to all three lexical aspectual classes. Her study was based on data collected among 76 college-level adult native speakers of English divided into two groups: second semester (n=32) and third semester (n=44). As was the case in Salaberry's (2003) study, Dinan used two multiple-choice tests differentiated according to narrative type (i.e., fictional and personal). The fictional narrative was based on a portion of the animated movie *Shrek*. It recounted a fairy tale with creatures such as dragons, ogres and a princess in a castle. The other multiple-choice test was based on a personal narrative, told in the first person point of view and narrating the story of a student's first day of school at the university. The number of words in each text was balanced, as was the distribution of verbs corresponding to different lexical aspectual classes. In particular, both texts contained 21 multiple-choice items (7 telic events, 7 atelic events and 7 states). Also, unlike in the study conducted by Salaberry, students were not provided with any movie prompt before they completed the fictional task. The findings from Dinan are summarized in Table 3.16.

From Dinan's results, it appears that the unexpected finding from Salaberry (2003) may have been an artefact of the unequal distribution of verb types in the fictional and personal narratives. That is, the data from the personal narrative task used in Dinan shows that the perfective form (i.e., Preterite) was the preferred marker of past tense across lexical aspectual classes. This is especially clear from the analysis of data from atelic verbs (i.e., activities and states). On the other hand, what was surprising in the findings from Dinan's study is that the Imperfect appears to be used in closer association with atelic verbs in the fictional rather than the personal narrative. Dinan speculates that the '[s]ubjects may have interpreted the

Table 3.16   Percentage of verbal endings in fictional and personal narrative

		Preterite		Imperfect		Other	
		Fictional	Personal	Fictional	Personal	Fictional	Personal
States	Second semester	38.1	**54.7**	42.6	32.0	19.3	13.3
	Third semester	23.3	54.1	60.1	39.2	16.5	6.7
Atelic	Second semester	38.6	**68.4**	31.2	24.4	30.2	7.2
	Third semester	34.8	73.4	44.7	25.0	20.5	1.6
Telic	Second semester	74.3	**75.6**	12.4	15.0	13.4	9.4
	Third semester	83.4	85.5	4.7	10.4	12.0	4.1

Based on data from Dinan (2007).

atelic events in the fictional narrative as being habitual or ongoing events, whereas the atelic events in the personal narrative could have been interpreted as completed actions in a one-time episode' (p. 18).

Finally, Salaberry (forthcoming) compared the relative effect of inherent lexical aspect and discursive grounding on the use of L2 Spanish Preterite and Imperfect using a written 40-item text-based forced-choice task. The text was an example of what Bardovi-Harlig (2000) categorized as a personalized fictional narrative. That is, the story was based on a native speaker's narrative of a cartoon in which the narrator was asked to play the role of the main character of the story. The task was completed by a group of 286 English-speaking learners of Spanish and a control group of 149 native speakers in their home country. This represents one of the largest databases of studies on the development of tense-aspect in L2 acquisition. The learners were classified into four levels of proficiency determined by course enrollment: second to fifth semester of instruction. The division of learners according to proficiency was further ascertained by the use of an independent test of Spanish (i.e., a modified version of the *Diploma de Español como Lengua Extranjera*). The text used in this study was a modified version of a native speaker's narrative of a cartoon from the popular graphic artist *Quino*. The original text was modified (1) to eliminate any vocabulary items that may have impeded the understanding of the text by the less proficient learners and (2) to maintain a good balance of verb types according to the classifications of grounding and lexical aspect. Out of 40 predicates selected as test items, 24 were classified as part of background clauses and the remaining 16 were categorized as part of the foreground of the story. The high proportion of backgrounded clauses (higher than in typical simple-plot fictional narratives) is due to two factors: (1) the content of the story in which the main character remembers several events from his childhood and (2) the fact that the narrator was asked to play the role of the main character. On the other hand, the proportion of lexical aspectual classes was fairly balanced with a slightly higher proportion allocated to the two ends of the continuum of lexical semantics: 14 states (10 in the background), 11 activities (9 in the background) and 15 telic events (5 in the background).

The analysis of learner data only revealed that both lexical aspect and grounding were directly correlated with the choice of past tense marker across all levels of proficiency in Spanish. On the other hand, the effect of lexical aspect and grounding did not reach the highest degree of association with past tense marking during the beginning stages of development. On the contrary, the association between lexical aspect and grounding with the use of Preterite and Imperfect gradually increased as proficiency in the L2 increased. In essence, these results provide additional empirical evidence against the first tenet of the LAH and furnish additional support for the claim of the DPTH. In essence, this study revealed a gradual increase in categorical choices (either Preterite or Imperfect) from second semester learners to native speakers according to both lexical aspect and grounding. For instance, Figure 3.3 shows how the use of Preterite becomes more associated with the foregrounded eventualities in the narrative at the same time that the Imperfect becomes more associated with the backgrounded eventualities in the narrative. Furthermore, there is also a noticeable trend towards the strong reliance on prototypical markers that surpasses the biases exhibited by native speakers (cf. Salaberry, 1999, 2002).

When we factor in the results from native speakers, some additional interesting trends are revealed. The statistical analysis of the findings showed that for the interaction between aspect and level, the only significant difference is given by the contrast between the native speakers and all groups of learners in association with activities only. That is, native speakers categorically preferred the use of the perfective form, whereas learners were more likely to use the imperfective form. There were no significant differences across groups for the analysis of grammatical marking with states or telic events. In contrast, the analysis of the interaction between grounding and level revealed a statistically significant difference between native speakers compared to all groups of learners in association with the use of grammatical markers of past tense in the foreground of the narrative. There was also a statistically significant difference between native speakers and all learners but the ones in the fifth semester in association with the use of grammatical markers of past tense in the background of the narrative.

Interestingly, native speakers were the most categorical in marking *telic events* with the Preterite in the foreground (a prototypical choice), while at

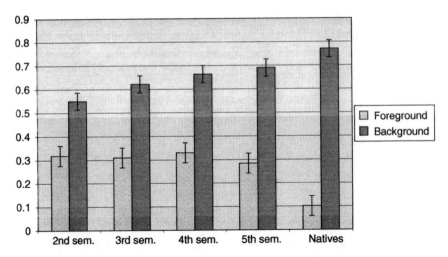

FIGURE 3.3 Distribution of means for foreground by level of proficiency (based on Salaberry, forthcoming). Y-axis = 0 corresponds to selections of Preterite and 1 to selections of Imperfect.

the same time they categorically marked *telic events* with the Imperfect in the background (a non-prototypical choice). The only learner group that patterned in their selections with native speakers was the group of fifth semester learners. In other words, it appears as if the learners in the lower levels of proficiency (second to fourth semester) are not yet marking *telic events* with grammatical markers in association with grounding as much as they mark them in association with lexical aspect. In fact, the selection of past tense markers associated with *states* reveals the same trend described for the marking of telic events (although this contrast was not statistically significant as was the association with telic events). That is, native speakers (as well as fourth and fifth semester students) marked *states* with the Preterite in the foreground (a non-prototypical choice), at the same time they tend to mark *states* with the Imperfect in the background (a prototypical choice). In sum, of the two independent variables (aspect and grounding), it appears that grounding is the one that more clearly distinguishes the performance of native speakers when compared to learners.

3.1.1.2 Data from advanced learners

Whereas most of the studies summarized previously posit the role of a default past tense during beginning stages of acquisition, empirical data indicates that highly proficient L2 learners may also rely on the use of a default marker of past tense (e.g., Antonio, 2007; Liskin-Gasparro, 2000; Lubbers-Quesada, 1999, 2007; Salaberry, 2005). From a theoretical point of view, this may indicate that English speakers in particular may be highly dependent on L1 transfer. Therefore, let us review some of the most significant studies in this regard.

Liskin-Gasparro (2000) analysed both personal and movie narratives as well as recall protocols of the use of past tense marking among eight advanced students of Spanish. The assessment of the proficiency level of the eight subjects On the American Council on the Teaching of Foreign Languages proficiency scale was as follows: Intermediate High (3), Advanced (3), Advanced High (1) and Superior (1). The personal narrative task was based on the interviewee's recounting of a significant event triggered by words about emotions (joy, fear, etc.) printed on a series of ten index cards used to prompt the informants' memory. The film retell was based on the well-known excerpt '*Alone and Hungry*' from the Chaplin film *Modern Times*. Both narratives were videotaped. The retrospective protocol session was conducted immediately after the participants finished their two narratives. During this last task, the researcher watched the videotaped narrative from each participant and stopped the tape at frequent intervals (especially when informants hesitated) to request their opinion as to the reasons for the use of Preterite or Imperfect.

Liskin-Gasparro analysed the data from all three tasks to investigate the effect of narrative type, lexical aspect, the role of the narrator and the effect of instruction. The analysis of the two narratives corroborated previous findings of a clear effect of type of narrative on the proportional use of Preterite and Imperfect in each narrative: a 60–40 per cent proportional use of Preterite–Imperfect in the fictional retell was reversed in the personal narrative with an equivalent 40–60 per cent use of the Preterite and Imperfect, respectively. Liskin-Gasparro comments that the difference in proportional distributions across narrative types is most likely due to the fact that film retells contain almost no evaluative elements. Thus, learners are likely to use fewer activity and state verbs. The analysis of data of the two narratives also provided additional empirical evidence to confirm the effect of lexical aspect on the selections of Preterite and Imperfect. Interestingly, however, the analysis of the recall protocols on the selection of past tense markers hints at the possible effect of a default value of past tense. In particular, Liskin-Gasparro mentions the case of Jason's (not his real name) 'default settings:' 'for state verbs – he opted for the imperfect' (p. 836) and what Rick labelled his 'safety things:' 'certain verbs are always to be encoded in the Imperfect, and others in the Preterite' (p. 837). For instance, after being asked why he used the Imperfect *había* in *había un accidente* (instead of Preterite *hubo*), Jason states:

I am not sure why, I think it's just conditioning, just that I am used to using a particular form, for some things I just tend to use the Imperfect more for *quería, había*, I don't think I like the *–o* in *quiso, hubo* (p. 837).

Finally, the effect of the narrator's choices on how to recount the stories and the effect of previous instructional rules of thumb are also evident in several comments from the students. For instance, Sam's response about the rationale for the use of the Imperfect in one scene but the Preterite in another similar sequence of events (as depicted in sentences 4 and 5) is very informative:

4. Una mujer joven estaba caminando (PROGR) por la calle. Estaba (IMP) sola, tenía (IMP) hambre. Le robó (PRET) un pedazo de pan de un camión.
   A woman was walking along the street. She was alone and hungry. She stole a piece of bread from a truck.
5. Entonces la joven con el pan corrió (PRET) por el parque y se chocó (PRET) con Charlie.
   Then the woman started to run with the bread towards a park and she stumbled upon Charlie.

Sam explains that his use of the Preterite in scene (5) but not (4) is 'because running is faster than walking. . . . And when I think about it now, it also makes sense that the running was interrupted. I guess the speed of it makes it a Preterite'. Liskin-Gasparro comments that 'what remained unarticulated in his misapplication of a common instructional rule was an awareness of the function of foregrounding and backgrounding in narrative'. Liskin-Gasparro further stated that learners effectively marked past tense aspect according to grounding, even though they refer to made-up rules that are post-hoc explanations.

Antonio (2007) replicated the findings from Liskin-Gasparro with a group of five near-native speakers of Spanish (also graduate students in Spanish as in Liskin-Gasparro's study). Antonio gathered the data through an informal oral interview, in which participants were asked to comment on their experiences (people they met, their expectations and their goals) after they first arrived to campus. The interview was audio-recorded and at the end of the interview, the researcher played back the tape and asked her informants for their rationale for the use of specific instances of Preterite or Imperfect. The researcher selected mostly uses of past tense in which the interviewees hesitated or paused during the interview. The range of requests for explanations about the uses of past tense varied from nine to thirteen instances per participant. The analysis of the explanations offered by her participants led Antonio to conclude there was an apparent use of preferred past tense markers with specific verbs. For instance, one of Antonio's participants articulated the following reason for his or her selection of the imperfective form with the state verb *estar* (to be):

> 'Estar' is one of those verbs I almost always use in the imperfect, it's automatic. I guess it's because it was over a period of time, I'm not really sure about them (verbs like 'estar'), and I think they're more commonly used in the imperfect [Participant 3] (p. 13).

Interestingly, Antonio concluded that '[t]he dominant reason for aspectual selection by advanced learners appears to be discursive in nature, followed by lexical [aspect] and finally instruction' (p. 9). Furthermore, Antonio points out that the learners seemed to recast their choices after they were asked to provide a rationale for them. For instance, one participant who had used the Imperfect stated: 'I guess, listening to it now, I would have used the Preterite because I thought it was over a period of years in the past, it's done now' [Participant 3] (p. 8).

In sum, the combined findings from Liskin-Gasparro and Antonio indicate that advanced learners may have difficulty to ascertain the use of past tense markers in association with specific verbs and, in particular, with states. At the same time, the data from both studies show that learners seem to be more accurate with their selections of past tense marking when they are based on grounding contrasts. Note that this contrasting trend in the use of past tense markers in L2 Spanish in association with lexical aspect, and grounding is mirrored by the results obtained from the analysis of data from Salaberry (forthcoming) reviewed in the previous section.

3.1.1.3 Data from study-abroad students

Whereas the studies reviewed earlier focused on data collected among strictly classroom students, some studies have gathered information from learners who have had exposure to L2 Spanish in the natural environment of communication (i.e., places where Spanish is the majority language). The results from these studies can be regarded as comparable, to some extent, to the findings of advanced students reviewed in the previous section. That is, these data provide additional information about possible effects of default past tense markers among advanced learners.

Lubbers-Quesada (1999) analysed written personal narratives from 32 university students after they had spent one month and a half in a language immersion programme in Mexico. The students already had one year of previous study in a classroom environment before their trip to Mexico. The analysis of past tense marking showed that the Preterite surpassed the use of the Imperfect in a proportion of 3:1, confirming a trend also reported in previous studies (e.g., Hasbún, 1995; Salaberry, 1999). More importantly, there were only six tokens of achievements marked with the Imperfect (out of 589 possible achievements). On the other hand, at the other end of the spectrum of lexical aspectual classes, statives were marked with both Preterite and Imperfect. For instance, the analysis of the six most common (typical) stative verbs shows that only the verbs *haber* (there is/are) and *estar* (to be) were marked with the Imperfect more often than the Preterite: 93 and 73 per cent, respectively. In contrast, the remaining four stative verbs (i.e., *hacer, querer, ser and tener*) were marked with Preterite as often as they were marked with the Imperfect: approximately 50 per cent. We should note that the verb *haber* is defective to the extent that it is not conjugated according to person or number: *Hubo* and *había* are the only past tense forms of this verb (except in non-standard varieties: *habíamos/habían cinco personas* – 'there were five people' instead of *había cinco personas* – 'there was five people'). As for the verb *estar*, it is in complementary distribution with the verb *ser*, at least in contrast with the use of the verb *to be* in English. In other words, the preference for the Imperfect with *estar* and *haber* may be explained as non-regularized typeS of past tense marking.

In a follow-up study, Lubbers-Quesada (2007) analysed data from oral narratives (as opposed to written narratives as reported in the previous study) among 30 L1 English study-abroad students divided into three groups according to previous experience with Spanish (one, two and three or more years of experience with the L2). The results replicate the previous findings from Lubbers-Quesada, in some cases showing even more categorical findings (e.g., learners with one year of experience with Spanish used the Preterite and Imperfect in a proportion of 9 to 1). Table 3.17 shows the relative distribution of past tense marking across all categories of verbs combined and with states only.

The analysis of these findings shows that the use of the Imperfect is biased towards the marking of states across all groups of learners by a large margin (from 79 to 89 per cent). For instance, 231 tokens of the Imperfect used among students with three years of experience were associated with states (i.e., 81 per cent rate). That is, there is no particular developmental trend

Table 3.17 Distribution of Preterite–Imperfect across all categories of verbs and *with states only*: across category analysis

	1 year	2 years	3 years	Natives
	all verbs/states	all verbs/states	all verbs/states	all verbs/states
Imperfecto	9/8	78/62	284/231	203/110
Pretérito	93/31	129/23	419/84	387/55
Total	**102/39**	**207/85**	**703/315**	**590/165**

Based on data from Lubbers-Quesada (2007).

Table 3.18 Distribution of Preterite–Imperfect *with states*: within category analysis

	1 year (%)	2 years (%)	3 years (%)	Natives (%)
Imperfect	20	73	73	67
Preterite	80	27	27	33

Based on data from Lubbers-Quesada (2007).

associated with the use of the Imperfect among learners. In line with previous studies, however, it appears as if learners radicalize their use of the Imperfect with states in comparison with the data from native speakers. The native speakers used the Imperfect with states at a 54 per cent rate, much lower than the approximately 89 per cent rate of learners. In contrast, the use of the Preterite reveals much lower percentages of association with states (between 20 and 33 per cent). The highest use of the Preterite with statives occurs among students with one year of experience: 31 out of a total of 93 tokens (33 per cent of the total). As a comparison, the percentage of use of the Preterite with other lexical aspectual classes was as follows: 17 per cent are activities, 23 per cent are accomplishments and 27 per cent are achievements (23, 84, and 55 tokens respectively). In other words, among beginning learners, the Preterite is used more often with states than with any other verb type. In essence, the Preterite seems to be acting as a default past tense marker with the least proficient learners only.

Another way of analysing these data is through an examination of past tense marking of states only (a within category analysis). Table 3.18 reveals a radical shift from one to two years of experience that completely reverses the proportional marking of states. That is, whereas states are marked with the Imperfect only 20 per cent of the time among students with one year of experience, they are marked with the Imperfect 73 per cent of the time among students with two years of experience. The reverse trend happens

Table 3.19   Tokens of use of Spanish past tense according to grounding

	Foreground			Background			
	PRET	**IMP**	**Total**	**PRET**	**IMP**	**Total**	**Total**
Learners	252	5	272	30	127	245	517
Natives	140	0	148	2	88	120	268
Total	**392**	**5**	**420**	**32**	**215**	**365**	**785**

Note. The number of tokens of Preterite and Imperfect do not add up to the total because the uses of present tense are not included in the table.
Based on data from Granda (2004).

with the use of the Preterite. The previous finding seems to provide empirical support for the claim of a default past tense marker among beginning learners only.

Granda (2004) specifically investigated the effect of foreground and background sections in written narratives from 15 L1 English speakers studying Spanish in Mexico. The learners had already taken the equivalent to 400 hours of class and were immersed in the natural environment of communication. The narratives were elicited with the use of the five-minute professional movie *El Héroe.* Ten native speakers acted as a control group. The following are the results of the analysis of the 785 tokens of past tense marking in the narratives of both native and non-native speakers. Contrary to the outcome of most other studies reviewed earlier, Table 3.19 shows that the number of tokens assigned to the foreground and the background of the elicited stories were almost proportional in length among both learners (272 versus 245 for foreground and background, respectively) and native speakers (148 versus 120 for foreground and background, respectively).

The interaction of grounding with the effect of lexical aspect is presented in Tables 3.20 and 3.21. With regard to the use of verbs in the foreground of the stories, Granda points out there are no significant discrepancies in the use of the Preterite across lexical aspectual classes: Highest use of Preterite with achievements and lowest use with states. The only minor exception to this trend would be the slightly higher use of Preterite with states among the native speakers (7 per cent) compared to the non-native speakers (3 per cent).

In contrast, the analysis of the use of the Preterite in the background of the elicited narratives among L2 learners is not equivalent to its use among native speakers. In fact, the only group that actually used the Preterite in the background was the group of L1 English speakers (30 tokens or 13 per cent). Among native Spanish speakers, the use of the Preterite was almost negligible (2 tokens or 2 per cent).

Table 3.20   Tokens of Preterite across lexical aspectual classes in the *foreground* clauses of the elicited narratives

	STA	ACT	ACC	ACH	Total
Learners	9 (3%)	39 (14%)	72 (26%)	132 (49%)	252 (92%)
Natives	10 (7%)	24 (16%)	40 (27%)	66 (45%)	140 (95%)

Based on data from Granda (2004).

Table 3.21   Tokens of Preterite across lexical aspectual classes in the *background* clauses of the elicited narratives

	STA	ACT	ACC	ACH	Total
Learners	21 (9%)	3 (1%)	4 (2%)	2 (1%)	30 (13%)
Natives	2 (2%)	0 (0%)	0 (0%)	0 (0%)	2 (2%)

Based on data from Granda (2004).

Granda points out, out of the 30 tokens of Preterite in the background of the narratives, 24 correspond to events and situations that are simultaneous to events mentioned in the foreground. Thus, the use of the Preterite was inappropriate. For the purpose of our discussion, note that 21 of the 24 incorrectly used Preterites are marked on statives. For instance, Granda mentions the following examples:

6. . . . vi a una chica que no *pareció* (PRET) cansada.
   . . . saw a girl that did not look tired.
7. *fue* (PRET) un hombre viejo que parecía solo
   there was an old man that seemed to be alone.
8. *hubieron* (PRET) dos hombres peleando.
   There were two men fighting.
9. . . . le dio cuenta que *hubo* (PRET) una muchacha enfrente de todas las otras personas.
   . . . he realized that there was a young girl in front of the other people.

The examples are revealing because these stative verbs are typically marked with the Imperfect. Thus, we cannot assume that these uses of the Preterite are the result of some distributional bias from the input data. Alternatively, it appears as if these L2 learners are trying to impose a morphological marker that clearly conveys the notion of past tense. That is, the Preterite, as argued earlier, appears to be regarded as a more appropriate carrier of past tense meaning.

Another study that evaluated the effect of the study-abroad experience among L2 learners was Güell (1998), which was based on data collected from 86 exchange students in Spain. Güell's informants represented a variety of native languages (as well as knowledge of other second languages) and 26 native speakers who acted as a control group. Güell classified the participants in her study into four levels of proficiency: 16 were classified as non-native speaker 1 (NN1) representing the lowest level of proficiency, 15 as NN2, 38 as NN3 and 17 as NN4.[12] Güell also classified learners according to previous background experiences in Spanish, and concluded that there were three distinct groups according to previous background. The first group (G1) was formed by exchange students in a translation programme from *Universitat Pompeu Fabra* in Barcelona, Spain. These students knew at least one second language apart from their native one (in most cases their L1 was English, French or German). Not surprisingly, these students were classified mostly in the upper levels of proficiency. Most important, 16 out of 17 students in level 4 (NN4) came from this group of students.[13] The other two groups of students had, on average, two years of previous study of Spanish. The main difference between these two remaining groups was their L1. G2 was composed of English-speaking students who were part of an exchange programme between Universidad de Barcelona and Knox University (USA). In contrast, G3 was composed of students who had a similar amount of previous study of Spanish as the US group, but unlike the US students, they spoke a variety of L1s.[14]

The test instrument used for the study was represented by four tasks: (1) a prompt-based written narrative, (2) a 32-item cloze test requiring the use of Preterite or Imperfect (the text was based on a native speaker's narrative from the first task), (3) a multiple-choice version of task 2 and (4) a grammaticality judgement task. I will comment on the results from the three most distinct types of tests used by Güell (i.e., tasks 1, 2 and 4). First, the narratives from both native and non-native speakers revealed a tendency to use the Preterite more often than the Imperfect. That is, native speakers used the Preterite on 62 per cent of verbal predicates and the Imperfect on 36 per cent of verbs. On the other hand, non-native speakers overall used the Preterite on 53 per cent of verbal predicates and the Imperfect on 41 per cent of verbs.[15] This result is not unexpected given that most sequential narratives show a similar trend.

The results from the 32-item cloze test are summarized in Table 3.22. The findings from the cloze test show that (1) native speakers' choices were categorical (i.e., Preterite was used in foreground clauses and Imperfect in background clauses), (2) the use of the Preterite is favoured in

Table 3.22 Selection of past tense marking in cloze test (Task 2)

	Background					Foreground				
	NN1 (%)	NN2 (%)	NN3 (%)	NN4 (%)	N (%)	NN1 (%)	NN2 (%)	NN3 (%)	NN4 (%)	N (%)
Imperfecto	**45**	49	76	86	90	14	22	17	5	0
Pretérito	**54**	36	17	6	0	66	54	78	92	100

Based on data from Tables 49 and 50 from Güell (1998, pp. 433–4).

foregrounded clauses, albeit this is a developmental trend and (3) students from the NN1 group favoured the use of the Preterite over the Imperfect in background clauses (in clear contrast to the selections of the other more advanced non-native speakers and the native speakers). The latter finding is worthy of further analysis given its potential towards the identification of a possible emergent tendency to mark tense instead of lexical aspect with verbal morphology.

Focusing on the data from the background section of the narrative only, there is a clear developmental trend in the proportional use of the Preterite–Imperfect. In fact, the ratios of use of the Preterite–Imperfect were 1.2, 0.73, 0.22 and 0.06 for the groups NN1, NN2 NN3 and NN4, respectively. That is, (1) the Preterite is the preferred initial marker of past tense for the NN1 group, (2) the Preterite is in competition with the Imperfect among members of the NN2 group and (3) the Preterite quickly loses out to the Imperfect among members of the NN3 and NN4 groups. We can substantiate the previous conclusion with additional evidence from specific verbs. For instance, Güell summarized the results across groups for one specific item (number 22) representing the stative *pasar* embedded in a background clause (as shown in its immediate narrative context in the following excerpt):

Era un día cualquiera en el centro del pueblo. La gente (1) PASEAR . . . El platillo (19) ACERCARSE hasta que (20) ESTAR tan cerca que incluso el perro y el gato (21) DEJAR DE JUGAR para mirar qué *era lo que (22) PASAR*. . . .

It was a regular day on the town square. People (1) STROLL . . . The UFO (19) TO GET CLOSER until it (20) TO BE so close that even the dog and the cat (21) STOP PLAYING to see what was that *(22) HAPPEN*. . . .

Güell points out that, native speakers categorically selected the Imperfect to mark *pasar*, non-native speakers of levels 1 and 2 split their choices into

Table 3.23 Selection of Preterite and Imperfect in the background clauses for item 22 in cloze task (Task 2)

	NN1 (%)	NN2 (%)	NN3 (%)	NN4 (%)	N (%)
Imperfecto	31	43	84	94	100
Pretérito	**50**	**43**	13	6	0
Otros	18	14	3	0	0

Based on data from Table 55 from Güell (1998, p. 439).

Table 3.24 Distribution of Preterite and Imperfect with telic/atelic verbs in grammaticality judgement task (Task 4)

	NN2	NN3	NN4	Natives
	Telic/Atelic	Telic/Atelic	Telic/Atelic	Telic/Atelic
Pretérito	80/40	85/28	95/6	95/14
Imperfecto	20/60	15/72	5/94	5/86

Summary from Güell (1998).

perfective and imperfective marking (Table 3.23). It is also interesting to note that *pasar* is preceded by a stative verb already conjugated in the imperfective form (i.e., *era*).

Finally, the results from the fourth test used by Güell (i.e., grammaticality judgement) summarized in Table 3.24 further confirm the increasing effect of lexical aspect in correlation with increasing levels of proficiency. An analysis of the selection of past tense marking with telic verbs across proficiency levels shows a constant increase in the use of Preterite with telic verbs (from 80 to 95 per cent) and a concomitant decrease in the use of the imperfective marker (from 20 to 5 per cent). Moreover, it appears as if the progression of change in morphological past tense marking moves towards native-like performance as clearly depicted in the exact correspondence of choices of native speakers and the NN4 group. A similar analysis of the selection of past tense marking with atelic verbs across proficiency levels shows the opposite effect we described for telic verbs: a constant decrease in the use of Preterite with atelic verbs (from 40 to 6 per cent) and a concomitant increase in the use of the imperfective marker (from 60 to 94 per cent). An interesting part of this analysis is that the range of variation in the use of past tense across proficiency levels for atelic verbs (approximately 34 percentage points) is twice as large as the range for telic verbs (approximately 15 percentage points). The wider range of change associated with atelic verbs reveals a large gap in proficiency to be traversed by learners in connection with atelic verbs.

3.1.2 Data from other languages

In this section, I review empirical findings from studies based on languages other than L1 English or L2 Spanish. Data collected with other combinations of first and second languages are important to ascertain the generalizability of the claim that L2 learners rely on the use of a default past tense marker. Furthermore, the studies reviewed here are based on data from fairly advanced L2 learners, thus providing additional evidence for the possible extension of the notion of a default past tense beyond beginning stages of acquisition.

3.1.2.1 Data from L1 Dutch and Danish speakers

There have been several studies on the acquisition of L2 Spanish past tense-aspect carried out with Dutch L1 and Danish L1 speakers. Among those studies, I review the findings from García and van Putte (1988), Martínez-Baztán (1994) and Cadierno (2000). García and van Putte (1988) compared data from a written task in Spanish from 20 L1 Dutch speakers, who were also L2 Spanish teachers, and 15 native speakers of Spanish from different countries (eight were Spaniards). At the time the study was conducted, the Dutch teachers were taking a postgraduate course at Leiden University. While García and van Putte do not describe the language background of their non-native informants (especially whether they had any experience living in a Spanish-speaking region), we must conclude that their subjects were, at a minimum, advanced speakers of Spanish. García and van Putte used the short story *El muerto* from the Argentinian writer Jorge Luis Borges as their test instrument. The original story is recounted in the historical present and it contains 185 verbal predicates. Both native and non-native speakers were asked to rewrite the story in the past tense. The distribution of choices made by both groups is presented numerically in Table 3.25. The information under native and non-natives on each row shows the number of items that were marked at specific percentages of Preterite or Imperfect. For example, among natives, 56 items were categorically marked with the Imperfect (100 per cent); whereas among non-natives, only 44 items were marked categorically with the Imperfect.

By and large, the profile of choices is very similar in both groups. This is not surprising considering that the non-native speakers were Spanish teachers. These numbers, however, are revealing of an important difference

Table 3.25   Distribution of uses of Preterite and Imperfect

% Imperfect	Natives (*N*=15)	Non-natives (*N*=20)
100	56	44
90–99	9	16
80–89	9	10
70–79	7	14
60–69	4	5
50–59	5	7
41–49	2	4
31–40	5	1
21–30	2	9
11–20	11	9
1–10	14	18
0	61	48
Total	**185**	**185**

Based on data from García and van Putte (1988: 266).

between groups. In particular, it is noticeable that native speakers were more prone to categorically choose a Preterite or Imperfect with 100 per cent agreement among all native speakers. In effect, adding up the two ends of the scale of each group, we obtain 63 per cent of categorical choices for native speakers (117 verbs out of a total of 185) compared to 50 per cent of categorical choices for non-native speakers (92 verbs out of a total of 185). More importantly, when García and van Putte analysed the verb choices that reflected a clear disagreement between groups, it was discovered that non-native speakers were less likely to use the Preterite. Let us review one particular example that the authors analyse in detail to illustrate this outcome:

> Otro año pasa antes que Otálora regrese a Montevideo. Recorren las orillas, la ciudad (que a Otálora le parece muy grande); llegan a casa del patrón; . . .
> Another year goes by before Otálora goes back to Montevideo. They stroll by the coast, the city (that in Otálora's view seems to be huge); they arrive to the boss' home; . . .

Non-native speakers mostly marked the verb *parecer* (seems) with the Imperfect (70 per cent). In contrast, native speakers rarely used the Imperfect (15 per cent) and favoured instead the Preterite. García and van Putte point out that natives interpret Otálora's impression (i.e., *le parece muy grande*) as part of the narrative line ('placeable in time by itself as an independent event'), whereas non-natives appear to perceive Otálora's impression as information about the place that Otálora is visiting (i.e., backgrounded). García and van Putte ask: 'Is the clause primarily about the town, or primarily about Otálora?' García and van Putte conclude that non-natives seem to 'heed only the local clues of lexicon and subordination', whereas the natives seem to have a broader view of the narrative 'preferring a Preterite to highlight the integration of the event parecer "*seem*" with the sequence of Otálora's experiences' (p. 272). García and van Putte conclude that non-native speakers have trouble assessing whether events are foregrounded or backgrounded. Furthermore, as the previous example shows, there also seems to be a possible strong effect of distributional biases associated with specific verbs, as also reported in Salaberry (1999, 2002).

Martínez-Baztán (1994) analysed the use of Spanish past tense in 30 written compositions from 15 L1 Dutch students who were taking their 'last language course' at Utrecht University in The Netherlands. The compositions were written as homework outside of class and the students were not warned that the focus of the analysis of their production would be on their use of past tense in Spanish. The analysis of the distribution of past tense forms in association with the lexical aspectual classes is presented in Table 3.26. There are some noticeable trends in these findings. First, there is an almost equal distribution of achievements and states: 260 achievements versus 253 states. That is, the compositions probably contained a significant amount of descriptions and evaluation relative to the typical fictional narratives. Second, the perfective marker was more commonly used than the imperfective in a proportion of 3:2: there were 398 Preterite forms versus 264 Imperfect forms.[16] Third, the distribution of the Preterite–Imperfect according to lexical aspectual classes seems to provide empirical

Table 3.26 Distribution of past tense markers by lexical aspectual class (percentage of appropriate use in parentheses)

Verb type	N	PRET	IMP
ACH	260	217 (*98%*)	43 (*74%*)
ACC	68	59 (*100%*)	9 (*78%*)
ACT	81	43 (*95%*)	38 (*79%*)
STA	253	79 (*80%*)	174 (79%)
Total	**662**	**398**	**264**

Based on data from Martínez-Baztán (1994).

support for the LAH. For instance, the Preterite is the preferred marker of past tense with telic events over the Imperfect: 217 versus 43 for achievements and 59 versus 9 for accomplishments. In contrast, the Imperfect is the preferred marker of past tense with statives over the Preterite: 79 versus 174 for Preterite–Imperfect marking, respectively. The distribution of past tense markers with atelic events, however, shows that the Preterite is in competition with the Imperfect: 43 versus 38 tokens, respectively.

On the other hand, the analysis of the appropriate use of both past tense markers revealed there were 22 inappropriate uses of the Preterite versus 57 inappropriate uses of the Imperfect. Given that the proportion of use of the Preterite was higher than the Imperfect, the analysis of errors in percentages is more accurate. In this respect, Table 3.26 shows that, whereas the inappropriate uses associated with verbs marked with the Imperfect were equally distributed across all four lexical aspectual classes (approximately 22 per cent), the inappropriate uses of the Preterite were restricted to one single lexical aspectual class: states with a 20 per cent error rate. Thus, the Preterite appears to be used correctly with all dynamic verbs, thus mirroring previous results that show the accurate use of the perfective form with dynamic verbs. On the other hand, the apparent difficulty of Martinez-Baztán's L1 Dutch speakers with the use of the Preterite with states extends and confirms a similar tendency already reviewed in Granda's study with L1 English speakers.

For her part, Cadierno (2000) studied the production of Preterite and Imperfect in narratives collected among ten native speakers of Danish. At the time of the study, Cadierno's subjects were taking a Spanish composition class. Their experience with Spanish was both extensive and varied. Apart from receiving instruction in Spanish for a period of two to three years (for 8 of the 10 subjects), all of them had spent time in a Spanish-speaking country. As a matter of fact, nine of them had spent time in Spain or Latin America for a period of six months to one and a half years. Cadierno's data were collected in the form of a written narrative and a semi-structured oral interview. The written narrative was based on the theme of the informants' unhappiest experience in their lives. In the oral interview, the Danish speakers talked about their happiest experience, what they had done over Christmas and an exciting trip they had taken. The results of Cadierno's study showed that her participants appropriately used both the Preterite and Imperfect in both the written and oral narratives with averages ranging from a minimum of 81.8 per cent of appropriate use of the Preterite in the oral task to a high score of appropriate use of the Imperfect of 86.9 per cent in the written task. When the use of Preterite and Imperfect was analysed according to lexical aspectual classes, the typical pattern of use from other studies also emerged: telic events were marked mostly with the Preterite (89 and 93 per cent for the written oral task, respectively), whereas statives were marked mostly with the Imperfect (70 and 75 per cent in written and oral tasks, respectively).

In terms of the appropriate use of the Preterite and Imperfect according to lexical aspectual class, the written task revealed there was a high degree of appropriate use of both past tense markers in their *prototypical* combinations (e.g., Preterite with achievements or Imperfect with states). That is, the Preterite in association with achievements was appropriately used 95 per cent of the time, whereas the Imperfect in association with states was appropriately used 91 per cent of the time. In contrast, non-prototypical associations (e.g., Preterite with states and Imperfect with achievements) were used appropriately only 60 per cent of the time. The results from the oral task, on the other hand, revealed that whereas the nonprototypical combination of states and the Preterite mirrored the findings from the written task (level of appropriate use of 64.6 per cent), the association of the Imperfect with achievements showed a departure from that trend with an 87 per cent level of appropriate use. Cadierno comments that achievements and states are prime candidates for natural prototypes because they differ with respect to all semantic traits (p. 37).

It is noteworthy that the aggregate data from Cadierno's study masked some important differences when the data were analysed according to each individual learner. The individual departures from the average tendencies exhibited by learners as a whole were regarded as important enough that Cadierno offered explicit commentaries on them. In particular, Cadierno points out that subjects 9 and 10 marked state verbs almost categorically with the Preterite in the written task (71 and 86 per cent, respectively for informants 9 and 10), but they were at the same time ambivalent about the choices of past tense in the oral task (48 and 75 per cent, respectively for informants 9 and 10). Cadierno notes that these two learners used a 'relatively small number of stative predicates repeatedly in the Preterite form' (p. 26). Interestingly, subjects 9 and 10 also marked achievements mostly with the Preterite in both the written task (86.2 and 100 per cent, respectively) and the oral task (97.2 and 87.5 per cent, respectively). In other words, these two advanced learners of Spanish were using the Preterite across all lexical aspectual classes.

3.1.2.2 Data from other Romance languages

The findings from studies that used Romance languages other than Spanish as the target language are obviously directly applicable to the analysis of the acquisition of L2 Spanish, given the close similarities in the representation of tense-aspect meanings across these languages. In this section, I review the findings from Wiberg's (1996) seminal study based on the analysis of Italian data, along with three recent studies focused on the acquisition of L2 Italian, L2 Catalan and L2 Portuguese. The Italian, Catalan and French tense-aspect systems are similar to that of Spanish with respect to the representation of perfectivity and imperfectivity. The main difference with Spanish in particular is that the Italian *Passato Prossimo*, and the French *Passé Composé* are compound forms that conflate perfective and perfect aspect and that both Italian and French use two auxiliary verbs (i.e., to be and to have). The Catalan Preterite is also a compound form that uses the verb *anar* (to go) as the auxiliary plus the infinitive form of the main verb (Comajoan, 2001, 2006). Thus, studies conducted with L2 Italian, L2 Catalan and L2 French are especially informative about the use of Preterite and Imperfect in Spanish. The Portuguese system is very much equivalent to the one of Spanish; minor differences are discussed in Salaberry (2005).

The first published article explicitly asserting the possible effect of a default past tense marker on the development of past tense verbal morphology was Wiberg (1996). Based on the analysis of data from adolescent learners of L2 Italian, Wiberg specifically argued that 'the *Passato Prossimo* is primarily a past tense, used with all types of verbs, while *Imperfetto*, used in a more limited way, shows a tendency to be restricted to states' (p. 1087). Wiberg's claim is mostly based on her analysis of data collected through dialogues with 24 Italian–Swedish bilingual children and adolescents aged 8 to 17. The children lived in Sweden and had one Italian and one Swedish parent. Nevertheless, Swedish was the children's dominant language. The conversations were conducted by Wiberg and were partially planned. Data from conversations with ten Italian native speakers (aged 10–14) from a secondary school in Rome were used as the native speakers' baseline data.

For the analysis of data, Wiberg classified the children into four levels of proficiency. Table 3.27 shows the distribution of *Passato Prossimo* and *Imperfetto* according to lexical aspectual class. What is most noticeable in the distribution of past tense marking is that for level 2, the *Passato Prossimo* is almost evenly distributed across all lexical aspectual classes. In contrast, the use of the *Imperfetto* is associated with statives with an initial spreading towards activities among students with the highest level of proficiency in Wiberg's data. Wiberg provided some excerpts of the data to illustrate the aforementioned tendency towards the use of the perfective marker across verb types. For instance, the following extract is a very revealing example of the prevalence of use of the perfective form: even though the interviewer

Table 3.27   Use of *Passato Prossimo* by lexical aspectual class and level
in tokens

Bilingual level	Passato Prossimo			Imperfetto		
	States	**Act.**	**Telic**	**States**	**Act.**	**Telic**
1	0	9	7	0	0	0
2	9	10	11	1	2	0
3	22	32	55	54	1	0
4	18	28	52	22	9	2

Based on data from Wiberg (1996).

prompts the use of the *Imperfetto* by the way in which she phrases her question, the learner (from level 3) ignores the prompt and uses the perfective
form in her response (in this case with the past participle only). This
finding has been shown in other studies reviewed earlier (e.g., Salaberry,
2003).

EVA:	che facevi (IMP) in Italia?	[habitual]
	What did you use to do in Italy?	
SIT:	mm # mangiato (Past Participle) salame e #st+ . . .[perfective]	
	mm # ate salami and st . . .	

The possible use of a default strategy to mark past tense is also evident in
the selection of the auxiliary (*havere* or *essere*). For instance, in the following
extract, the learner (level 2) uses the auxiliary *havere* even though the interlocutor uses *essere* in her question (additional evidence about the use of the
auxiliary *avere* presented by Rocca (2005) will be discussed later in text).

EVA:	eh tu ci sei mai stata (Past Participle) a Napoli?	
	Have you ever been to Naples?	
SIT:	sí, ho stata (Past Participle).	[wrong auxiliary]
	Yes, I have been.	

Wiberg concluded that 'the most important feature of the *Passato Prossimo*
. . . is the transmission of the meaning [+past]. The distinction between
Passato Prossimo and *Imperfetto* is therefore a secondary opposition, less frequent and more sensitive to the inherent semantics of the verb' (p. 1110).
That is to say, the perfective form is used as a default past tense marker,

whereas the imperfective form is introduced in association with specific few and frequent verbs (i.e., stative).

Whereas Wiberg proposed that the Italian compound past (i.e., *Passato Prossimo*) acts as default past tense marker for L2 Italian learners, Rocca (2005: 176) extended this claim arguing that her data revealed 'both the bare past participle (e.g., *andato*, past participle of the verb *to go*), and the compound past (e.g., *ho andato*, have gone = went) function as default past tenses'. Rocca analysed data from three L1 English-speaking girls (ages 7–8) learning Italian as an L2 in Italy. At the beginning of data collection, the participants had been living in Italy for 4 years and 9 months. Rocca collected data during 15 sessions over a period of six months. She used three tasks in each session: personal stories about what the children had done in the past on specific occasions, movie-based retell narratives (animated cartoons) and oral cloze tasks (the 'beep' game). The combined data from all three tasks rendered a total of 1,308 verb tokens. Most of those verb tokens were marked for past tense (i.e., 1,198). Moreover, the use of past tense revealed a strong preference for the use of the perfective form: out of a total of 1,198 past tense tokens, less than one-fourth were instances of the *Imperfetto* (278). On the other hand, perfective meaning was conveyed mostly with the bare past participle and the compound past: almost half of the total of verbs marked for past tense (i.e., 557) with the perfective were in the form of bare past participles, whereas the compound past represented about one-third of the total (i.e., 363). The most common form of perfective past tense marking (i.e., bare past participle) was used mostly with telic predicates. The compound past, in contrast, was used in approximately equal proportions among telic and atelic predicates.

Moreover, children seemed to favour the use of the auxiliary *avere* in cases where *essere* was the correct choice. This outcome is more significant in the case of verbs denoting change of location (*andare* 'go', *venire* 'come', *arrivare* 'arrive', *cadere* 'fall') that, according to Sorace (2000), are core unaccusatives, thus they should systematically trigger the use of *essere*. Rocca concludes: 'In these L2 Italian learners, *avere* functions as a default auxiliary also occurring with intransitive telic and stative predicates, which would normally select *essere*' (p. 152). Rocca speculates it is possible that the overgeneralization of *avere* derives from the transfer of the English present perfect auxiliary 'have'. However, as suggested by Duffield (2003: 112), the auxiliary *have* acts as default value among native speakers as well. Another interesting outcome of the analysis of the use of auxiliaries is that the past participles preceded by *essere* agreed in gender and number with the subject, whereas the ones preceded by the auxiliary *avere* did not show agreement.

Interestingly, one subject used the *Imperfetto* mostly with states. The other two children, however, marked states with the imperfective only during the first half of the sessions, whereas during the second half, they marked states mostly with the compound past and to some extent the bare past participle. This result is striking given that data from L1 Italian children show that the *Imperfetto* is often overextended at the expense of the *Passato Prossimo*. Rocca surmises that the overproduction of the *Imperfetto* with activities and the concomitant underproduction with states may be prompted by transfer from the children's L1 (i.e., English) in which the Progressive is normally used with activities, but typically not used with states.

Turning our attention to Catalan, Comajoan (2001, 2005b, 2006) studied the emergence of Preterite and Imperfect morphology among three learners of Catalan. Two specific aspects of the research design of Comajoan's study are worth mentioning. First, unlike the majority of previous studies, Comajoan's data were collected over a period of seven months (i.e., it was a longitudinal study). Second, the three informants were L1 English speakers who had achieved an intermediate or advanced level of Spanish and French. Moreover, two of the learners (i.e., Robert and Barbara) had some knowledge of a third Romance language (Romanian and Italian). Comajoan analysed written narratives based on three different types of prompts: a movie clip from the film *Modern Times* already used in several previous studies (*Alone and Hungry*), two storybook narratives (*The Legend of the Knight Saint George* and *The Berenstain Bears' New Baby*) and two comic strips (*Jep and Fidel* and *The Magician*). Comajoan argued that the use of past tense forms among his informants provided empirical support for the aspect hypothesis, 'because achievement and accomplishment predicates in general were inflected for Preterite morphology more frequently than were activity and state predicates, and the opposite was found for the emergence of Imperfect morphology' (p. 2001). Comajoan's conclusion, however, is debatable given that he grouped all types of narratives together. This is important because the data from each type of narrative was collected under very different conditions. For instance, some of the informants' retellings of *The Legend of the Knight Saint George* were preceded by a similar past tense narrative produced by the researcher. The narratives from the film *Modern Times*, in contrast, were not prompted by any previous rendition of the same narrative task.

For the sake of comparison with data from previous studies, let us review the data collected with the movie prompt, which is the only one for which conditions of data collection did not vary from one session to the next

Table 3.28 Use of Preterite, Imperfect and total tokens in the narrative based on the *Modern Times* story

	STA	ACT	ACC	ACH
	Pre-Imp-Oth	Pre-Imp-Oth	Pre-Imp-Oth	Pre-Imp-Oth
Daniel	4 - 3 - 21	6 - 5 - 34	12 - 1 - 38	36 - 6 - 76
Barbara	14 - 1 - 32	9 - 2 - 36	10 - 2 - 66	30 - 0 - 96
Robert	11 - 2 - 17	12 - 3 - 21	16 - 6 - 39	30 - 0 - 59
Total	**29 - 6 - 70**	**27 - 10 - 91**	**38 - 9 - 143**	**96 - 6 - 231**

Note: Pre = Preterite, Imp = Imperfect, Oth = Other
Summarized from Table 8 in Comajoan (2006: 233).

(2006: 221). The summary of findings based on the narrative from the film *Modern Times* is presented in Table 3.28. The analysis of the narratives based on the *Modern Times* film excerpt reveals a clear trend towards the use of the perfective form across all lexical aspectual classes. For instance, within the class of statives, the use of the Preterite (29 tokens total) surpassed the use of Imperfect (6 tokens total) five times to one. Looking at specific cases, we note that Barbara marked states 14 times with the perfective form and only once with the imperfective form. Barbara also used preponderantly the perfective form with other lexical aspectual classes. Furthermore, the proportional use of non-past forms to past forms in Barbara's data is proportionally equivalent across lexical aspectual classes: 15 to 32 tokens with states versus 30 to 96 for achievements. In essence, these data seem to show that the Preterite is overextended to all lexical aspectual classes. In fact, this finding is even more surprising given that these students already knew another Romance language other than Catalan. Notwithstanding the previous claim, it is also the case that telic events (accomplishments and achievements) were overwhelmingly marked with the perfective form.

Finally, Salaberry (2005) analysed data from 70 English–Spanish bilinguals studying L2 Portuguese and 16 native speakers of Portuguese in order to investigate the possible transfer of the aspectual distinctions from one non-native Romance language (i.e., Spanish) to another non-native Romance language (i.e., Portuguese). The analysis was based on L1 English–L2 Spanish learners studying L3 Portuguese. The participants were divided into two groups according to their previous knowledge of Spanish: High and low. Fifty-six students (out of the grand total of 70) were enrolled in a first semester accelerated Portuguese course for Spanish speakers and the remaining 14 students were enrolled in a third semester course for more advanced students. Given that the participants in the study had more experience with the use of aspectual distinctions in Portuguese through their previous knowledge of Spanish, Salaberry analysed his findings according to the categorical selections of past tense marking. Thus, it was determined that all verbs that received combined scores of 80 per cent or higher in favour of the Preterite were regarded to be categorical selections of the perfective marker. In contrast, all verbs that received combined scores of 80 per cent or higher in favour of the Imperfect were considered to be categorical selections of the imperfective. Categorical selections of one or the other marker are indicative of a stable representational system of aspectual distinctions. That is, whenever a group as a whole tends to agree on one or the other marker categorically (i.e., high level of homogeneity of responses), we conclude that group of speakers shares a common representational meaning of the target item.

Table 3.29 shows the number of predicates that were classified unambiguously as Preterite or Imperfect across all three groups. The findings from Salaberry's study provide evidence for two main conclusions. First, there was a clear contrast in the number of categorical choices made by native and non-native speakers. That is, native speakers were, as expected, the most categorical in their choices of perfective or imperfective marker. In contrast, both groups of learners made clear choices of selection of one or the other aspectual marker in approximately two-thirds of the 30 items used in the test. Furthermore, the findings from this study reveal a clear association of the use of the Preterite with mostly telic events across all groups. For instance, out of a total of 15 categorical uses of the Preterite for native speakers, ten of those items were associated with telic events. Similarly, among the more advanced group of L2 Spanish speakers, 9 out of a total of

Table 3.29 Categorical selections of past tense marking (Preterite/Imperfect) across verb types and groups

	Telic	Atelic	Statives	Total
Native speakers	10/3	2/4	3/6	15/13 = 28/30
Spanish-high	9/3	2/4	0/4	11/11 = 22/30
Spanish-low	8/4	2/4	0/2	10/10 = 20/30

Adapted from Salaberry (2005).

11 items categorically marked with the Preterite corresponded to telic events. Thus, learners seem to have clear intuitions about the use of both the Preterite and the Imperfect when using them with dynamic events (non-statives).

On the other hand, the analysis of the use of past tense markers restricted to the category of states only revealed an interesting developmental trend. That is, the less knowledge of Spanish, the more likely the selection of past tense endings with states was non-categorical. For instance, among the members of the Spanish-low group only 2 out of a total of 10 statives received a categorical marking of either Preterite or Imperfect. Spanish-high students made five categorical choices, out of a total of ten options. Finally, native speakers had clear intuitions about the use of one or the other past tense marker in 9 out of 10 instances. In conclusion, among proficient speakers of a Romance language as L2, the marking of states in another Romance language as L3 continues to be challenging. In turn, the difficulty with the marking of states may be associated with the fact that the Imperfect is prototypically associated with states. In other words, the actual learning challenge may be the use of the imperfective form. The latter position is in line with the proposal of the role of a default past tense marker (i.e., the perfective form).

3.2 Syntactic approaches

The more recent studies conducted within the Minimalist perspective (the SSH) introduce both theoretical and methodological differences with previous studies carried out within the purview of the analysis of lexical aspect or narrative grounding. In line with the main claim advanced in the previous two chapters with respect to the definition of aspectual meanings represented in Spanish Preterite and Imperfect, I critically review the findings from studies focused on a strictly syntactic definition of aspect. The evaluation of the data from syntactic analyses of tense-aspect data will be useful to substantiate the contextualized definition of aspect described in Chapter 2. In essence, the extended discussion of these findings will be useful to incorporate them into a broader model of tense-aspect development among L2 Spanish speakers. This section focuses on the analysis of findings that have been advanced to argue for (1) the distinct syntactic and pragmatic meanings of aspect, (2) the distinction between iterativity and habituality, (3) the distinct meaning of generic versus episodic meanings and (4) the development of aspectual contrasts based on accretion or stage-wise progression.

3.2.1 (Selective) effects of pragmatic coercion

Among the first studies to test the role of Universal Grammar on the acquisition of temporality markers in L2 Spanish, Slabakova and Montrul (2002a) analysed data on tense-aspect knowledge among 60 English-speaking learners of Spanish subclassified into 33 intermediate and 27 advanced learners. Two tests were used to classify the participants by proficiency level. The first one was a written test adapted from the *Diploma como Lengua Extranjera* (DELE) exam comprising 50 items: 20 cloze items and 30 multiple-choice vocabulary items. The second test was a 30-item multiple-choice morphology recognition test to determine to what extent the participants were able to use the Preterite and Imperfect. Seventeen native speakers acted as a control group.

The main elicitation task was a sentence conjunction judgement task that required participants to judge the combinatorial felicity of two conjoined clauses on a five-point scale. The possible scores for each sentence spanned a range from [−2 = illogical] to [+2 = logical] with a neutral middle point of 0. The test consisted of 56 sentences (half logical and half illogical) equally divided into four sets of 14 sentences: three sets corresponding to the lexical aspectual classes of achievements, accomplishments and states plus a fourth category of distractors.[17] The sentences were presented in scrambled order. The following are examples of logical and illogical sentences from the categories of states and achievements, respectively.

10a. La clase *era* a las 10 pero empezó a las 10:30. [Logical]
The class was (IMP) at 10, but started (PER) at 10:30
−2 −1 0 1 $\boxed{2}$

10b. La clase *fue* a las 10 pero empezó a las 10:30. [Illogical]
The class was (PRET) at 10, but started (PER) at 10:30
$\boxed{-2}$ -1 0 1 2

11a. Los González *vendían* la casa pero nadie la compró. [Logical]
The González sold (IMP) their house but nobody bought it.
−2 −1 0 1 $\boxed{2}$

11b. Los Gonzalez *vendieron* la casa pero nadie la compró. [Illogical]
The González sold (PRET) their house but nobody bought it.
$\boxed{-2}$ −1 0 1 2

The objective was to investigate whether learners were aware of the semantic implications (logical entailments) of the use of each past tense marker (i.e., Preterite or Imperfect) in the first clause of each sentence. The earlier examples show that the sentences with the Imperfect (i.e., *era* and *vendían*) are compatible with a negation of the event expressed in the second clause of each sentence. This is because the event is not viewed as bounded (thus, a response of +2 is expected). In contrast, the sentences with the Preterite in each pair render the combinations contradictory (thus, a response of –2 is expected). The same instrument was also used to test the LAH. That is, L2 learners were expected to be more accurate identifying that the Preterite would be illogical with accomplishments and achievements than the illogical use of the Preterite with states. This is because the grammatical markers are associated with some lexical aspectual classes at first (i.e., perfective with telic events and imperfective with states). The opposite predictions were made for the judgements about the use of the Imperfect: L2 learners would be more accurate with states than with the eventive classes.

The results of the morphology test confirmed that learners knew how to use Preterite–Imperfect verbal morphology. Furthermore, the statistical analysis of the results of the sentence conjunction judgement task (summarized in Table 3.30) revealed a significant difference in the selections of Preterite and Imperfect with accomplishment, achievement and stative predicates for all the groups (native, advanced and intermediate). That is, both groups of learners knew both the morphology and the semantic entailments associated with each verbal form instantiated in all aspectual classes tested (states, accomplishments and achievements (p. 385).

On the other hand, there was no evidence in the learners' data of an asymmetry of responses consistent with the predictions of the LAH. In other words, it was not the case that states in the Imperfect and achievement and accomplishments in the Preterite were judged more acceptable than the opposite combinations. As a possible explanation for this outcome, Slabakova and Montrul propose that the learners in their study were already too advanced to detect any effects of lexical aspect on the selection of past tense morphology.

Table 3.30 Responses to sentence conjunction test according to 5-point scale

	ACH		ACC		STA	
	PRET	**IMP**	**PRET**	**IMP**	**PRET**	**IMP**
Control (*n*=17)	–1.67	1.39	–0.98	1.34	–1.50	1.56
Advanced (*n*=27)	–1.80	0.26	–1.05	1.19	–0.94	0.84
Interm (high) (*n*=30)	–0.85	–0.30	–0.27	0.26	–0.27	0.24

Based on data from Slabakova and Montrul (2002a).

A quick glance at the results across lexical aspectual classes for all groups of subjects shows that overall, native speakers accepted all sentences marked with the Imperfect and rejected all sentences with the Preterite. In contrast, learners' reactions varied but, overall, their responses were tentative as their average scores tended to concentrate on the neutral middle of the five-point scale (around 0).[18] This is true of the analysis of the data from the intermediate learners, with the possible exception of their rejection of achievements in the Preterite with an average of –0.85. The latter score for the intermediate learners stands in contrast with the averages of –1.8 and –1.7 for advanced and native speakers, respectively. As pointed out by Slabakova and Montrul, the only case in which both groups of learners (not just the intermediate one) did not accept the use of the Imperfect was in the case of achievements (0.26 and –0.30 on the scale of –2 to 2 for advanced and intermediate learners, respectively).

In their discussion of this finding, the authors suggest that '[t]he results of the advanced and intermediate learners with achievements are unexpected, and deserve some comment. Our participants as a group tend to reject achievements in the Imperfect, although they rate achievements in the Preterite even lower, thus demonstrating knowledge of a contrast. This is indeed an intriguing interaction between viewpoint and situation aspect' (p. 387). With respect to the use of the imperfective form with achievements, Slabakova and Montrul correctly point out that 'the process leading up to [the] moment of change' in an achievement 'can be extended, e.g., *reach the top, win a game*. They further note that English native speakers already know how to shift achievements into accomplishments by making reference to the process that precedes the *telos* of the event (e.g., I am reaching the summit). Accordingly, they surmise that the 'process of extending the period leading up to the change of state in achievements is a matter of pragmatics, and more precisely, of aspectual coercion'. Therefore, Slabakova and Montrul 'tentatively conclude that pragmatics is outside of Universal Grammar, and *acquisition of pragmatic contrasts are not guided by the same principles that guide the acquisition of the viewpoint contrast*' (p. 387, stress added).

I believe this conclusion may be premature for two reasons. First, learners did not necessarily reject the combination of the Imperfect with achievements. Rather, they were agnostic in their choices: the scores of both advanced and intermediate learners mostly clustered around the neutral marker of 0 on the five-point range of the –2 to +2 scale (+0.26 for the advanced group and –0.30 for the intermediate group). Native speakers, on the other hand, clearly accepted achievements marked with the Imperfect (average score of +1.39, slightly short of the maximum score of +2 on the five-point scale). Thus, we could argue that learners did not necessarily reject certain answers, but rather, that they provided a tentative response. In other words, the findings from the marking of achievements in particular do not necessarily show that learners knew the semantic contrast represented in the target sentences with achievements.

Second, the proposed division between pragmatic knowledge and grammatical knowledge is theoretically questionable. This is especially relevant for the assessment of whether the definition of aspectual meanings can be represented at the syntactic level or at a discursive level. In this respect, note that if we were to assume that the interpretation of the Imperfect with achievements is a matter of pragmatics, we should logically conclude that the interpretation of the Preterite with states is a matter of pragmatics as well. Basically, if coercion is a process that shifts lexical aspectual classes, it should do so with several (non-prototypical) combinations of lexical and grammatical aspect. Thus, as much as we can focus on the fact that achievements can add a process stage that precedes their inherent endpoint, it is also possible to remove the focus on the process that leads to the inherent endpoint of an accomplishment. In fact, this is quite likely the reason why some of the sentences with accomplishments in the perfective form were rejected categorically by both advanced learners as well as native speakers (−1.05 and −0.98, respectively on a scale of −2 to +2: see Table 3.30).

To test this hypothesis, let us analyse an accomplishment verb in the imperfective (i.e., *corría*) as shown in example (12).

12. Joaquín corría (IMP) la carrera de fórmula 1, pero no participó (PRET).
    Joaquín was going to participate/was running in Formula One race
    but he didn't take part in it.

The grammatical marker (Imperfect) focused the informants' attention on the process leading up to the inherent end point of *running the Formula One race*, thereby shifting the accomplishment to an activity. In essence, the use of the verb *correr la carrera de fórmula 1* in the imperfective (sentence 12) is logical because the inherent end point corresponding to the accomplishment has been subtracted (we only focus on the process).[19] Additional support for the view herein proposed is provided by Michaelis (2004), who argues that the use of the Progressive with accomplishments reveals the effect of contextual coercion in which there is no focus on the inherent end point of the verb. Michaelis claims that 'Progressive sentences containing telic VP complements are instances of coercion. . . . In interpreting the sentence *They were baking a fruitcake,* the interpreter *must derive an interpretation of the VP complement which is compatible with the activity feature that the construction imposes* on its complement daughter' (p. 38, stress added). Thus, why would learners be able to successfully apply pragmatic coercion in one case (i.e., accomplishment into activity) but not in another case (i.e., achievement into activity)?

In fact, the analysis of statives yields a similar outcome to the analysis proposed for accomplishments and achievements. Notice that in sentence (13), the stative verb in focus (i.e., *saber*) – marked with the Imperfect (i.e., *sabía*) – is a stative according to the typical operational tests (e.g., cumulativity, divisability). In contrast, when the verb in focus is marked with the Preterite (i.e., *supo*), it effectively focuses the informant's attention on the transitional state, thus shifting the lexical aspectual category of state to telic event (for additional analysis of the classification of lexical aspectual classes and shifted categories see Chapter 2).

13a. Sabía (IMP) la verdad.
     (S/he) knew the truth.
13b. En ese momento, supo (PRET) la verdad.
     At that moment, (s/he) discovered the truth.

In sum, the pragmatic-discursive coercion mechanism that Slabakova and Montrul propose for the interpretation of coerced achievements as accomplishments appears to be necessary to account for coerced accomplishments and coerced states as well. In the case of achievements, the use of the imperfective form shifts its interpretation to an accomplishment reading of the verb phrase, whereas in the case of accomplishments and states, the use of the Preterite shifts their interpretation to a telic event reading in both cases. This conclusion, however, makes the argument about the access to syntactic contrasts versus pragmatic contrasts less tenable because the data show that in two cases, learners are able to use the proposed pragmatic mechanism (i.e., with accomplishments and states), but they fail with the other one (i.e., they do not correctly mark achievements with the imperfect). Therefore, at a minimum, we must conclude that learners had access to and used the pragmatic knowledge adduced to be behind the interpretation of coerced accomplishments and states. At the same time, however, we conclude that learners failed to access such type of knowledge to correctly interpret coerced achievements.[20] In conclusion, the distinct outcome for (coerced) accomplishments and states versus the (coerced) achievements may be accounted for by the fact that the close semantic association between (telic) achievements and the (bounded)

Preterite is too strong for learners to overcome. In other words, these findings may provide empirical support for the proposed bias towards inherent lexical aspect in the selection of past tense marking (cf. the LAH), at least at one end of the spectrum where the main prototype of past tense is located (cf. Andersen and Shirai, 1994, 1996). This is also in keeping with the proposal of a default value of past tense.

As an extension of the previous study, Montrul and Slabakova (2002) used the same test instruments as in Slabakova and Montrul (2002a) to investigate whether knowledge of Preterite–Imperfect morphology correlated with the acquisition of the bounded/unbounded semantic opposition of the features [± perfective]. The study was based on data collected among 71 English-speaking learners divided into two subgroups according to proficiency level as determined by the DELE test described earlier. Out of 71 participants, 42 learners were classified as intermediate and 29 as advanced learners. There was also a control group of 23 Spanish native speakers from various Spanish-speaking countries. The average scores obtained in the sentence conjunction judgement test for each group are presented in Table 3.31.

The data show the results for the intermediate group subdivided into two subgroups according to the scores, they obtained in the 30-item morphology test referenced earlier. Students who scored 80 per cent or more correct responses (24 out of 30 items correct) in that test were deemed to know the morphology associated with Preterite–Imperfect. The students who scored below the cut-off point of 24 items correct were considered not to have attained a good understanding of how to use past tense morphology in Spanish. All advanced students, but one, were part of the high-scorers and so were 18 out of 42 intermediate learners.

Table 3.31 Responses to sentence conjunction test according to 5-point scale

	Achievements		Accomplishments		States	
	Pret	**Imp**	**Pret**	**Imp**	**Pret**	**Imp**
Control (n=23)	−1.67	1.39	−0.98	1.34	−1.5	1.55
Advanced (n=28)	−1.79	0.25	−1.1	1.23	−0.9	0.92
Interm (high) (n=18)	−0.86	−0.03	−0.20	0.42	−0.32	0.53
Interm (low) (n=25)	−0.57	0.75	−0.24	0.24	−0.25	0.12

Based on data from Montrul and Slabakova (2002).

The results, similar to the previous study, show that all groups (natives, advanced and intermediate learners) discriminated between the semantic entailments of Preterite and Imperfect with all combinations of lexical aspectual classes (state, accomplishment and achievements). For the learners who did not know the morphology (intermediate low), however, there was a statistically significant contrast in the test of semantic interpretations between Preterite and Imperfect with accomplishment predicates only. That is, the responses from the least proficient students did not show a statistically significant contrast in the selection of Preterite and Imperfect with achievements and states. Despite the statistically significant results, the average responses from the intermediate learners tend to cluster around the middle score of 0 (i.e., neither Preterite nor Imperfect). Not surprisingly, the most categorical responses (i.e., biggest difference between Preterite and Imperfect choices for each verb class) correspond to the native peakers.

3.2.2 *Iterativity*

Slabakova and Montrul (2002b, 2007) investigated learner's judgements of grammaticality/acceptability of verbal predicates that shift their lexical aspectual class in accordance with grammatical versus pragmatic conditions (see discussion of shifted lexical aspectual classes in Chapter 2).[21] For instance, as an example of a pragmatically induced shift, Slabakova and Montrul argue that option (14b) represents a case of 'implicit coercion' of the lexical aspectual class of an achievement verb (i.e., *llegar*) into a habitual activity, prompted by the use of the adverbial clause that precedes it (e.g., *durante muchos meses*).[22]

14a. Ayer el tren del mediodía llegó (PRET) tarde.
Yesterday the 12 o'clock train arrived late.
14b. Durante muchos meses el tren del mediodía llegó (PRET) tarde.
For months the 12 o'clock train arrived late.

Other examples of proposed pragmatically induced shifts are animacy (sentences 15a and 15b), and the use of the adverbial 'for X time' or 'in X time' (sentences 16a and 16b).

15a. *El río corrió (PRET) por la montaña.
The river ran through the mountain.
15b. Roberto corrió (PRET) por la montaña.
Roberto ran through the mountain.

16a. *El jardinero cortó (PRET) el pasto en una hora y todavía lo sigue cortando.
     The gardener mowed the lawn in an hour and he is still mowing it.
16b. El jardinero cortó (PRET) el pasto (por) una hora y todavía lo sigue cortando.
     The gardener mowed the lawn for an hour and he is still mowing it.

In contrast, Slabakova and Montrul argue that 'grammatically-induced shifts signal aspectual transitions by means of overt grammatical elements' (p. 633). For instance, tense markers trigger the change from a state interpretation of *saber* to a telic event interpretation.

17a. Juan sabía (IMP) la verdad.   [state]
     Juan knew the answer.
17b. Juan supo (PRET) la verdad.   [telic event]
     Juan found out the answer.

Similarly, the addition of a direct object such as *a mile* provides an inherent end point that serves to transform an activity into an accomplishment.

18a. Juan corrió (PRET) en el parque.   [atelic event]
     Juan ran in the park.
18b. Juan corrió (PRET) una milla.   [telic event]
     Juan ran a mile.

Finally, the addition of the aspectual particle *se* adds a telic meaning to an otherwise atelic event as shown in sentence (19a), thus making it ungrammatical with the adverbial *por una hora* (19b).

19a. Juan leyó (PRET) el libro (por una hora).   [atelic event]
     Juan read the book (for an hour).
19b. Juan se leyó (PRET) el libro (*por una hora). [telic event]
     Juan read the book (completely) (*for an hour).

Slabakova and Montrul's objective was to determine whether the judgements of L2 learners differ from the judgements of native speakers, and if they do, whether such distinct response 'is due to pragmatic processing abilities or to differences in the operation of grammatical principles' (2002b: 632). Taking as a point of departure Piñango et al.'s (1999) prediction of higher computational cost for coercion, Slabakova and Montrul specifically investigated 'whether aspectual shifts triggered by grammatical aspectual operators like direct objects, the telicity marker *se*, and tense inflection *are easier to acquire* than aspectual shifts triggered by discourse pragmatic signals, such as adverbials. . . .' (p. 635, stress added).

Slabakova and Montrul analysed data from 60 English native speakers and 27 native Spanish speakers. The English native speakers were divided into two groups according to their proficiency in Spanish based on the DELE test reviewed earlier: 27 advanced learners and 33 intermediate learners. The test instrument was a grammaticality judgement test that consisted of 49 pairs of sentences testing six conditions of shifted aspectual interpretations and one set of seven distractor sentences. The sentences were presented in pairs to test the meaning contrast of verbs with a basic and a shifted interpretation brought about by grammatical or pragmatic means. The grammatically based shifted interpretations investigated were (1) stative–eventive shifts with the use of the Preterite–Imperfect (sentences 17a and 17b), (2) activities into accomplishments by the addition of a direct object (sentences 18a and 18b) and (3) activities into accomplishments with or without aspectual *se* (sentences 19a and 19b). The pragmatically based shifted interpretations investigated were (1) achievements into habituals with the addition of an adverbial (sentences 14a and 14b) (2) animate versus inanimate subject with eventive predicates (sentences 15a and 15b) and (3) accomplishment into activities with the addition of an adverbial (sentences 16a and 16b).

Informants judged all sentence pairs on a five-point scale from 1 (unacceptable, 'I would never say this') to 5 (perfect, 'I would say this'). The results of the study revealed that all three groups reliably distinguished meaning shifts of an accomplishment to an activity (pragmatically induced), and in sentences that contained the particle *se* as a telicity marker (grammatically induced). Intermediate learners failed to distinguish the difference in meaning represented in all other contrasts in the study. Thus, Slabakova and Montrul concluded there was no obvious primacy of grammatical over pragmatic effects among the intermediate learners. On the other hand, the pattern of responses of advanced learners was indistinguishable from the responses from native speakers in statistically significant ways, except for one condition: telic events that have been iterated (e.g., *Durante muchos meses el tren del mediodía llegó tarde*, For months the 12 o'clock train arrived late). Slabakova and Montrul argue that 'this result is a tentative indication that pragmatic and grammatical knowledge may differ in interlanguage grammar' (p. 641).

This study is very important in that it is the first one to show that L2 learners are not aware of the meaning of iterativity conveyed through the

Preterite in Spanish (as opposed to the meaning of habituality that is conveyed with the Imperfect). However, the claim about the separation of grammatical and pragmatic shifts for the theoretical representation of the grammatical marking of temporality in L2 acquisition may be overly strong given both theoretical and methodological constraints of the study. Let us review the findings in detail to assess the proposed separation of grammatical and pragmatic components of aspect. First, the results of the shift in aspectual meaning triggered by durative adverbials when added to sentences with telic events are important, although not necessarily for the reasons that Slabakova and Montrul adduce. Essentially, the findings show that both advanced and intermediate learners as well as the native speakers consistently accepted the use of the Preterite with sentence (14a) in which the single arrival of the train is depicted. The scores for intermediate and advanced learners and natives were 4.33, 4.88 and 4.88, respectively. That is, measured on the five-point scale, all groups strongly agreed with the grammaticality of that sentence.

In contrast, the two learner groups rated iterated achievements (exemplified in sample sentence 14b) two points lower than native speakers on the grammaticality scale: average scores of 2.89 and 3.05 for intermediate and advanced learners, respectively versus a score of 4.47 for the native speakers. Interestingly, the difference in scores for the single-event versus the iterated-event sentences among the intermediate learners was smaller than the difference among the more advanced group of informants: a 1.29 differential score for the intermediate learners versus a 1.99 differential score for the advanced learners. Thus, it appears that the advanced learners have more trouble than the intermediate ones accepting the use of the Preterite with iterated events. One could speculate that the reason for this unexpected outcome is that the more experienced learners are moving towards a representation of the Preterite as a form strongly associated with telic events only (also documented in Hasbún, 1995; Ramsay, 1990; Salaberry, 1999). Moreover, the fact that learners confuse habituality with iterativity may simply be due to the fact that the representation of that aspectual distinction is not formally taught. And we can add that, as a consequence, it is not learned.

We should also note some methodological caveats about Piñango et al.'s (1999) claim about the computational costs of processing the semantic meanings of aspectual distinctions (see Section 2.5.2). First, it is not entirely clear that Piñango et al.'s claim about the higher computational cost of coercion on semelfactives can be extended to the analysis of findings in the Slabakova and Montrul study.[23] In the latter study, the lexical aspectual classes used in their target sentences span a broader range than the lexical classes used in Piñango et al.'s (1999) study (i.e., only semelfactives). Thus, it is an empirical question whether such computational costs apply to other lexical classes as well. Second, it is open to question whether a larger contextualization framework could actually eliminate the aforementioned computational cost. That is, in principle, it is possible that the computational costs of processing a larger context of reference would make negligible the effect substantiated by Piñango et al. for an analysis of data restricted to the effects at the verb-phrase level. Third, it remains to be empirically verified that such computational costs are valid for second language learners as well. The latter is not a trivial question if we were to assume that the linguistic representational system among natives and non-natives are not qualitatively equivalent (cf. comparative fallacy: Bley-Vroman, 1983; Lardiere, 2003; Shirai, 2007). Finally, Slabakova and Montrul acknowledge that their stimuli may have not been appropriate to test the intended contrast between grammatically versus pragmatically induced shifts: 'Since all the test sentences (and most natural language sentences, for that matter) contain (non-)quantized objects, and aspectual tense cues, it is hardly possible to tease apart their contribution from the contribution of the pragmatic cues, especially in the conditions testing pragmatic contrasts' (p. 641). In other words, it is difficult to ascertain what extrasentential meanings participants may have brought to bear for the analysis in order to make sense of the decontextualized sentences. This is not unlike what Coppieters found in his study with regard to the responses from native and near-native speakers (i.e., Coppieters used decontextualized sentences).

Another study that investigated the representation of iterativity among non-native speakers was Pérez-Leroux et al. (2007). The authors argued that learners' problems with complex aspectual representations such as habitual versus iterative contexts can be better accounted for by feature activation or selectional restrictions (see Section 2.5.2). Their analysis was based, primarily, on the effect of explicit and implicit triggers of iterativity as shown in sentences (21b) and (21c), respectively.

20. Jugaban en el parque.
     The children (habitually) played in the park.   [habitual, imperfect]
21a. Los niños se cambiaron de asiento (una vez).
     The children changed seats (once).   [punctual event, Preterite]

21b. Los niños se cambiaron de asiento repetidamente.
The children changed seats repeatedly.   [iterative adverbial,
                                                 Preterite]
21c. Los niños se cambiaron de asiento por horas.
The children changed seats for hours.   [iterative coercion,
                                                 Preterite]

Pérez-Leroux et al. point out that past habitual sense is expressed with the Imperfect in (20), whereas iterative sentences depicted in (21a, b and c) are expressed with the Preterite. Non-iterative, single telic events (21a) are proto-typically expressed with the perfective as well. Pérez-Leroux et al. point out that as far as knowledge about the effects of iterativity on verbal marking, '[g]rammatical instruction does not distinguish between these senses, it merely states that "repetition in the past is expressed in the Imperfect form"'. In other words, if learners have access to only explicit instruction to develop their L2 system, we should expect them to mistakenly use the imperfective marker with iterated, non-habitual events (cf. sentences 21b and 21c).

Pérez-Leroux et al. analysed data from 41 students and ten native speakers on the effects of unique, habitual and iterated situations with the use of a 50-item grammaticality judgement task and an 18-item translation task. The learners were divided into two levels of proficiency based on course enrolments in second or third year. There were two different conditions that triggered an iterative interpretation: explicit with the use of an iteration adverbial (e.g., *repetidamente*) and implicit with the use of a duration adverbial (e.g., *por días*). The unique situation was acceptable with the Preterite, the habitual with the Imperfect, and both iterated situations were acceptable with the Preterite only. The following are samples of the test sentences used by Pérez-Leroux et al. in their study:

22a. En su niñez, jugaban (√ IMP) en la calle por las tardes.
22b. En su niñez, jugaron (#PRET) en la calle por las tardes.
     In their childhood, they used to play/played in the streets in the afternoon.
23a. El terremoto sacudió (√PRET) la ciudad a las 8.
23b. El terremoto sacudía (#IMP) la ciudad a las 8.
     The earthquake shook the city at eight.
24a. El terremoto sacudió (√PRET) la ciudad por días.
24b. El terremoto sacudía (# IMP) la ciudad por días.   [iterative,
     implicit coercion]
     The earthquake shook the city for days.

25a. El terremoto sacudió (√PRET) la ciudad repetidamente.
25b. El terremoto sacudía (#IMP) la ciudad repetidamente. [iterative, explicit coercion]
The earthquake shook the city repeatedly.

The results of the data analysis revealed that both groups of learners accepted the prototypical combinations of perfective marker with unique punctual event and imperfective marker with a generic habitual event. In contrast, learners failed to reject the ungrammatical use of the Imperfect with both implicit and explicit iterated events. Furthermore, contrary to the results of Slabakova and Montrul (2002b), the findings from Pérez-Leroux et al. show that the advanced learners accept the use of the Preterite with iterated events more than the intermediate learners. These findings lead Pérez-Leroux et al. to consider the possible explanation that '[t]he two instructed conditions elicited better performance in L2 speakers (unique and habitual) than the non-instructed iterative contexts' (p. 449).[24]

Pérez-Leroux et al. note, however, a hierarchical sequence of acquisition: 'non-native speakers find it easier to identify the association between Preterite and unique events. Next, they show mastery of preference for the imperfective with the habitual condition. Because they did not actively reject the Preterite in habitual contexts, they failed to reach native-speaker levels of contrast' (p. 448). Pérez-Leroux et al. thus conclude that the aspectual restrictions associated with the Preterite are learned separately from the ones that correspond to the Imperfect: 'If a learner has determined that the Preterite selects eventualities, but has not determined the selection of the Imperfect, we would expect patterns of results such as those encountered'. In other words, at the same time that learners demonstrate knowledge of the prototypical associations of grammatical markers of past tense and lexical aspect (consistent with the tenets of the LAH), they also seem to consider the Preterite as an overall marker of past tense that works across lexical aspectual classes.

3.2.3 Genericity

Slabakova and Montrul (2003) were the first researchers to test the distinct meanings of genericity and habituality conveyed by the Spanish Imperfect. Their study was intended to show that learners have 'unconscious knowledge of abstract properties of the grammar' (p. 180) that cannot be accessed through general cognitive, non-modular processes. Slabakova and Montrul claim that 'If L2 acquisition is regulated by domain specific grammatical constraints, then we expect L2 learners to be more accurate on the generic/specific subject interpretation of Preterite and Imperfect sentences than on the correct choice of habitual/episodic contexts' (p. 180).

To substantiate their claim, Slabakova and Montrul analysed data from 69 English-speaking learners of Spanish (42 intermediate and 27 advanced learners) and 18 Spanish native speakers who acted as a control group. The classification by proficiency level (i.e., intermediate and advanced) was accomplished with the same two tests used in their 2002 study reviewed earlier (i.e., the adaptation of the DELE test and the morphology recognition test). The main experimental test was a Truth Value Judgement task in which participants had to read 80 short-paragraph stories and decide whether the sentence that followed each story was true or false. The stories tested the following conditions: (1) habitual versus one-time events and (2) generic versus specific interpretations with impersonal constructions. The following two examples tested the habitual versus one-time event condition. Participants had to indicate whether a sentence with the verb in the Preterite or Imperfect was true or false in the context provided by the written story. Slabakova and Montrul posit that for the one-time event context, the Preterite is the right choice (i.e., T for true). Conversely, they propose that for the story with the habitual context, the Imperfect is the right choice.

Context: One Time Event

Panchito era muy tímido y no tenía muchos amiguitos con quien jugar. Panchito pasaba todo el tiempo en su casa con su mamá. Ayer Panchito se reunió por primera vez con sus vecinitos para jugar y pasaron un rato muy agradable. Hoy Panchito se quedó nuevamente con su mamá.

Panchito jugaba (IMP) con sus vecinos.	F
Panchito jugó (PRET) con sus vecinos.	T

'Panchito was (IMP) very shy and he did not have (IMP) friends to play with. Panchito would spend (IMP) time at home with his mother. Yesterday, for the first time, he got together (PRET) with his neighbors to play and they had (PRET) a very pleasant time. Today Panchito stayed (PRET) with his mother again'.

Panchito played (IMP) with his neighbours.	F
Panchito played (PRET) with his neighbours.	T

Context: Habitual

Laurita tenía muchos amiguitos y después de la escuela pasaba el tiempo en la casa de sus vecinos. Ayer se quedó en casa con su mamá y pasó un rato muy agradable.

Laurita jugaba (IMP) con sus vecinos.	T
Laurita jugó (PRET) con sus vecinos.	F

'Laurita had (IMP) many friends and after school she would spend (IMP) time at his neighbors' house. Yesterday Laurita stayed (PRET) at home with her mother and had (PRET) a very good time'.

Laurita played (IMP) with his neighbors.	T
Laurita played (PRET) with his neighbors.	F

The responses provided for the one-time event stories show that both the advanced and the intermediate learners were more accurate using the Preterite (97 and 81 per cent, respectively) than with the Imperfect (74 and 41 per cent, respectively). That is, they were more accurate in correctly *accepting* the use of Preterite with one-time events than in correctly *rejecting* the Imperfect with one-time events. Similarly, the findings from the responses provided for the habitual stories show that both the advanced and the intermediate learners were more accurate in using the Preterite (93 and 81 per cent, respectively) than using the Imperfect (70 and 47 per cent, respectively). That is, they were more accurate in correctly *rejecting* the use of Preterite with habituals than in correctly *accepting* the Imperfect with habituals. The authors conclude that the combined analysis of these results shows that the semantic knowledge associated with the Imperfect develops later than the semantic meaning associated with the Preterite.

The second condition tested in this study (i.e., generic versus specific interpretations with impersonal constructions) was implemented with the following examples. In the generic case, only the imperfective choice is possible, whereas in the specific condition, both the Imperfect and the Preterite are possible choices.

Context: Generic

Según el periódico, el restaurante de la calle Jefferson era muy bueno y el servicio era excelente. Lamentablemente el restaurante cerró el verano pasado y nunca tuvimos la oportunidad de ir.

Se comía bien en ese restaurante.   T
Se comió bien en ese restaurante.   F

'According to the newspaper the restaurant on Jefferson Street was (IMP) very good and the service was (IMP) excellent. Unfortunately the restaurant closed (PRET) last summer and we never got to go (PRET)'.

One ate (IMP) well at that restaurant.   T
We ate (PRET) well at that restaurant.   F

Context: Specific

Según la mayoría de la gente, el restaurante de la calle Jefferson era muy bueno y el servicio era excelente. Fuimos a celebrar el cumpleaños de Carlos y a todos nos gustó mucho.¡Qué lástima que lo cerraron!

Se comía bien en ese restaurante.   T
Se comió bien en ese restaurante.   T

'According to most people's opinion, the restaurant on Jefferson Street was (IMP) very good and the service was (IMP) excellent. We went (PRET) there to celebrate Carlos's birthday and we all liked (PRET) it a lot. It's a pity that it closed!'

One ate (IMP) well at that restaurant.   T
We ate (PRET) well at that restaurant.   T

The responses provided for the generic stories show that the advanced learners were equally accurate in correctly *accepting* the Imperfect and in correctly *rejecting* the use of the Preterite (86 and 85 per cent, respectively). In contrast, the intermediate learners were more accurate in correctly *accepting* the Imperfect (82 per cent) than in correctly *rejecting* the use of the Preterite (66 per cent). On the other hand, the results from the specific stories show that both the advanced and the intermediate learners were more accurate in using the Preterite (85 and 74 per cent, respectively) than with the Imperfect (64 and 46 per cent, respectively). As previously mentioned, both options (i.e., Preterite and Imperfect) are possible with the specific stories. The results for both sets of tests are summarized in Table 3.32.[25]

The statistical analysis of the findings revealed significant differences among groups for the first condition (i.e., habituals versus one-time event), whereas there were no statistically significant differences among groups for the data from the second condition (i.e., generic versus specific events with

Table 3.32 Selection of Preterite–Imperfect by groups and testing condition in percentages (differential points in parentheses)

			Natives	Advanced	Intermediate
Habitual	IMP	T	88 (−10)	70 (−23)	47 (−34)
	PRET	F	98	93	81
One time	IMP	F	89	74	41
	PRET	T	96 (+7)	97 (+23)	81 (+40)
Generic	IMP	T	92 (+4)	86 (+1)	82 (+16)
	PRET	F	88	85	66
Specific	IMP	T	81	64	46
	PRET	T	90 (+9)	85 (+21)	74 (+28)

Based on data from Slabakova and Montrul (2003).

impersonal verbs). In other words, only the second condition failed to differentiate the performance of native speakers and non-native speakers. Slabakova and Montrul, thus argue that the use of aspectual *se* with specific 'we' or generic 'one' suggests that L2 learners may be able to learn properties of the grammar that are not explicitly taught in language classrooms (i.e., generic interpretations). More specifically, Slabakova and Montrul conclude that 'the results of the present study suggest that adult learners of a second language reveal unconscious knowledge of abstract properties of the grammar that are *unlikely* to be derived from observation of the primary linguistic data, from their native grammar directly, or on the basis of straightforward (1) analogy with their native grammar, or with (2) what they are taught' (p. 192, stress added).

I would argue, however, that the alternative explanations considered by Slabakova and Montrul (i.e., analogy with the L1, induction from primary linguistic data and instructional effects) cannot be summarily dismissed. The first option (i.e., analogy with the native grammar) is discussed in detail by Slabakova and Montrul. The authors note that there is an obvious correlation between the English Simple Past and the Progressive on the one hand, and the Spanish Preterite and Imperfect on the other hand. Thus, one possible working hypothesis for the English-speaking learners is to 'map the Imperfect tense on their native Progressive tense, and the Preterite on their native past simple [*sic*]' (p. 188). Slabakova and Montrul conclude, however, that the Progressive form in English does not have an equivalent generic subject interpretation (which is indeed true). Alternatively, they propose that the possible English equivalents for the target sentence in Spanish with the generic interpretation are as follows:

26a. Se comía bien en casa de la abuela.
      Se eat-IMP well in house of the grandmother.
      One/We would eat well at Grandma's.
27a. ?You were eating well at Grandma's.
27b. *One was eating well at Grandma's.
27c. One/you ate well Grandma's.

Note, though, that Slabakova and Montrul disregard the possibility that learners may use (as a heuristic or rule of thumb) the structure typically used to convey habituality in the past in English (i.e., *used to/would*) to translate the target sentence. In fact, that option is actually represented in the translation of the previous target sentence but not considered by Slabakova and Montrul as a possible option entertained by the learners.

Thus, let us review the most likely options considered by the L2 learners when faced with the previous target sentence with a generic meaning. First, learners are unlikely to give up on the fairly transparent correlation of English Simple Past with Spanish Preterite. Hence, faced with the dilemma that their alternative past tense form in English (i.e., the Past Progressive) may not be adequate to convey the meaning of genericity expressed by the Spanish Imperfect, learners will look into an option that is neither the Simple Past nor the Past Progressive. That third alternative is the periphrastic *used to/would* that conveys past habituality in English. In fact this form is typically equated with the Imperfect in most instructional settings. It would be very surprising if learners were not to extend the two most basic rules of thumb they are taught in most academic programmes (i.e., habituals versus completed actions) to the contrasts exemplified in the generic versus specific interpretations. In sum, we cannot rule out the possibility that learners may rely on the periphrastic *used to/would* to approximate the meaning of the generic subject interpretation conveyed by the Imperfect in Spanish. Of course, this argument does not deny the possibility that learners may consider other 'rules of thumb' as well, even if they are not target-like.

Finally, I note two methodological factors inherent to Slabakova and Montrul's research design that may have affected the results of the study. First, the wording of the stories may have primed students towards the right responses. For instance, in the story depicting the generic interpretation with an impersonal subject, the prompt sentence includes two clues for the learners to infer that right response. In effect, the two verbs conjugated in the Imperfect (i.e., *era*) may have led the learners to accept the use of the Imperfect in the test sentence.

28. El restaurante de la calle Jefferson *era* [IMP] muy bueno y el servicio *era* [IMP] excelente.

Intermediate learners had an acceptance rate of 82 and 66 per cent for the selections of the Imperfect and the Preterite, respectively, in the story prompting the generic interpretation. In contrast, when students analysed the specific context story, there is a sentence that includes two clues to infer the right response as well. That is, there are two verbs (i.e., *fuimos* and *gustó*) already conjugated in the Preterite in the prompt sentence:

29. *Fuimos* [PRET] a celebrar el cumpleaños de Carlos y a todos nos *gustó* [PRET] mucho.

Even though both the answers with the Imperfect and the Preterite were acceptable in the context of the specific interpretation story, intermediate learners had an acceptance rate of 74 and 46 per cent for the selections of Preterite and Imperfect, respectively. Granted, whether the learners used those clues present in the test sentences (and whether they were able to use them consistently) or not is speculative, but subject to empirical verification in future studies.

A second methodological constraint is also related to the possible effect of the test instrument. Slabakova and Montrul point out that although the native speakers 'had judged correctly 4 out of 6 story-sentence combinations, or achieved 66% accuracy, *we accepted that percentage* as the cutoff point for successful acquisition for the learners' (p. 185, stress added). This appears to be a rather low level of achievement for a native speaker. While it is true that not all native speakers performed at that low level, there is a significant degree of variability in the native speakers' responses. Such variability contrasts with the type of homogeneity that has been the expected response among native speakers both theoretically and empirically. One way to account for the low percentage of correct responses obtained by at least some native speakers is that the test instrument may have introduced a significant degree of uncertainty in the required responses. Slabakova and Montrul do consider that possibility for the results of another part of their test (cf. habituals and one-time events) when they state that 'the performance of the advanced learners may be partly attributable to the actual test items, and partly to later development of the grammatical knowledge' (p. 187). As to why the test instrument may have negatively affected the responses of the native speakers in particular, Slabakova and Montrul argue that the decontextualized sentences may have compromised 'the most natural context for the Progressive reading. This fact alone may explain the native speaker and learner preferences discussed above' (p. 192).[26]

3.2.4 Constructionism

As mentioned earlier, Constructionism represents a distinct theoretical strand within the syntactic-based proposals mostly due to its claim about the gradual nature of acquisition. Herschensohn (2000: 109–110), in particular claims that 'L2 parameter setting . . . is not an all-at-once phenomenon, but Progressive learning, construction by construction'. Schell (2000) is one study that has used the framework of Constructionism to analyse the acquisition of past tense marking in L2 Spanish. Schell investigated the development of past tense markers in Spanish among five students (selected from a group of 15) who spent nine months in the natural setting of a study-abroad programme in Spain. The selection of the five informants was based on the students' consistent participation in the study, their seriousness performing the tasks and their 'overall attitude towards learning Spanish' (p. 73). In other words, the participants were highly motivated and dedicated to studying Spanish. Thus, they cannot necessarily be regarded as representative of an average population of Spanish college students (not to mention the fact that students who decide to do a nine-month study-abroad programme are already a self-selected group). Two learners (Alice and Kate) had completed two years of Spanish at the university level and three (Mitch, Tim and Beth) had completed three years of college-level Spanish by the time they travelled abroad. Their overall length of exposure to Spanish studies, however, was actually much longer if we also count their studies before college.

Schell collected data in the form of written passages in which learners had to select the past tense form of infinitives at three different time periods: before travelling to Spain, three and a half months into the stay and at the end of the nine-month period.[27] Table 3.33 summarizes the data from all five students. The data in the three written passages were purposefully manipulated by Schell to obtain different match-ups of lexical and grammatical aspects (i.e., prototypical choices). Specifically, the prototypical selections of Preterite or Imperfect were 93, 64 and 82 per cent for Times 1 to 3, respectively. Notice that native speakers tend to select the Preterite and Imperfect on an even basis, except for the first test in which there is a preference for the use of the imperfective form. Interestingly, the selections of most non-native speakers (i.e., Alice, Kate and Mitch) in favour of the Preterite (from 63 to 75 per cent) contrast clearly with the native

Table 3.33   Accuracy rates in the selection of Preterite–Imperfect

	Time 1		Time 2		Time 3	
	Preterite	**Imperfect**	**Preterite**	**Imperfect**	**Preterite**	**Imperfect**
Natives	40	60	47	53	51	49
Alice	*63*	*37*	*65*	*35*	54	46
Kate	*63*	*37*	50	50	44	56
Mitch	*75*	*25*	*59*	*41*	54	46
Tim	55	45	*71*	*29*	51	49
Beth	35	65	*56*	*44*	51	49

Based on summary of data from Schell (2000).

speakers' choices. The preference for the perfective, counter to the native speakers' choices continues in the second test but almost disappears completely by the time of the third and final test.

Tables 3.34 and 3.35 show the choices of past tense marking for states and telic events, respectively. The selections of past tense marking with telic events show an almost exact match-up between native and non-native speakers' choices, and, in particular, a strong preference for the Preterite. In contrast, the use of past tense markers with states shows that three out of five students prefer the perfective marker with statives during the first time of data collection, which occurred right before they travelled abroad. For example, in the following example from Schell (p. 138), all five subjects used the Preterite with all three verbs incorrectly (items in bold are all statives):

'*Hay un día en particular que recuerdo muy bien. Yo *tuve que estudiar, mi mejor amigo Ricardo *necesitó cuidar a su hermano, y mis primos Juan y Alfredo no *fueron a hacer nada, pero al final decidimos ir a una fiesta*'.

There is one day in particular that I remember very well. I had (PRET) to study, my best friend Richard had to (PRET) take care of his brother, and my cousins John and Alfred were not going to (PRET) do anything, but in the end we decided (PRET) to go to the party.

Schell argues that her data show that 'the production of L2 learners does not display a matching of lexical to grammatical aspect at the early stages (or in the case here, at the early intermediate stages), but rather at the late intermediate to early advanced stages of learning' (p. 142). This finding is supportive of the claim advanced by the DPTH.

Table 3.34   Accuracy rates in the selection of Preterite–Imperfect *with states only*

	Time 1		Time 2		Time 3	
	Preterite	**Imperfect**	**Preterite**	**Imperfect**	**Preterite**	**Imperfect**
NS	2	8	3	8	3	12
Alice	*5*	*2*	*10*	*1*	*5*	10
Kate	6	4	2	9	2	13
Mitch	8	2	3	8	4	11
Tim	2	8	4	7	5	10
Beth	0	10	5	6	3	12

Based on summary of data from Schell (2000).

Table 3.35   Accuracy rates in the selection of Preterite–Imperfect *with achievements only*

	Time 1		Time 2		Time 3	
	Preterite	**Imperfect**	**Preterite**	**Imperfect**	**Preterite**	**Imperfect**
NS	15	1	13	3	16	4
Alice	11	2	10	6	15	5
Kate	14	1	13	3	13	7
Mitch	16	0	13	3	16	4
Tim	16	0	13	3	16	4
Beth	10	6	13	3	16	4

Based on summary of data from Schell (2000).

Furthermore, Schell accounted for her findings with a developmental model that seems to go beyond the claim of a strictly syntactic hypothesis. She argues that learners appear to be going through at least three stages of development of inflectional markers. During the first stage, there is evidence of transfer from the L1; during the second stage, lexical aspect seems to have an effect and finally, learners are able to use either one of the past tense markers with every verb type (p. 133). Interestingly, the definition of the different stages of development of L2 knowledge about the Spanish Preterite–Imperfect adduced by Schell focuses on the effect of non-modular processes. Moreover, the description of the third stage of acquisition points in the direction of a contextualized definition of tense-aspect meanings along the lines of the definition that I proposed in Chapter 2 and that I develop in more detail in Chapter 4.

4. Conclusion

Andersen (2002: 102) proposed there are two important research questions that needed to be addressed in future studies:

> [First], '[h]ow does the learner discover the form to meaning relation encoded by the marker when the learner first begins to productively use it in natural communication?' A second and equally important question is, 'How does this mechanism account for the initial use of the morpheme *as well as* its development over time as it expands in function and breadth?'

I believe that each question has become the focus of attention of different research paradigms. The first question (i.e., form-meaning match up) has become the primary target of syntactic approaches. The second question (i.e., the initial use and development of tense-aspect markers) has been addressed primarily by semantic-discursive approaches. In line with Andersen's perspective, I take the position that both questions are important. Thus, in this chapter, I have dedicated significant attention to an in-depth review of findings from studies that have analysed both of the research targets specified by Andersen. Ultimately, however, I argue that the theoretical representation of tense-aspect meanings requires a discourse-based definition.

In sum, I outlined the major hypotheses that account for the L2 acquisition of tense-aspect knowledge and I reviewed some relevant empirical data that support those positions. Given that the previous literature on this topic already provides a fairly substantive analysis of the claims advanced by the LAH and the DH, I focused the discussion of previous studies on the ones offered in support of more recent claims such as the DPTH and the proposals based on the SSH. I further argued that these two proposals are worthy of a detailed discussion since they are based on two seemingly orthogonal lines of research based on distinct definitions of tense-aspect knowledge: a discursive one (i.e., the DPTH) and a syntactic one (i.e., the SSH).

Two main arguments were advanced in this chapter. First, I have analysed empirical evidence that serves to substantiate a contextual definition of tense-aspect meanings is generally uncontroversial. For instance, the findings of studies that were reviewed in support of the DPTH rely on a mostly contextual definition of aspect (e.g., Granda, 2004; Lubbers-Quesada, 1999, 2007; Salaberry, 1999, 2002, 2003, 2005, forthcoming). From the specific perspective of the DPTH, Salaberry (forthcoming) proposes that the gradual increase in categorical selections of Preterite–Imperfect may be directly related to the constant incorporation of contextual elements into the learner's evolving grammar to better and more appropriately define the meanings of the Preterite–Imperfect. In contrast, the studies reviewed under the heading of syntactic theories tend to rely on a definition of tense-aspect meanings restricted to, mostly, the verb-phrase level. The latter assertion is, however, overly broad. In particular, the contrastive analysis of empirical data collected across the three different theoretical strands representing syntactic theories (i.e., feature-based, selectional-based and Constructionism) serves to qualify the claim that tense-aspect meanings can be defined strictly at the syntactic level.

For instance, Schell (adopting a Constructionist perspective) explicitly argues for the relevance of the inclusion of a developmental stage in which the 'true' meaning of the Preterite–Imperfect contrast (i.e., Smith's viewpoint aspect) is incorporated into the definition of the dependent variable (knowledge of tense-aspect contrasts in Spanish). Furthermore, the notion that a continuum of contextual elements is necessary to define tense-aspect meanings has related theoretical consequences. Thus, Pérez-Leroux et al. (adopting a selectional perspective) argue that the available empirical evidence shows that learners do not seem to acquire the meanings associated with both perfective and imperfective morphology simultaneously. As a consequence, Pérez-Leroux et al. highlight the gradual nature of the process of learning tense-aspect contrasts and propose that learners are 'developmentally' slowed down, given that some components of the composition of aspectual meanings will take longer than others to be incorporated into their evolving interlanguage. A gradual progression towards native-like performance may be indicative of a non-native system that is developing according to a process of accretion (cf. Sharwood Smith and Truscott, 2005). In particular, the lack of evidence for any particular shift in the developmental system of L2 learners (thresholds) could be taken as evidence against the argument about categorical grammars (e.g., Bybee, 1995b).

A second major argument proposed in this chapter is that the DPTH (as defined in previous sections) provides a more viable theoretical account for the empirical findings referenced in this chapter. This argument can be substantiated along the lines of the theoretical representation and the comprehensiveness of the DPTH. At a theoretical level, the DPTH is predicated on the notion of direct transfer from L1 English to L2 Spanish given that (1) English marks tense only at the inflectional morphological level (i.e., Simple Past) and (2) the Preterite is the default marker given that it is temporally located. That is, both English Simple Past and Spanish Preterite convey the representational meaning of tense (e.g., Doiz-Bienzobas, 1995,

2002). I argued further that the DPTH may provide a more comprehensive alternative to the one offered by the LAH or the DH. In general, within the DPTH, the effects of lexical aspect and discursive grounding are associated with ever-increasing levels of proficiency in the L2. Thus, to some extent, the rationale that underlies the proposal of a default marker of past tense is also based on basic notions underlying the LAH and the DH. For instance, the notion of a default past tense represented in both source and target language (i.e., Spanish Preterite and English Simple Past) is compatible with the theoretical underpinnings of the LAH. That is, the learner may rely on the One to One Principle (Andersen, 1989) and use the Preterite to convey past tense reference with verb phrases of all lexical aspectual classes. In contrast, the Imperfect may mark temporality in association with particular lexical items (lexical learning).

There are, however, important theoretical distinctions between the LAH and the DPTH. For instance, I concluded that some of the recent studies on tense-aspect learning provide initial evidence about the use of a default past tense marker not only among beginning learners, but among advanced learners as well (e.g., Antonio, 2007; Liskin-Gasparro, 2000; Salaberry, 2005). Thus, let us review in detail the theoretical significance of the use of a default marker of past tense among proficient learners. For instance, let us focus on the analysis of data from the two ends of the continuum of lexical aspectual classes (i.e., states and telic events). Let us first assume that the data showed that advanced learners (at least sometimes) fall back on the incorrect use of the Preterite with statives, although they rarely or never use the Imperfect incorrectly with telic events (i.e., achievements and accomplishments). The differential outcome in the incorrect use of perfective with states and (mostly) correct use of the imperfective marker with telic events can be accounted for by the DPTH. That is, the Preterite is the default past tense marker, and thus it is naturally overextended to contexts in which it should not be used. This is particularly true in cases of verbs that are aspectually complex for students to assess. In principle, the LAH could possibly account for the finding that the state verbs are incorrectly marked with the Preterite under the assumption that the Preterite has not yet completely spread in its uses to the other end of the continuum of lexical aspectual classes. The LAH would have difficulty, however, accounting for the concurrent correct use of the Imperfect with telic events given that the Imperfect is, supposedly, the last marker to make 'its journey' towards the other end of the lexical aspectual continuum.

In sum, the analysis of empirical data from this chapter falls in line with the arguments about definitional concepts of tense-aspect meanings developed in the previous chapter. That is, I argued that (1) there is an apparent effect of a broadly contextualized concept of aspectual knowledge and (2) the representational meaning of tense-aspect being developed by L2 Spanish learners is highly constrained by L1 transfer effects as well as L2 representational meanings. In the following chapter, I focus on the discussion of a theoretical framework that can be used for the analysis of the acquisition and development of tense-aspect knowledge in L2 learning. The description of the proposed theoretical framework will be based on the integration of information about the theoretical definition of tense-aspect presented in Chapter 2 and the critical review of selected previous findings presented in this chapter.

Chapter 4

The L2 Acquisition of Invariant-Contextualized Meanings of Tense-Aspect

1. Introduction

The analysis of theoretical definitions of aspect (Chapter 2) and the review of empirical findings on the acquisition of aspectual knowledge (Chapter 3) provide the foundation for the theoretical framework of acquisition of tense-aspect to be outlined in this chapter. In Chapter 2, I concluded that one of the current debates on the L2 acquisition of temporality is the possible dissociation between syntactic and discursive-pragmatic components of the overall make-up of the concept of tense-aspect: core and peripheral grammar (e.g., Herschensohn, 2000) or syntactic and pragmatic aspect (e.g., Slabakova and Montrul, 2002b, 2007). In this chapter, I take as a point of departure the idea of a continuum of representational levels of tense-aspect meanings to argue that the dichotomy of core-peripheral grammar or syntactic-pragmatic representations of aspect can be reconceptualized as invariant and contextualized meanings (cf. Binnick, 1991; Doiz-Bienzobas, 1995, 2002). The argument will be made for both the levels of lexical and grammatical aspect.

Even though, in principle, one could argue that the proposed reconceptualization amounts to a change of labels, I believe that there is a substantial difference given that the invariant-contextualized contrast is predicated on the notion of a continuum of tense-aspect meanings. Thus, it represents a single-construct approach as opposed to a categorical break from one category to the next (cf. Smith, 1991/1997). For instance, the invariant concept of boundedness becomes imbued with specific aspectual meaning when placed in context, thus serving to communicate that an event is bounded or unbounded. Similarly, the invariant concept of iterativity becomes imbued with specific aspectual meaning when placed in context, thus serving to communicate that an event is iterative or habitual. More importantly, the specific meanings of invariant concepts in context are associated with specific grammatical markers. For instance, in Spanish, both bounded and iterated events are typically marked with the Preterite, whereas unbounded and habitual events are typically marked with the Imperfect.

With regard to the acquisition of aspectual meanings, I specifically propose that L1 English speakers are not necessarily challenged by the concept of aspectual contrasts in L2 Spanish. English speakers already mark aspectual meanings with the past progressive in contrast with the simple past, periphrastics such as *used to* in contrast with simple past, narrative grounding and so on. Thus, their developmental difficulties with Spanish Preterite and Imperfect must reside in a different realm. One possible area of difficulty is the actual mapping of aspectual concepts and inflectional morphology. In essence, English speakers may have difficulty, not necessarily with the conceptual understanding of aspectual distinctions in the L2 per se, but rather with the representation of aspectual contrasts through inflectional endings (cf. Slobin, 1996a, 1996b). I further argue that adult L2 learners transfer their L1 representational system to process L2 information. As a consequence, L2 learners are constrained by the features already available in their L1. In particular, I argue that the DPTH discussed in Chapter 3 represents a viable theoretical hypothesis to analyse tense-aspect acquisition data not only during beginning stages of acquisition, but also among advanced learners.

2. Contextualized Meanings

The proposed separation between syntactic and pragmatic components of tense-aspectual knowledge is correlated with the prototypical versus non-prototypical combinations of lexical and grammatical aspect respectively. De Swart (1998), for instance, notes that the following examples show some prototypical combinations of past tense and lexical aspectual classes:

1a. Anne était (*Imparfait*) malade.
1b. Anne was ill.
2a. Anne écrivit (*Passé Simple*) une lettre.
2b. Anne wrote a letter.

De Swart claims that 'given that the French sentences in (1a) and (2a) are equivalent to their English counterparts in (1b) and (2b), we can conclude that the same combination of aspectual class and a past tense operator is sufficient to derive the proper interpretation of the sentence'. She further states that '[t]he Passé Simple is thus used exclusively to locate events in the past, whereas the Imparfait locates states or processes in the past'. (p. 368). There-fore, de Swart (1998: 372) rejects 'the treatment of the *Imparfait* and the *Passé Simple* as aspectual operators, for, unlike the Perfect and the Progressive, they do not specify one particular aspectual transition'. Surprisingly, however, de Swart leaves out of her analysis the non-prototypical combinations of French past tenses with eventuality types exemplified in sentences (3a) and (4a).

3a. Anne *fut/a été (Passé Simple/Passé Composé)* malade.
3b. Anne was ill.
4a. Anne *écrivait (Imparfait)* une lettre.
4b. Anne wrote a letter.

Note that both the perfective and imperfective options in French may ren-der one single translation into English as shown by examples (3b) and (4b). In other words, it is not that these examples from French should be equated with the ones from English to conclude that the 'semantic contribution of the perfective and imperfective aspect reduces to zero [and should be] descriptively characterized as "unmarked" cases'.[1] In the final analysis, what is relevant for our purpose is the fact that de Swart recognizes that ". . . only French makes the fact that the state is presented as an event visible in the morphology of the verb" (p. 371). That is, from the point of view of acquisi-tion, what matters for the learner is that whenever a state is presented as an event in French (or other Romance languages for that matter), there are morphological correlates that signal this shift.

The previous discussion of de Swart's examples highlights the fact that, for learners to acquire a complete representational system of tense-aspect knowledge, they need to move past the prototypical combinations of lexical and grammatical aspect (e.g., states with the Imperfect). In this respect, the discrepancies identified by Coppieters (1987) in his comparison of native and near-native speakers led him to conclude that near-native speakers may have trouble with components of the grammar that lie outside of any Universal Grammar (UG) capacity. In essence, Coppieters argued that the problem learners face is that they cannot properly incorporate into their analysis of aspectual meanings the role of contextual factors (see also García and van Putte, 1988). Let us review this argument in more detail.

2.1 Context relevant for all theoretical accounts

The choice of grammatical aspect is not arbitrary. In Spanish, in particular, the use of either Preterite or Imperfect is not capricious. On the other hand, the choice to use one or the other inflectional ending is not necessarily deterministic: any given verbal predicate is embedded in a particular context that guides the choices made by native speakers. Interestingly, the effect of context on the selection of the Spanish Preterite and Imperfect is also accepted by researchers working within the parameters of a formal syntactic theory. For instance, in Chapter 3, we reviewed the empirical findings from Schell (2000) with L2 Spanish learners in a study abroad context. Even though Schell conducted her analysis within the Minimalist framework (e.g., Giorgi and Pianesi, 1997; Zagona, 1994), she concluded that '[w]hether the imperfect or preterit will be used depends on factors such as adjuncts within the same clause, subordinate or main clauses, or previous context that specifies a telic or atelic reading' (p. 35). That is, when Spanish native speakers used the Preterite or the Imperfect, their choices reflected the influence of components beyond the minimal description of a verb-phrase (i.e., internal and external arguments). Not taking into account the aforementioned sentential and extrasentential factors in the analysis of the selection of Preterite–Imperfect would constrain our theoretical representation of the L2 system of temporality marking. Effectively, discounting the effect of adjuncts as well as the effect of the larger context beyond the verb-phrase constitutes an analysis of the effect of lexical aspect on grammatical marking. On this point, Schell explicitly states that '[i]n an isolated mono-clausal sentence in which there are no adjuncts or aspectual references, the grammatical aspect assigned will automatically match the perfectivity (or imperfectivity) of the Inner Aspect Phrase' (pp. 35–36).

Montrul and Slabakova (2002: 8) also agree with the argument about the relevance of discourse for the appropriate characterization of aspectual meanings. For instance, they argue that the following sentence is not usually felicitous in the Imperfect because achievements have an inherent end point whereas the Imperfect implies an unbounded situation.

5a. El hielo se derretía (IMP).
      The ice melted.

Montrul and Slabakova specify, however, that sentence (5a) is acceptable in the context of a larger piece of discourse as shown in (5b).

5b. Durante la primavera, el hielo se derretía (IMP).
      During the spring, the ice melted.

Perhaps the strongest claim about the contextual nature of tense-aspect meanings comes from Coppieters (1987), who explicitly stated that the marking of tense-aspect meanings may not necessarily be part of the core grammatical properties of language. Coppieters argued that the data from his analysis of native and near-native speakers' judgements of decontextualized sentences representing the aspectual distinctions conveyed by French *Passé Composé* and *Imparfait* (equivalent to the aspectual distinction between Spanish Preterite and Imperfect):

> do carry some information; but, by and large that same information can readily be extracted from the context, and does not need to be explicitly expressed through grammatical means. In such circumstances, it may be difficult (particularly one whose native language does not formally mark the category or distinction in question) *to separate contextual from grammatical information* (p. 567, stress added).

In the final discussion of his findings, Coppieters concluded that the near-native speakers' intuitions diverged mostly in areas of functional or semantic knowledge, but not so much in areas of formal aspects of French grammar.

2.2 Grammatical knowledge is contextual knowledge

The conclusion to gather from the previous section is that, irrespective of theoretical framework, there seems to be common agreement about the fact that knowledge about tense-aspect meanings transcends the realm of the verb phrase. Where theoretical frameworks part company, is in their views about how to characterize the aforementioned two levels of representation of aspectual meanings. Thus, one important question in this regard is: How do we characterize the meaning shifts of specific verbs in isolation when they are placed in specific discursive contexts?

The following examples from Smith (1997: 51) provide some context to this dilemma:

6a. Last year, the train arrived late.
6b. For months, the train arrived late.
7a. Last year, John fed the cat.
7b. For months, John fed the cat.
8a. Last year, John moved to a new apartment.
8b. For months, John moved to a new apartment.

In both (6b) and (7b), there is a straightforward (default or prototypical) interpretation of the verb phrase as a derived activity, or multiple event activity (cf. Smith, 1997): there were multiple arrivals of the train and multiple feedings of the cat. Sentences (6a) and (7a), on the other hand, require some pragmatic knowledge to make sense of the most likely meaning of the sentence, because the adverbial *last year* may ambiguously signal a one-time event or multiple events of the same type. Thus, our pragmatic knowledge about the nature of the activities involved (i.e., train schedules and feeding pets) leads us to believe that the multiple event activity is to be preferred in both instances. Sentence (8), however, presents us with an interesting conundrum. That is, the same pragmatic knowledge we used with sentences (6a) and (7a) leads us to infer that (8a) refers to one single event of moving (as a whole). In contrast, (8b) conveys the same overall meaning of (8a). Sentence (8b), however, contributes an additional piece of information: John's move, as a whole, may have required several trips (in principle, as many as there were train arrivals or feedings of the cat). Therefore, the verbal predicate *to move* can be classified as a telic event.[2]

Ziegeler (2007: 999) points out that the solution of using syntactic means to resolve semantic conflicts (i.e., coercion) is not adequate and argues instead for a process of grammaticalization and historical change.[3] For instance, she contends that the generalization of the use of the English progressive with dynamic verb types (e.g., *she was winning, he was dying*) can be regarded 'as part of the shift towards the verb end of the noun-to-verb continuum' in the transition of English (p. 1020). In fact, even if some of the information about aspectual knowledge were to be regarded as 'pragmatic' in nature (i.e., conventional meanings in Smith's terms), it could eventually become part of the grammatical system. On this point, Ziegeler surmises that 'transitory pragmatic inferencing strategies may eventually be adopted and generalised across entire populations of users, and across entire paradigmatic domains of usage, where they may become conventionalised in usage, and henceforth no longer identifiable as changes' (p. 1022). Thus, we need to consider that what may be a historically based continuum (i.e., grammaticalization), may also be analysed as a conceptually based continuum of tense-aspect knowledge as well (i.e., an invariant-contextualized continuum of meanings).

In this regard, a potential expansion of Ziegeler's proposed process of grammaticalization of meanings can be instantiated in particular uses of the Spanish Preterite and Imperfect in association with the notions of iterativity and habituality. For instance, let us review the distinct representation of these two aspectual notions in sentences (9) and (10).[4]

9a. Durante mi infancia, el tren del mediodía llegaba (IMP) tarde.
    During my childhood, the 12 o'clock train arrived late.
9b. ?Durante mi infancia, el tren del mediodía llegó (PRET) tarde.
    During my childhood, the 12 o'clock train arrived late.

10a. ?Durante muchos años, el tren del mediodía llegaba (IMP) tarde.
   For years, the 12 o'clock train arrived late.
10b. Durante muchos años, el tren del mediodía llegó (PRET) tarde.
   For years, the 12 o'clock train arrived late.

Sentence (9a) prototypically represents a habitual and as such it is marked with the Imperfect, whereas sentence (10b) represents iterativity, thus it readily accepts the use of the Preterite. Notice, though, that switching the adverbials between sentences makes the alternatives (9b) and (10a) less acceptable. Why would this be the case? A possible answer is that these particular associations represent a first stage of grammaticalization by which specific adverbials are associated with specific aspectual concepts (not unlike the association of some relative clauses with the subjunctive). There is a second observation about the representation of iterativity and habituality in these sentences that is relevant in the context of the argument about a continuum of grammatical representation of tense-aspect meanings. Notice that the only potential difference in meaning between these adverbial clauses is the magnitude of the time-span denoted by each one (i.e., *mi infancia* versus *muchos años*). Interestingly, however, it is not possible to offer any categorical response to the question of which time span is longer (cf. Comrie, 1976; Michaelis, 2004). For instance, while *my childhood* (*mi infancia*) could comprise a period of time starting at age 1 or 2 (after one is a baby) until age 12 or so (when one becomes an adolescent), the phrase *for years* (*muchos años*) may refer to 10, 20 or 30 years.

In sum, in the absence of any extralinguistic information, I conclude that sentences (9a) and (10b) are mirror images of each other in terms of syntactic structure. Their major differences are in the realm of lexical knowledge (as represented by the time magnitude conveyed by the adverbial) and morphological (as represented by the use of perfective or imperfective marker on the verb). Thus, it is not possible to claim that in one case (i.e., 9a) the selection of past tense marking is due to a morphosyntactic factor, whereas in the other one (i.e., 10b) the selection of past tense marker would be due to pragmatic factors. In essence, the interpretation of both sentences is determined by the same phenomena, whether it is morphosyntactic or pragmatic.

2.3 Computational costs of processing aspectual knowledge

The specific categorization of the basic (invariant) and contextualized meanings of tense and aspect has important repercussions for the analysis of the L2 development of tense-aspect meanings (e.g., a definition of the dependent variable). For instance, the analysis of the computational processing of aspectual meanings is inherently predicated on the specific definition of tense-aspect. In this respect, de Swart's (1998, 2000) argument about the principled separation of grammatical and pragmatic information at the level of the theoretical representation of tense-aspect meanings has been extended to the realm of acquisition studies. In particular, it has been argued that the processing of pragmatic information is more costly than the processing of grammatical information (cf. Piñango et al. 1999). More specifically, Slabakova (2002: 184) makes a case for the importance of computational costs associated with the processing of pragmatic information (coercion) towards developing an understanding of the representation of tense-aspectual knowledge among L2 learners:

> . . . when the *passé simple* combines with a process or stative eventuality description, or when the *imparfait* combines with an event, two operations apply instead of one. In addition, when a simple tense operator applies on an eventuality description, the interpretation process is within the realm of syntactic composition; when aspectual coercion applies in addition to the tense operator, the process involves the pragmatic module as well as the syntactic module.

Slabakova's argument can be analysed in terms of both theoretical and methodological factors. First, Slabakova equates syntactic composition to prototypical selections of past tense marking (e.g., Preterite with punctual event or Imperfect with states), while, at the same time, she associates pragmatic knowledge with the marked choices in which the lexical aspect of a verb phrase does not match up with the aspectual meaning of the grammatical marker (e.g., Preterite with a state or Imperfect with a punctual event). In essence, equating syntactic composition with unmarked choices and pragmatic coercion with marked choices amounts to stating that syntactic composition represents an extension of the values of lexical aspect. Although this is a theoretically plausible option (e.g., de Miguel, 1992; de Swart, 1998, 2000; Michaelis, 2004), it is a position that carries a serious disadvantage given that we lose explanatory power to account for the principled selection of the perfective–imperfective marker (e.g., Spanish Preterite and Imperfect) with all lexical aspectual classes.[5] That is, if our theoretical model is only capable of accounting for the types of sentences in which there is a match up of situation aspect and viewpoint aspect (using Smith's 1997 labels), we fail to account for the most obvious dilemma faced by L1 English speakers learning L2 Spanish. To put it more bluntly, if we set out to investigate what constitutes one of the most difficult representations of Spanish past tense aspect, but eventually settle for an explanation that only accounts for the 'easy' conditions of our target objective, we have not addressed the main research goal we set out to investigate in the first place.

Second, it is questionable that the proposed computational costs of the coercion operation actually account for the empirical findings from Slabakova and Montrul (2002b, 2007). Piñango et al. (1999: 396) specifically point out that when they 'refer to aspectual coercion, the "aspectual" part of it is restricted to situational aspect [i.e., lexical aspect]'. Piñango et al. emphasize that '[a]spectual coercion is strictly local. It operates over the verb-phrase only' (p. 401). That is, their analysis does not pertain to the meanings conveyed by viewpoint aspect. As argued earlier, however, such a restrictive definition of tense-aspectual knowledge cannot account for the aspectual meanings conveyed by Spanish Preterite–Imperfect.

Third, the study from Piñango et al. is focused on data about one single lexical aspectual class. Note that the verbs that received 'enriched semantic composition' in the sample sentences used by Piñango et al. should actually be classified as semelfactives (cf. Smith, 1997), and not as activity verbs (i.e., atelic events). More specifically, Piñango et al. argue that '*jump*, as a point-action activity – that is, as an activity with an intrinsic beginning and an end – is by definition not compatible with any kind of additional temporal boundary otherwise imposed. This incompatibility should in principle yield an ungrammatical sentence' (p. 397). In fact, semelfactives are perfectly acceptable with boundaries because they share features of both telic and atelic events (i.e., they are both durative and instantaneous). Smith (1997: 37), for instance, points out that both Vendler (1967) and Dowty (1979) defined semelfactives as a special atelic subclass of achievements.[6] More importantly, Ziegeler (2007: 991) points out that the semelfactive verbs used by Piñango et al. 'seem to be almost conventionalised to the point of no longer appearing to be coerced in any way'.

Fourth, we need to understand why the higher computational cost associated with the processing of coercion would have an effect among non-native speakers, but not affect native speakers. In this respect, Montrul and Slabakova (2002: 142) argue that, even though both English and Spanish speakers coerce in their respective languages,

coercion might be peripheral to UG competence, and thus harder to acquire. That is, non-native speakers have the morphosyntactic and interpretative properties of AspP fully intact but, unlike native speakers, they might not have the pragmatic ability to coerce so as to avoid conflict between the semantic features of lexical aspectual class (telic) and those of aspectual tense (unbounded).

Assuming, thus that L2 learners already possess the ability to coerce in the L1, should they be able to transfer that ability to the processing of the target language? If not, how can we account for that failure to transfer processing knowledge that, unlike linguistic knowledge per se, would be hard to categorize as modular? (see Clarke, 1980 for an account of a related phenomenon associated with the transfer of reading skills to the processing of L2 data).

Finally, it is premature to assert that the addition of more linguistic information is directly correlated with higher computational costs. I believe that computational costs, as a matter of cognitive processing, may affect more than one component of the L2 grammar (i.e., from lexical to discursive factors). Thus, in principle, one could argue that what is computationally costly is not the processing of an extended piece of discourse, but rather the processing of decontextualized sentences without enough contextual information. In fact, the thrust of Birdsong's (1992) critique of Coppieters' (1987) analysis of past tense morphology was predicated on the idea that decontextualized sentences were not adequate to represent tense-aspect meanings, thus one would argue they were more difficult to process. In essence, one can argue that the true cost of computational processing is felt in decontextualized rather than contextualized sentences.

In sum, Piñango et al.'s proposal about computational costs is worth replicating with a larger sample of lexical aspectual classes embedded in a more expanded contextual space. In essence, the claim about computational costs to process tense-aspect information is not incompatible with a definition of tense-aspect meanings predicated on a continuum of contextualized levels of representation. In fact, in subsequent sections of this chapter I explicitly argue that L2 learners are better able to process and convey tense-aspect meanings in more contextualized rather than less contextualized settings.

3. Invariant Meanings and Default Values

To recapitulate, definitions of tense-aspect restricted to low levels of contextualization (e.g., at the verb-phrase level) categorize non-prototypical combinations of lexical and grammatical aspect as phenomena outside of the scope of a theory of grammatical knowledge. That is, non-prototypical choices, such as those triggered by the effect of adverbials are determined by pragmatic knowledge. As an example, achievements such as *llegar* (to arrive) are assumed to shift into habitual activities with the addition of temporal adverbials as in (11).

11. Por meses el tren llegó (PRET) tarde.
    For months the train arrived late.

Ironically, the aspectual concept conveyed with the use of a larger contextualization frame may constitute one of the most basic meanings of aspect. In the case represented in sentence (11) the concept of an iterated event would not be possible without the information contributed by the adverbial. At the most basic level of analysis, the previous example is another instantiation of the basic principle that lexical aspect and grammatical aspect are two distinct dimensions.

Similarly, the concept of boundedness is not necessarily associated with telic events only. Thus, like iterativity, boundedness can be expressed in prototypical or non-prototypical ways. For instance, in sentence (12) the Preterite provides temporal specification with reference to speech time irrespective of the lexical aspectual classification of the verb (cf. Doiz-Bienzobas, 1995, 2002). Thus, the situation of *knowing* is bounded. On the other hand, that states tend to be marked with Imperfect (cf. *sabía*) is a reflection of the fact that verbs have a default interpretation outside of context (sentence 13).

12. Siempre supo (PRET) la verdad.
    (S/he) always knew the truth.
13. Sabía (IMP) la verdad.
    (S/he) knew the truth.

As described in Section 6.4 of Chapter 2, lexical aspectual classes should be more precisely defined as default classes (i.e., prototypes) that are further specified in context. That is, Klein's (1994) maxim of minimality (put as little as possible into the lexical content) leads us to believe that verbs are typically perceived as belonging to a specific aspectual class by default (unmarked or prototypical reading).

In sum, even though the selection of the past tense aspectual endings in Spanish is based on the effect of the context in which a verbal predicate is embedded, there are invariant aspectual meanings associated with the Preterite and Imperfect (e.g., boundedness, iterativity, genericity). This argument is based on Doiz-Bienzobas' (1995: 29) claim that the 'contextual uses of the

	Invariant	Contextualized
	◄--►
Lexical aspect	breathe (air)	breathe air-a poisonous substance
	build (a house)	build a house-houses
Grammatical aspect	boundedness	bounded-unbounded
	iterativity	iterative-habitual

FIGURE 4.1   Continuum of invariant to contextualized meanings.

Imperfect and the Preterite are instantiations of their general meanings'. Furthermore, in line with Klein's (1994) maxims of minimality and contrast, we can posit the existence of default lexical aspectual classes that are further defined in the context of a larger piece of discourse as needed for communicative purposes. Figure 4.1 presents a graphical depiction of the continuum of meanings from invariant to contextualized for both the categories of lexical aspect and grammatical aspect.

In essence, there are default values instantiated in two distinct dimensions roughly equivalent to the traditional dichotomy of lexical aspect and grammatical aspect. In Chapter 2, I discussed in great detail the relevance of default values to understand how lexical aspectual classes acquire specific meanings in a range of minimally specified contexts to highly contextualized ones. In the remainder of this section, I discuss in more detail the invariant aspectual meanings of boundedness, iterativity and genericity.

3.1 Boundedness as a grammatical concept

The notion of boundedness is one of the most basic aspectual concepts conveyed by perfective–imperfective morphology (e.g., Comrie, 1976; Depraetre, 1995; Smith, 1997). Boundedness is essentially a grammatical concept, or, at a minimum, a concept that can have a grammatical representation. It has been argued, however, that boundedness can be expressed both grammatically and pragmatically. For instance, Slabakova and Montrul (2002b) illustrate the distinction with the following examples:

14a. Mary looked at Bill. He smiled.
14b. Mary looked at Bill. He was smiling.

Slabakova and Montrul (2002b: 632) propose that 'nothing in the overt grammatical form of these sentences suggests that in the case of (14a) the two events are sequential while in (14b) one event in progress overlaps with the first-mentioned momentary event'. Thus, they conclude that such knowledge is part of our pragmatic competence. Their analysis is not without merit, although I believe that there is an alternative interpretation also worth considering. That is, it can be argued that it is precisely the *distinct* 'overt grammatical form' used in these two sentences what triggers the two possible sequences of events described above. Notice that in sentence (14a) *smile* is conjugated in Simple Past, whereas in sentence (14b) it is marked with the Progressive Past Tense. Indeed, we cannot but conclude that there is at least a very enticing correlation between grammatical form and semantic interpretation in the previous two sentences. That is, in one case the Simple Past conveys clearly the notion of aspectual boundedness, whereas in the other one, the Past Progressive conveys the notion of unboundedness.

In fact, the aforementioned examples are reminiscent of the examples used by Kamp and Rohrer (1983) to account for the choice of grammatical aspect as part of their discourse representation structure (DRS). The latter is predicated on the application of construction rules to each adjacent pair of sentences (e.g., precedence relation, overlap relation and interpretation relation). For instance, in sentence (15a), the use of the imperfective form (i.e., *Imparfait*) conveys the idea that Marie was on the phone when Pierre entered the room, whereas in (15b), Marie made a phone call (inceptive point).[7]

15a. Pierre entra (*Passé Simple*). Marie téléphonait (*Imparfait*).
     Pierre came in. Marie was making a phone call.
15b. Pierre entra (*Passé Simple*). Marie téléphona (*Passé Simple*).
     Pierre came in. Marie made a phone call.

The previous examples show that the choice of perfective or imperfective verbal ending serves to convey a very specific aspectual meaning associated with boundedness. Note, however, that the argument about the pragmatic nature of some aspectual meanings is more feasible in the case of aspectual contrasts not directly correlated with grammatical markings. For instance, according to Hinrichs (1986), in the following examples, the imperfective form serves to advance narrative time, whether we use an adverbial (*maintenant*) or not.

16a. Pedro éteignit (*Passé Simple*) la lumière. Maintenant il faisait
     (*Imparfait*) absolument noir.
     Pedro turned off the light. Now it was dark.
16b. Jean tourna (*Passé Simple*) l'interrupteur. La lumière l'éblouissait
     (*Imparfait*).
     John turned on the switch. The bright light dazzled him.

The aspectual meaning conveyed by the second clause of each one of Hinrich's examples (16) indicates the inception time of an eventuality (i.e., *to be dark* and *to dazzle* respectively). The aforementioned construal of aspectual meaning may be regarded as indirect given that in both cases, it is the imperfective form that advances narrative time. That is, unlike the examples in sentences (15a) and (15b), the inception of the second eventuality is not marked by the use of the perfective form. Thus, the indirect understanding of the boundedness of the eventuality is the result of (pragmatic) inference.

3.2 Iterativity as a grammatical concept

The aspectual notion of iterativity is another basic aspectual concept conveyed through perfective–imperfective past tense morphology in Spanish. As is the case with boundedness, iterativity has been regarded to be part of pragmatic knowledge – as opposed to grammatical knowledge. For instance, as discussed in Chapter 3, Slabakova and Montrul (2002b, 2007) consider that the iterated events depicted in sentences (17b), (18b) and (19b) are interpreted through the process of pragmatic (implicit) coercion of the lexical aspectual class of an achievement verb (i.e., *llegar, acordarse* and *notar*). Pragmatic coercion is adduced to be prompted by the use of the adverbial clause that precedes the verbal predicate (e.g., *durante muchos meses, por muchos años* and *todo el día*).

17a. Ayer el tren del mediodía llegó (PRET) tarde.
Yesterday the 12 o'clock train arrived late.
17b. Durante muchos meses el tren del mediodía llegó (PRET) tarde.
For months the 12 o'clock train arrived late.
18a. En ese instante Julia se acordó (PRET) del accidente.
At that moment, Julia remembered the accident.
18b. Por muchos años Julia se acordó (PRET) del accidente.
For many years, Julia remembered the accident.
19a. De pronto, Juan notó (PRET) que Mónica estaba distraída.
Suddenly, Juan noticed that Mónica was not paying attention.
19b. Todo el día Juan notó (PRET) que Mónica estaba distraída.
All day long, Juan noticed that Mónica was not paying attention.

One wonders, however, why would habituality be defined as a grammatical concept whereas iterativity is defined as a pragmatic concept? First, in the cases of both habituality and iterativity, we have essentially the same process: an eventuality is iterated (e.g., Comrie, 1976). More importantly, both habitual and iterated eventualities are atelic given that they both satisfy the additivity and cumulativity tests. Despite their apparent common features, however, we cannot fail but notice that iterativity is prototypically marked with the Preterite, whereas habituality is prototypically marked with the Imperfect. Moreover, the association of habituality and iterativity with distinct grammatical markers (i.e., Imperfect and Preterite respectively) is reflected in the fact that habituality can be contrasted with iterativity as shown in sentences (20a) and (20b).

20a. Cuando era niño, el tren del mediodía siempre llegaba
   (IMP) tarde.   [habitual]
   When I was (IMP) a child, the 12 o'clock train always arrived late.
20b. Por muchos años, el tren del mediodía llegó
   (PRET) tarde.   [iterative]
   For years, the 12 o'clock train arrived late.

One possible reason that has led to the view that habituality is a more basic aspectual concept (thus, a grammatically represented concept) may be due to the fact that habituality is traditionally compared with boundedness to show aspectual contrasts conveyed through the Preterite and Imperfect. If, on the other hand, both iterativity and habituality are regarded as grammatical concepts, we should be able to find their effects in data about the development of the L2. In fact, this is the case, given our analysis of the findings from Slabakova and Montrul (2002b, 2007) and Pérez-Leroux et al. (2007) reviewed in Chapter 3. In essence, even advanced learners have difficulties in grasping the conceptual knowledge of iterativity conveyed through the Preterite as opposed to the concept of habituality conveyed by the Imperfect. If replicated with very advanced learners, this would represent evidence against the claim that L2 learners can achieve ultimate attainment in the representation of tense-aspect meanings.

The challenge posed by the contrast of habituality and iterativity is not surprising given the apparent complexity of the input data available to L2 learners. To ascertain that the input data are complex, let us review in more detail the empirical findings regarding the effects of iterativity gathered by Güell (1998), a study that I reviewed in Chapter 3. Güell analysed the responses of native and non-native speakers to events that had been iterated with the use of a sentence-grammaticality test. Sentences (21) and (22) provide two examples of the sentences used by Güell as prompts (p. 487).

21. Cada dos años, Vicente ganaba/ganó (PRET-IMP) algún premio.
    Every two years, Vicente won some award.
22. Los martes, el profesor de matemáticas paseó/paseaba (PRET-IMP)
    por la playa.
    On Tuesdays, the math professor strolled along the beach.

It is important to note that the iteration of events represented in Güell's sentences correspond to habituality (as opposed to iterativity). In fact, as shown in Table 4.1, the findings reveal that native speakers categorically used the Imperfect in both (21) and (22). In contrast, the least proficient learners (NN1) were ambivalent about their selection of either Preterite or Imperfect.

Furthermore, note that the learners with the highest level of proficiency (i.e., NN4) revert to marking iterated events with the perfective marker. This is shown in the increase in the use of the perfective form among NN3 learners (8 per cent) to NN4 learners (14 per cent). These results seem to confirm the apparent U-shaped behaviour in performance also represented in the findings from Slabakova and Montrul (2002b, 2007).

Güell also investigated whether these results could be strongly related to the information about lexical aspectual values. That is, it is possible that sentence (21) containing a telic event (*ganar*= to win) was primarily marked with Preterite, whereas sentence (22) containing an atelic event (*pasar*= to stroll) was primarily marked with Imperfect. Table 4.2 shows the same results presented in Table 4.1, but separated according to the telicity of the verbal phrase.

It appears that the least proficient non-native speakers in Güell's data are sensitive to the telic nature of the verb: telic verbs are primarily marked with Preterite (70 per cent for NN2) while atelic events are marked with Imperfect (61 per cent for NN2). This may be because non-native speakers tend to disregard the aspectual information provided by the sentence beyond the basic verb constellation (i.e., the verbal predicate and its

Table 4.1   Selection of verbal ending with iterated verbs in percentages

	NN2 (%)	NN3 (%)	NN4 (%)	N (%)
Pretérito	52	8	14	0
Imperfecto	48	92	86	100

Based on data from Güell (1998).

Table 4.2   Selection of verbal ending with
iterated *telic-atelic* verbs in percentages

	NN2 (%)	NN3 (%)	NN4 (%)
Pretérito	70/38	17/4	24/4
Imperfecto	30/61	83/96	76/96

Based on data from Güell (1998).

arguments). That is, non-natives made their selections of Preterite–Imperfect in accordance with the telicity nature of the verbal predicate. Further support for this argument is provided by the responses of natives and non-natives to sentences in which an iterated atelic eventuality is temporally circumscribed within a specific interval of time. For example, sentence (23) presents an atelic verb (*pasear*) that has been iterated with an adverbial (*cada día*), and which has been further circumscribed within a specific time period (*la semana pasada*).

23. La semana pasada Antonio paseó/paseaba (PRET/IMP) por
    el parque cada día.
    Last week Antonio strolled in the park every day.

Non-native speakers overwhelmingly preferred the imperfective form, indicating that their responses matched the atelicity of the verbal predicate (i.e., Imperfect in association with an atelic event). Native speakers, in contrast, showed great variation in their responses with a 50/50 selection of Preterite or Imperfect. In other words, the consideration of three levels of aspectual information – from the verbal predicate to the sentence level – triggered some uncertainty among native speakers about which component(s) of the overall composition of the aspectual meaning of the sentence to favour. That is, native speakers were affected in their responses by the addition of a higher level of contextualization of the basic sentence. Non-natives apparently remained unaffected by this higher level of contextualization of aspectual meanings (see also García and van Putte, 1988 for a similar claim based on the analysis of their data).

The scarce empirical evidence available so far leads to the following two conclusions. First, L2 learners seem to have great difficulty understanding the difference between iterativity and habituality, whereas native speakers show a high level of systematicity in their interpretations (unless the context becomes too complex). Second, the input data available to L2 learners is not very consistent, and at times, it contradicts most rules of thumb given to learners (e.g., an event that is durative should be marked with the Imperfect). In sum, the incomplete acquisition of iterativity coupled with the lack of consistent input data may substantiate the claim that L2 learners do not have access to any modular (UG-guided) learning process, but rely instead on general cognitive processes.

3.3 Genericity as a grammatical concept

As discussed in Chapter 2, an additional concept that is crucial to identify the aspectual meanings conveyed by the Preterite and Imperfect is the notion of genericity – as opposed to specificity. Genericity in Spanish is always conveyed with the use of the Imperfect, whereas the reference to the actual instance(s) of an event (specific) with the Preterite has no formal equivalent in English.

24a. Los niños de mi barrio jugaban (IMP) al fútbol.   [generic]
     The children in my neighborhood played soccer.
24b. Los niños de mi barrio jugaron (PRET) al fútbol.   [specific]
     The children in my neighborhood played soccer.

Previous analyses of genericity have actually regarded the distinction as grammatical and not pragmatic (e.g., Slabakova and Montrul, 2003). This perspective stands in contrast with the position advocated for the characterization of iterativity as pragmatic already discussed in the previous section. It has been assumed, however, that genericity is not available to L2 learners from input data. For instance, based on information from teachers and the analysis of textbook data, Slabakova and Montrul (2003: 174) claim that 'the generic/specific meanings of the Preterite and Imperfect are not taught and are not very frequent in the input'. Thus, Slabakova and Montrul argue that the lack of information about the generic/specific meanings of past tense markers in Spanish in the primary linguistic input, 'present[s] a poverty of the stimulus situation for language learners'. This argument is controversial, however, given both methodological and theoretical factors (see Chapter 3). In fact, one could argue that the generic meanings conveyed with the Imperfect are represented in the input data available to L2 learners in a more systematic manner than is the case for the representation of iterativity. Thus, one could argue that, despite the apparent aspectual complexity of genericity, L2 learners would be able to apprehend generic meanings conveyed with the Imperfect.

Irrespective of the theoretical position one may take with regard to the possible availability of information about the aspectual meaning of genericity in the input data available for L2 learners, genericity represents an essential component of a definition of aspectual meanings. Unfortunately, except for the study conducted by Slabakova and Montrul (2003), there is no other L2 acquisition study on this topic. Future studies should address this research void with the use of multiple research designs.

4. Mapping Aspectual Knowledge onto Grammatical Form

Thus far, I have argued that English speakers have a representation of aspectual concepts by and large equivalent to the one that Spanish native speakers have (e.g., iterativity, boundedness, narrative grounding and so on). Early on, however, Bull (1965: 170) noted that the Simple Past is 'completely ambivalent, and speakers of English, as a result, are not trained to observe aspectual differences'. His observation is important because it points to a possible representational problem for L1 English speakers attempting to learn how to mark aspectual distinctions through Spanish past tense inflectional endings. More importantly, the notion that the difficulty to learn the L2 system of tense-aspect meanings is represented by the possible mismatch between meaning and form seems to be a point of agreement among many researchers. Slabakova and Montrul (2003: 178), for instance, state that 'Spanish aspectual morphology carves the semantic space differently from English aspectual morphology'. Similarly, Ayoun (2005: 100) claims that 'the difficulties that L2 learners may encounter lie in the mapping of the abstract features to the appropriate L2 surface morphology'. In this section, I discuss the mapping problem faced by L2 learners from the perspective of a Cognitive Grammar perspective.

4.1 Thinking-for-speaking

According to Langacker (1999), linguistic structures are inherently defined by the nature of general cognitive processes. Thus, grammar is defined as the structuring and symbolization of conceptual knowledge. One important consequence of this definition is that conceptual knowledge may be moulded on particular grammars. In fact, Cognitive Grammar in general leads us to conclude that the language that we speak directs our attention to various features of situations and thus filters our experiences of the world. Langacker (1987: 6–7), in particular, proposes that 'the semantic value of an expression does not reside solely in the inherent properties of the entity or situation it describes, but critically involves as well the way we choose to think about this entity or situation and mentally portray it'.

Along the same lines, Sebastian and Slobin (1994) and Slobin (1996a, 1996b) have specifically proposed that different language typological patterns represented in the first language of speakers may influence their conceptualization and expression of motion events in particular (a neo-Whorfian hypothesis along the lines of Lucy, 1992). According to Sebastian and Slobin (1994: 611) when children acquire their L1, they also learn particular ways of thinking-for-speaking. In other words, the child 'learns to attend to particular aspects of experience and to relate them verbally in ways that are characteristic of that language'. In essence, Slobin's (1996a: 76) thinking-for-speaking entails that speakers focus on '. . . those characteristics of objects and events that (a) fit some conceptualization of the event, and (b) are readily encodable in the language'. Slobin's thinking-for-speaking proposal is very enticing to assess the status of the development of tense-aspectual knowledge in a second language. It is possible that, in principle, L1 English speakers have a distinct conceptualization of past tense aspectual meanings that have already been 'moulded' on the specific representational system of tense-aspectual knowledge of their L1. This theoretical argument would account for the common problem that L2 Spanish learners seem to have with the acquisition of the representation of tense-aspectual knowledge conveyed through the Preterite–Imperfect.

There are, however, two arguments – one empirical and one theoretical – against the viability of this proposal. First, there is no compelling empirical evidence to substantiate Slobin's proposal with regard to the concept of motion events in particular. Cadierno (2004) was the first study to empirically assess the validity of Slobin's proposal with regard to L2 acquisition processes. Cadierno's conclusion, however, revealed some inconsistencies with respect to the role of the learners' L1 in the expression of motion events in an L2. In particular, she did not find support for the hypothesis concerning the differences between the L2 learners and the Spanish native speakers on the use of event conflation and the allocation of attention to movement and setting. In fact, the findings from a follow-up study carried out by Cadierno and Ruiz (2006: 205) further corroborate the limited role of Slobin's L1-thinking-for-speaking in L2 development. Cadierno and Ruiz specifically point out that 'the influence of the L1 thinking-for-speaking patterns might be stronger at the initial and intermediate stages of language acquisition, but that it gradually disappears as the acquisition process advances'.

Second, the aspectual concepts expressed through Spanish Preterite–Imperfect morphology are already part of the representation of aspectual knowledge among L1 English speakers. For instance, English speakers have a conceptual notion of iterativity distinct from habituality and are capable of formally expressing this contrast in their L1. Thus, the difficulties of English speakers to convey iterativity as opposed to habituality with the use of Spanish Preterite–Imperfect must be related to something other than the concept itself. I would argue that the problem resides not in the representation of the concept, but in the mapping of form and concept. That is, L2 Spanish speakers have difficulties conveying tense-aspectual notions through grammatical carriers that are not already part of the concept-to-form mapping enabled by their native language.

In sum, the data from the acquisition of tense-aspect meanings represented in Spanish Preterite–Imperfect can be accounted for by Slobin's thinking-for-speaking proposal, if the latter is viewed as the actual mapping of specific concepts (e.g., temporal concepts) to formal means that are characteristic of a specific language (e.g., verbal morphology). Interestingly, Cadierno and Ruiz (2006: 205) note that 'learners might be inadvertently transferring an L1 pattern to the L2, possibly as a result of a shared conceptual system underling [sic] both their L1 and L2 structures . . ." Thus, why would L2 learners not be able to successfully express a concept (e.g., iterativity) in the L2 that is part of the representational system of both the source and target language?

4.2 Mapping concepts to forms

To further evaluate the relevance of the interpretation of Slobin's thinking-for-speaking, let us analyse the learning scenario provided by the Imperfect. A possible working hypothesis for the English-speaking learners is to 'map the Imperfect tense on their native progressive tense, and the Preterite on their native past simple' (Slabakova and Montrul, 2003: 188). Of course, this hypothesis can only go so far because there are some aspectual meanings represented in the Imperfect that are not represented in the progressive form in English. For instance, the progressive form in English neither has an equivalent generic subject interpretation, nor does it convey the notion of habituality. English speakers are thus forced to further refine their initial hypothesis about the strict correspondence of the English Past Progressive and the Spanish Imperfect. The problem, however, is not one of creating a new aspectual concept for the meanings of habituality or genericity. English provides a representation of genericity and habituality, even though these meanings are not conveyed with the same marker that signals progressivity. For instance, the periphrastic form *used to/would* and even the simple past convey the aspectual notion of habituality. In other words, English speakers do not need to learn new aspectual concepts. Rather, they need to learn how to map them onto a single linguistic carrier (i.e., Spanish Imperfect).

The contrastive use of the Imperfect and the Preterite brings up another challenge for English native speakers given that the Imperfect may be used in non-prototypical ways as shown in (25), an example provided by Comajoan (personal communication, 14 August 2007).

25. Esta mañana llegaba (IMP) a Madrid el presidente de EEUU.
     This morning, the US president was arriving (arrived) to Madrid.

The use of the Imperfect in (25) is non-prototypical to the extent that it takes over the basic tense information that is normally conveyed with the use of the Preterite. This use of the Imperfect creates a temporal setting (Doiz-Bienzobas, 1995: 97) that conveys the notion that the arrival occurred at some time in the morning without specifying the exact time or its time span. It is important to note that the use of the Imperfect in the context of (25) is actually fairly common. Thus, the Imperfect represents a challenge for non-native speakers not only due to the range and complexity of aspectual notions conveyed with it, but also because it can replace the Preterite in some of its normal functions.

Let us focus now on the use of the Preterite, and in particular, the adduced inability of English speakers to convey iterativity with it. Why would English speakers not be able to simply transfer their use of the Simple Past to convey iterativity from English? If transfer were successful, we would expect L1 English speakers to (correctly) mark iterativity in Spanish with the Preterite given that the latter is the most likely equivalent for Simple Past. In principle, learners should be able to make this simple positive transfer. One caveat to keep in mind, however, is that by the time learners start to cope with iterativity in their L2, they have already started to modify their original working hypothesis. As mentioned above, their first hypothesis was based on the almost direct equivalence of the English Past Progressive with Spanish Imperfect, and the English Simple Past with the Spanish Preterite. This hypothesis soon proves to be falsified by the fact that habituality in Spanish is also conveyed with the Imperfect.

As a consequence, one of the (usually successful) adaptations of the learners' working hypothesis is to assume that the iteration of all eventualities (both telic and atelic) requires the use of the Imperfect. Obviously, the unconstrained application of this assumption will lead to overgeneralization, and eventually lead learners to (erroneously) mark iterativity with the

Imperfect. For instance, the marking of the verbs *descubrir* and *entender* in sentences (26) and (27) contradicts that rule of thumb.[8]

26. A través de los años Carmen descubrió (PRET) el verdadero carácter de su marido.
    Throughout the years Carmen discovered the true character of her husband.
27. Gradualmente, Otálora entendió (PRET) que los negocios de Bandeira eran (IMP) múltiples . . .
    Gradually, Otálora understood that Bandeira's affairs were manifold . . .

In a small pilot study intended to elaborate on the findings from Slabakova and Montrul's (2002b) study, Salaberry and Scholes (forthcoming) asked L2 Spanish learners to succinctly verbalize their reasons for rejecting (or not) iterated achievement verbs marked with the Preterite. Their responses were fairly homogeneous. Worded in various ways (although mostly paraphrasing traditional grammar rules), learners regarded the use of the Preterite as incompatible with the 'durative' nature of iterated predicates (whether telic or atelic).

In fact, the difficulty that L2 learners have with some uses of the Preterite is not restricted to the notion of iterativity, but, more importantly, to the notion of boundedness as well. Sentences (28a) and (28b) from Güell (1998: 102) show the effect of boundedness on the selection of Preterite or Imperfect, irrespective of the value of the components of lexical aspect. That is, the use of the adverbial *durante mucho tiempo* in (28a) does not have an effect on the selection of the Preterite. Learners, however, are normally led to focus on the aspectual role of adverbials.

28a. Lo supo (PRET)/*sabía (IMP) durante mucho tiempo.
     (S/he) knew it for a long time.
28b. Lo *supo (PRET)/sabía (IMP) desde hacía mucho tiempo.
     (S/he) knew it from a long time ago.

In line with Doiz-Bienzobas' (1995, 2002) argument, Güell claims that sentence (28a) is temporally delimited, thus it requires the use of the Preterite to mark a tense contrast. In turn, sentence (28b) is not delimited temporally, thus it is acceptable with the Imperfect only. The examples shown in (28a, b) are important because they provide evidence against the claim that the Preterite is exceptionally used with states when the latter convey inchoativity (i.e., the beginning of the state) only. In fact, in Chapter 2 we reviewed several uses of the Preterite with non-inchoative meaning of stative verbs as shown by the following examples gathered by Bybee (1995a):

29. Supe (PRET) Latín.
    I knew Latin.
30. Primero hizo (PRET) sol y luego llovió (PRET).
    First it was sunny and then it rained.
31. Estuvimos (PRET) allí tres horas y después fuimos (PRET) al cine.
    We were there for three hours and then we went to the movie theatre.

This apparently unusual use of the Preterite with states (at least for many non-native speakers) is accounted for by Doiz-Bienzobas' theoretical framework: the Preterite is the only true tense marker, thus it serves to mark temporal delimitation (see Chapters 2 and 3). In essence, thus, the difficulty experienced by adult native English speakers learning Spanish is not necessarily attributable to the expression of aspectual concepts of iterativity, or genericity or boundedness. Their major problem is matching up the aspectual concepts with the appropriate morphological carriers of those meanings.

4.3 Summary: Mapping aspectual knowledge onto grammatical form

The argument developed thus far indicates that L2 Spanish learners have difficulties with the appropriate *marking* of invariant aspectual concepts (e.g., boundedness, iterativity) with inflectional morphology. This conclusion leads us to reassess previous claims about L2 learners' limitations to incorporate the effect of contextual factors to the appraisal of the aspectual value of any given predicate (e.g., Coppieters, 1987). For instance, the selection of the imperfective form among non-natives to mark the verb *entender* in sentence (27) leads us to conclude that L2 learners put too much weight on the contribution of the adverbial that accompanies the predicate (i.e., *gradualmente*) to determine the selection of inflectional marker. Thus, L2 learners are assessing the aspectual value of the verb according to information above the verb phrase. Interestingly, Spanish speakers give less importance to the aspectual value of the adverbial.

In this respect, note that due to its more 'impoverished' inflectional system, English relies on the use of adverbials to mark aspectual distinctions (e.g., Lubbers-Quesada, 2006). Most dramatically, whereas state verbs in Spanish can be marked with either Imperfect or Preterite, states in English are generally marked exclusively with Simple Past. The aspectual distinction between the imperfective and perfective meaning of states in English must rely on the contribution of other contextual information. Thus, relative to Spanish speakers, English speakers, due to L1 transfer, will privilege the presence of the adverbial in order to select the target inflectional marker (i.e., Preterite or Imperfect). Essentially, English speakers experience a mapping problem caused by the L1 representation of tense-aspectual meanings.

Interestingly, Gabriele, Martohardjono and McClure (2005) substantiate the previous claim based on the analysis of L2 English data produced by L1 Japanese speakers. Gabriele et al.'s findings show that Japanese speakers have more difficulties with the interpretation of the Progressive (*be* + *ing*) than with the interpretation of the Simple Past. More specifically, Japanese speakers incorrectly accepted sentences with a progressive meaning as having a perfective meaning. For instance, they apparently interpreted the meaning of *My niece was singing two songs* as equivalent to *My niece sang two songs*. In this respect, Gabriele et al. note that the equivalent progressive structure in Japanese *te-iru* has both a perfective and a progressive meaning. Thus, they conclude that the difficulties of Japanese learners with the interpretation of the Progressive in L2 English are probably because 'the perfective is actually a default interpretation in the mental representation of *te-iru* . . ." (p. 822). The relevance of this finding is that whenever more than one aspectual concept is subsumed within one single grammatical marker in the L1, it is a challenge to associate this bundle of aspectual meanings into separate grammatical markers in the L2. In the following section I discuss the effect of the L1 in further detail and in so doing I further substantiate the case for role of default values to process L2 tense-aspect information.

5. The Effect of the L1

The challenge for English-speaking learners is to match the use of aspect-bearing past tense inflectional morphology in L2 Spanish with aspectual distinctions with which they are already familiar in their native language. Thus, we could logically surmise that L1 learners will be *initially* inclined to transfer whatever inflectional or periphrastic markers of aspectual meaning they have in their native language.[9] The relative role played by L1 transfer, however, varies across different proposals both in terms of its weight vis-à-vis other factors and also with regard to which components of the L1 are transferred.

The LAH, for instance, has primarily favoured the role of a universal tendency to convey aspectual distinctions over tense distinctions, irrespective of the learners' L1. Substantiating this point, Shirai (2007: 58) argues that except for a few recent studies '[t]he AH studies so far have not paid much attention to the effect of the L1 . . . , placing more emphasis on the universal aspects of tense-aspect acquisition' Shirai adds, however, that '[t]his in fact is a historical accident, and the field is now ripe for inquiries into this important area'. Similarly, most studies on the acquisition of tense-aspect conducted within a strictly syntactic approach such as Minimalism have favoured the effect of UG-based processes leading to the argument that 'the formal features associated with the functional category AspP are fully acquirable and "unimpaired" in SLA' (Montrul and Slabakova, 2002: 38). The theoretical reliance on the effect of UG processes during adult L2 acquisition leads to discounting the effect of L1 transfer (see reviews in Chapter 3). It should be noted, however, that studies that do not support the 'full-access' view shun the effect of UG factors, favouring instead the strong influence of L1 transfer (e.g., Hawkins and Chan, 1997; Hawkins and Liszka, 2003).

Despite the possible 'underweighting' of L1 transfer effects, most researchers tend to agree that L1 transfer may have important consequences on the L2 development of tense-aspect knowledge. Thus, Slabakova (2002: 186) proposes that 'much more precise research questions can be formulated if L1 transfer is taken into account and only properties that differ in the L1 and the L2 are investigated'. In agreement with Slabakova, Shirai (2004: 1) argues that the 'prototype past (i.e., past tense with telic events) is frequent in the input, and the learners' L1s tend to have a similar prototype'. Shirai goes on to propose that, in principle, both the effects of input and native language could account for the bias towards using perfective morphology, especially during the beginning stages of acquisition. Thus, it is important to analyse in more detail the possible effect of L1 transfer on the development of past tense aspectual knowledge in L2 Spanish.

5.1 English Simple Past

The analysis of possible transfer of knowledge about aspectual meanings from the L1 to the L2 with regard to the specific pairing of L1 English–L2 Spanish leads us to conclude that one important challenge for L1 English speakers is that aspectual contrasts in English are not systematically marked on verb endings, as is the case in L2 Spanish Preterite–Imperfect. In essence, English expresses tense but not aspectual distinctions through inflectional morphology (see Chapter 2). There is substantial agreement on this point. For instance, Ziegeler (2007: 1023) argues that English does not have two representational meanings associated with the simple past (i.e., aspectual and tense meanings), but rather 'one prototypical use that is likely to have related to its historical development (perfectivity), and . . . any nonprototypical uses are extensions via pragmatic inferencing (past temporality)'. Similarly, de Swart (1998) explains that '. . . the simple past in English is *aspectually neutral* and the aspectual nature of the eventuality is inherited from the aspectual class of the sentence' (p. 368).[10] Finally, in his last revision of the original aspect hypothesis, Andersen (2002: 89) argues that 'although Past is a tense category and Perfective is an Aspect category, the two appear to have almost the same prototype'.

A corollary of the fact that English Simple Past marks tense and not aspect is that it is natural for L2 Spanish learners to simply equate Simple Past with Spanish Preterite, as proposed by the DPTH. As learners become more experienced with the L2, they are able to accommodate the use of two alternative past tense markers. The change of a system based on one single marker of past tense to one with two complementary markers (i.e., Preterite and Imperfect) will be supported by several factors. For instance, the lexical aspectual meanings of different verbs will be more closely associated with either the Preterite or the Imperfect (cf. the LAH). Similarly, specific distributional tendencies in the input data will favour the use of one or the other Spanish past tense marker with specific verbs (cf. the distributional bias hypothesis). Moreover, discourse grounding will guide learners towards associating one or the other marker with the foreground or background of a narrative. Finally, there are possible instructional sequences that may favour the use of the perfective form as the prevalent past tense marker.[11]

The previous description is, however, an oversimplification because there are mismatches not only in the explicit marking of tense-aspectual meanings through inflectional endings, but in the range of aspectual concepts as well. Olsen (1997: 68), for instance, argues that the 'progressive imperfective has narrower interpretation than general imperfective (ongoing event than ongoing event or state) it is semantically marked and more likely to be expressed periphrastically'. Thus, the Spanish Imperfect is conceptually more difficult than the English Past Progressive, because it spans a wider range of semantic concepts than the English Past Progressive (e.g., continuity, habituality and genericity), and as such the Imperfect is more ambiguous. More importantly, this challenge is not restricted to the Imperfect, since the aspectual representation of the Preterite is also affected by the extensive range of aspectual concepts conveyed by the Imperfect. An example of this effect is the response of L1 English speakers to the marking of iterativity with the Preterite. That is, even though L1 English speakers may express iterativity with the Simple Past, they fail to accept the same expression of iterativity through the Preterite. This is an important finding that will require more empirical data than what is currently available to investigate L2 learners' development of that essential concept of tense-aspect meanings.

5.2 English marks tense only: Are states special?

One interesting case to assess the possibility that the difficulty of L1 English speakers resides in the match-up of aspectual concepts with aspectual morphology is the marking of statives in L2 Spanish. Kihlstedt (2002), for instance, argues that dynamicity instead of telicity explains the use of perfective across all dynamic classes in French L2 data (see also Bergström, 1995 and Salaberry, 1998). Salaberry (2005: 208) specifically claimed that English-speaking 'learners will have a harder time using both perfective and imperfective markers with [–dynamic] verbs than they would with [+dynamic] verbs'. In fact, several studies show that learners have difficulty in appropriately marking *states* with past tense morphology (e.g., Cadierno, 2000; Granda, 2004; García and van Putte, 1988; Salaberry, 2005; Schell, 2000). Furthermore, the empirical evidence seems to indicate that, even at fairly advanced stages of development, L2 Spanish learners struggle with the appropriate inflectional marking of statives (e.g., Granda, 2004; Hawkins and Lizska, 2003; Liskin-Gasparro, 2000; Lubbers-Quesada, 1999, 2007; Salaberry, 2005). Moreover, from a theoretical point of view, states are less clearly demarcated as a lexical aspectual class, thus making the dynamic verbs a sort of default lexical aspectual class. For instance, Olsen (1997: 38) claims that '[s]tates . . . have both stative and dynamic interpretations. In contrast, [+dynamic] verbs are always interpreted as dynamic, independent of stative constituents or pragmatic contexts'.

On the other hand, English speakers can rely on their L1 to mark aspectual meanings on statives in Spanish. That is, L1 English speakers have one important piece of knowledge about aspectual contrasts in their L1 that, although not exactly equivalent to the aspectual contrast conveyed by Spanish Preterite–Imperfect, is nonetheless fairly close to it. More specifically, even though English does not mark the perfective–imperfective aspectual contrast (i.e., Simple Past is a tense marker only), it does convey an aspectual contrast with the use of the Past Progressive–Simple Past pairing. That is, L2 learners may possibly associate the aspectual value conveyed by the Imperfect in Spanish with the one conveyed by progressivity in English. Thus, in principle, transfer from L1 English can account for the use of the imperfective form with states. Several researchers, however, discount the option that learners use L1 transfer to successfully mark statives with the Imperfect. Montrul and Slabakova (2002: 40), for instance, show that stative verbs are marked with the Spanish Imperfect when they are incompatible with the Progressive in English. Although Montrul and Slabakova's findings represent an important piece of empirical evidence to substantiate the search for an account other than the one of L1 transfer, I believe it is still premature to discount the value of transfer. I discuss some of those reasons.

First, at a theoretical level of analysis, statives are not necessarily incompatible with the progressive marker either in Spanish or in English (see examples from Olsen, 1997 in Chapter 2). More importantly, the marking of states with the progressive is not necessarily due to pragmatic coercion effects. For instance, Ziegeler (2007: 1019–20) specifies that 'in its Old English uses, the progressive was often used to refer to situations of both a more permanent or generic nature and a durative, temporary nature – i.e., it was a general imperfective marker'. In present day English, however, the use of the Past Progressive with states is not as prevalent as before (recessive) given that the Progressive has become more strongly attached to dynamic verbs. As a consequence, Ziegeler argues that 'the apparent coercion we see in today's uses is reflective of the historical development of the progressive, and of a gradual diachronic development, rather than an instantaneous, on-line shift'.

Second, L1 English learners may rely on the aspectual meaning conveyed by the progressive to approximate the aspectual meaning conveyed by the imperfective in Spanish. This is a heuristic procedure that, by definition, does not have to be based on exact equivalencies. Finally, the fact that English speakers are not used to marking states with the Past Progressive (e.g. *I was knowing, *I was loving) as often as Spanish speakers tend to mark states with the Imperfect may not necessarily discourage English speakers from transferring the notion of progressivity. That is, L2 learners may assume that the L2 is different from the L1, thus they may be more willing to 'bend' structural and semantic restrictions prevalent in the L1 when processing L2 information (cf. Pienemann et al., 2005).

On the other hand, states may also be marked with the Preterite (as opposed to the Imperfect). More importantly, in many cases, L2 learners tend to overextend the use of the Preterite with states to contexts in which it is not appropriate. For instance, Granda (2004) showed the unusual contrast in the use of Preterite in background clauses and how that use was the only significant contrast in the use of Spanish past tense markers between native and non-native speakers. Most previous analyses have not provided a theoretical account of the inappropriate use of the perfective form with states among L2 Spanish learners. Among one of the few explicit analyses of this important finding, Schell (2000) claims that in the following use of the Preterite form, *fue* 'seems to indicate that this was a direct translation from English'.

32. *Fue (PRET) las 8:31 cuando nosotros llegamos (PRET).
    It was 8:31 when we arrived.

This particular use of the stative verb *to be* is important because, according to the theoretical framework proposed by Giorgi and Pianesi, the [+perfective] feature does not apply to statives. Moreover, statives are prototypically associated with the Imperfect. Thus, why would L2 learners use the perfective form with states? To account for this outcome, Schell argues that '. . . the high frequency of the Preterite with states is due to the transfer of the [+FINAL] [feature] from the English morphology used to modify them in the L1' (p. 131). This argument, however, stands in contrast with the proposal advanced by Giorgi and Pianesi with regard to the contrastive analysis of English and Spanish already discussed in Chapter 2 (i.e., English does not mark perfectivity at the grammatical level, but rather at the lexical level). At a minimum, Schell's account seems to add some degree of unnecessary redundancy to the theoretical explanation. On the one hand, it is claimed that states start out as [−perfective] at the lexical level, but are eventually marked as [+perfective] by Simple Past. On the other hand, eventive verbs marked as [+perfective] at the lexical level, are marked again as [+perfective] at the grammatical level.

5.3 The hypothesis about a default past tense

I believe that the hypothesis that most directly addresses the inappropriate use of the Preterite with states is the DPTH (default past tense hypothesis). I turn to a more extended discussion of this hypothesis in this section.

5.3.1 Main theoretical tenets

If we consider the case of the L1 English–L2 Spanish pairing, there are at least four different factors that substantiate the learners' reliance on the use of the Preterite as a default marker of past tense during the initial stages of the L2 development. Those factors are (1) only tense is represented in English past tense inflectional morphology (i.e., Simple Past), (2) conversely, the Preterite is the basic past tense marker in Spanish, (3) distributional biases in the L2 and (4) specific teaching paradigms that highlight the use of the perfective form as a carrier of tense by excellence. I have already discussed the relevance of the fact that the English Simple Past only marks tense distinctions and how this factor constrains the options entertained during the acquisition of L2 Spanish.

A second factor to be considered is that the Spanish Preterite may also function as a tense marker. Despite the fact that most learners (and sometimes teachers) talk about the Spanish Preterite and Imperfect as two tenses, the majority of theoretical treatments define them in qualitatively distinct ways. More specifically, the Preterite is regarded as the basic past tense marker, whereas the Imperfect is a more straightforward aspectual marker. In fact, this is an argument made for the perfective–imperfective contrast in general. Comrie (1985: 121) argues that in the past tense the perfective aspect is the unmarked member of the dichotomy. Similarly, Fleischman (1990) argues that in narratives the perfective is the unmarked form and the imperfective, the marked form (for more details on the notion of markedness, see Waugh, 1990). With regard to the Preterite–Imperfect Spanish contrast in particular, Guitart (1978: 142) claims that the Preterite 'states that an occurrence took place before the moment of speaking', whereas the Imperfect tells about an occurrence which happened before the time of speaking, in which some other situation took place or was taking place'. Finally, within the perspective of Cognitive Grammar, Doiz-Bienzobas (1995) substantiates the argument that the Preterite is the only inflectional marker of past tense in Spanish that conveys the notion of time specification. That is, the Preterite is a more prototypical marker of past tense than the Imperfect.

To substantiate the previous claim, let us review in the context of this analysis some examples introduced in Chapter 1 and repeated here.

33. SABÍA (IMP) la verdad.
    (S/he) knew the truth.
34. En ese momento, SUPO (PRET) la verdad.
    At that moment, (he) discovered the truth.
35. Siempre SUPO (PRET) la verdad.
    (S/he) always knew the truth.

The use of the Imperfect in (33) and the Preterite in (34) is largely uncontroversial: the Imperfect is the prototypical marker used with homogeneous states, whereas the Preterite is used to focus on the inception of the state of knowing (event). The use of the Preterite in sentence (35), however, puzzles many English speakers. In fact, although it is not inconceivable that the use of the Preterite is triggering the concept of iterativity, it is not very likely. That is, the interpretation of the verb *saber* is more likely along the lines of its basic stative meaning (homogeneous). In fact, notice that the English translation of saber in (34) is *discovered*, but in both (33) and (35) is *knew*. That is, the use of the Preterite in (26) is not conveying the meaning of an iterated event. I believe that the best theoretical account for the interpretation of the use of the Preterite in sentence (26) is offered by Doiz-Bienzobas (1995, 2002). That is, the Spanish Preterite acts as the 'default aspectual form for the expression of past events . . .' (Doiz-Bienzobas, 1995: 92).

A third factor that may lead learners to rely on the use of the Preterite as a default marker of past tense is represented by distributional tendencies in the input data (including the distributions according to lexical aspectual semantics). Distributional tendencies in input data may be regarded as part of *cognitive processing* factors that lead learners to focus on certain verbs or certain inflectional endings more than others. Obviously, the lexical semantics of the verbal predicate and its associated arguments and adjuncts is one powerful factor that will guide learners' attention to specific features of the linguistic representation of a situation. In this respect, the findings from Lubbers-Quesada (2006) reveal that L2 learners seem to rely heavily on the meaning of adverbials to process aspectual information in Spanish. By the same token, narrative grounding is a textual feature of both written and oral discourse that will help learners focus their attention on specific characteristics that are associated with the use of various past tense markers. Furthermore, as discussed in previous chapters, another causal factor that can account for particular developmental stages of L2 acquisition of verbal morphology is the role of the perceptual saliency of verbal endings (i.e., irregular morphology) and their frequency in the input (e.g., Bayley, 1994; Klein et al., 1995; Lafford, 1996; Salaberry, 2000b; Wolfram, 1985).

Finally, the role of instruction is also relevant to assess the possible effect of default past tense markers. In particular, the use of 'rules of thumb' provides learners with an efficient procedure to counteract the role of defaults when the latter is not adequate to mark past tense. For instance, the findings of studies focused on the lack of use of the Preterite with iterated events (e.g., Salaberry and Scholes, forthcoming; Slabakova and Montrul, 2002b, 2007) are probably due to the indiscriminate use of the rule of thumb that states that any eventuality that occurred a series of times is durative, thus it requires the use of the Imperfect. In other words, instruction leads learners to over-rule the general use of the default marker of past tense. Ironically, in the case of the use of the imperfective form with iterated events, instruction leads students to incorrectly avoid the use of the perfective form. I return to the analysis of the effects of instruction in more detail in Chapter 5.

5.3.2 Reconciling competing hypotheses

Shirai (2004) contends that the findings that apparently contradict the LAH are mostly restricted to data associated with irregular and frequent morphology. He further argues that this outcome is predicated on the fact that adult second language learners possess a greater capacity for rote memory learning compared to L1 learners (i.e., children). Thus,

> . . . the weaker association between past and achievements or between progressive and activities observed with L2 learners at lower proficiency levels is due to the use of these high-frequency forms that learners access and produce without really knowing or controlling the semantics of the morphological forms associated with them (p. 102).

In other words, Shirai adduces that a dual system approach may account for some studies showing departures from the expected association of past tense markers with lexical aspectual classes. The assumption made by Shirai is that the use of memorized forms (likely represented by frequent irregulars) is not indicative of the true representational system of learners.

Shirai's account theoretically reconciles the existence of a dual system with the LAH by claiming that one dimension of that system (i.e., memorized storage of irregulars) does not constitute part of the actual representational knowledge of tense-aspect. In other words, the memorization of irregulars is like a developmental 'crutch' that will allow L2 learners to achieve functional competence until true representational competence in the L2 system of temporality is acquired. In turn, the representational system of temporality will comply with the developmental sequences proposed by the LAH. Shirai's proposal, however, is contradicted by the findings of Buck (2007, in press) who showed that, contrary to previous findings, the effects of irregular endings actually increase along with proficiency in the L2 (see Chapter 3 for an extended discussion).

In contrast, the DPTH has been regarded as empirically inconclusive given the actual outcome of most tense-aspect acquisition studies (e.g., Bardovi-Harlig, 2000; Comajoan, 2006). In effect, if Spanish L2 learners indeed relied on the use the Preterite as a default past tense form – as the DPTH claims – we should be able to find evidence of the Preterite being used as the only marker of past tense across all lexical aspectual classes (including statives), at least at some stage in the developmental process. This could be regarded as the most stringent test of a default past tense hypothesis (see Bardovi-Harlig, 2000: 266 and Comajoan, 2006). Alternatively, we could argue for a less stringent empirical test if we consider the concomitant influence of other relevant factors (described in the previous section) that affect the use of past tense marking in L2 Spanish. For instance, even though the Preterite may be the default past tense marker, distributional biases favour the use of the Imperfect with specific verb types (most notably high-frequency verbs such as *ser, estar,* etc.). However, positing that both the Preterite and the Imperfect may be used concurrently could become overly constraining as far as the testing of the hypothesis is concerned. Thus, there must be a way to falsify the claim that the Preterite is the actual default past tense marker. In this respect, the question is whether the Imperfect is the first past tense marker and the Preterite then 'spreads' from achievements towards statives as the LAH would predict, or whether the Preterite was the first marker to be used with statives.

The available data reviewed in Chapter 3 seem to indicate that both the Preterite and the Imperfect are in competition with each other for the marking of statives from the very beginning. In consequence, instead of witnessing a categorical use of the Preterite across all lexical aspectual classes, we find a lopsided distribution of past tense marking, in which the Preterite competes with the Imperfect during the preliminary stages of marking of statives. Comajoan (2006) provides a persuasive account of this outcome. Comajoan claims that the imperfective may not spread to other aspectual classes of verbs because it is associated with a limited number of verb types (p. 253). Comajoan bases his argument on Ellis' (2002) claim that type frequency (as opposed to token frequency) is more likely to lead to strong associations of morphological endings with a restricted class of verbs. This is even more relevant if the number of verbs of a given category is not too large as is the case for states. I believe that Comajoan's argument provides further support for the claim that the Preterite and the Imperfect are processed in a different manner (i.e., generative versus associationistic processing respectively), and thus that the Preterite acts as a default marker.

5.3.3 Expanding the DPTH

Interestingly, some of the available data on the marking of temporality among advanced learners seem to indicate that the use of a default past tense is not restricted to the beginning stages of acquisition. Rather, the use of the Preterite as a default past tense shows up in the use of advanced learners when the application of the target language 'rule' becomes too complex (e.g., Antonio, 2007; Granda, 2004; Liskin-Gasparro, 2000; Schell, 2000). This finding, if confirmed with additional empirical evidence, raises important theoretical questions. For instance, how do we explain the resilience of the enduring effect of a default tense marker even after lexical aspect and discursive grounding appear to have been incorporated to the learner's evolving grammar? One possible answer is that L2 Spanish learners never 'give up' on the use of default past tense form. Other factors that may guide the use of past tense markers (e.g., lexical aspect) are simply added to the system, as the learner's grammar is capable of further complexification.

Thus, it is possible that, contrary to previous assertions (Wiberg, 1996; Salaberry, 1999), the existence of a default marker of past tense is relevant across all levels of proficiency including near-native speakers. In fact, the idea that a default past tense marker remains active in the L2 system – even after the imperfective form has already been incorporated to the system of past tense contrasts – may help account for the elusive findings that contradict most previous hypotheses (e.g., the inadequate use of the Preterite with states in García and van Putte, 1988 and Granda, 2004 inter alia). The possible role of a default past tense marker among more advanced stages of acquisition is also in line with more recent proposals such as Labeau's (2005) claim that the development of aspectual knowledge can be metaphorically represented as the movement of a pendulum. The latter would more accurately describe the constant adjustments, failed attempts and wrong hypotheses that persist even among near-native speakers. The notion of instability of the L2 system proposed by Labeau parallels the earlier claim advanced by Coppieters based on the heterogeneous responses of near-native speakers relative to the homogeneous responses of the native speakers. That is, the highly proficient near-natives of Coppieters are likely making adjustments and committing mistakes (cf. Labeau's pendulum) because their L2 grammatical systems are not stable.

Finally, the claim that the Preterite acts as a default past tense marker among more advanced stages of acquisition raises questions about the possibility of achieving native-like knowledge of tense-aspectual marking in Spanish. On the point of possible developmental stages, Sharwood Smith and Truscott (2005: 225) argue that '[I]f actual growth was truly stage-like, one would expect a rapid disappearance of all signs of the former stage as soon as (rapidly emerging) new features in learner performance have signaled the learner's arrival in a new stage'. To some extent, some of the studies mentioned above show that the signs of a default past tense marker do not totally disappear from the L2 learner's grammar. Thus, we could argue that, at least with reference to the levels of proficiency represented in those studies, native-like knowledge of tense-aspectual marking in Spanish is not attainable. The proposal about the lack of ultimate attainment of native-like competence in tense-aspect knowledge first advanced by Coppieters (1987), and later revived by Labeau (2005) is associated with a non-modular view of second language acquisition.

6. Modular Versus General Learning Processes

6.1 Modular learning in L2 acquisition

Several researchers have argued that adult learners of a second language can acquire unconscious knowledge of abstract properties of the L2 grammar even in cases when there may not be direct evidence either from the L1 or input knowledge. Thus, full acquisition of new functional categories (e.g., AspP) and their associated features (e.g., [–perfective]) is possible (e.g., Schwartz and Sprouse, 1996; Vainnika and Young-Scholten, 1996). In their various publications, Montrul and Slabakova extend the previous argument stating that native-like competence is possible in the specific area of tense-aspect knowledge as well. On the other hand, Slabakova and Montrul (2002a: 387) 'tentatively conclude that pragmatics is outside of Universal Grammar, and acquisition of pragmatic contrasts are not guided by the same principles that guide the acquisition of the viewpoint contrast'. That is, pragmatic knowledge is regarded as essentially a non-language specific ability that is not part of our genetic endowment. Thus, it follows that pragmatic knowledge is prone to increased variability in competence throughout cognitive development. Slabakova and Montrul (2002b, 2007, inter alia) distinguish grammatical versus pragmatic knowledge according to two major criteria: domain-specificity and innateness. Let us review these two factors in more detail.

First, we need to decide whether innateness and modularity should be regarded as a single construct. Bates and Goodman (1999), in particular, specifically point out that the innateness argument has to be separated from the modularity argument. As they explain, it is the latter that is the more controversial one. Second, Bates et al. (1998: 599) propose that '[t]he same facts can be explained by replacing innate knowledge (i.e. representations) with architectural and temporal constraints that require much less genetically specified information'. For instance, Bates and Goodman (1997: 508) propose that vocabulary and grammar 'may be acquired and processed by a unified processing system, one that obeys a common set of activation and learning principles'. Furthermore, it is theoretically possible that a modular dissociation between grammar and the lexicon emerges over time. That is, even though language acquisition may not be modular at first, general cognitive processes may quickly specialize and become modular as learning unfolds. In other words, modularity is the outcome of the process of learning, rather than its cause (e.g., Karmiloff-Smith's, 1992 'modularization' process). Irrespective of the position that one may take on the issue of modularity to assess the developmental process of tense-aspect knowledge in L1 acquisition, it is not guaranteed that L2 acquisition will be modular even if that were the case for L1 acquisition. Thus, let us discuss in more detail the claim advanced for a non-modular process to learn aspectual distinctions.

6.2 General learning processes

Among the earliest and most clearly articulated proposals about the non-modular nature of L2 acquisition, Bley-Vroman's (1989) fundamental difference hypothesis (FDH) attributes the differences between child and adult language acquisition to the adult learners' lack of direct access to the principles and parameters of UG. That is, as cognitively mature individuals, adult learners have a full-fledged linguistic system in place when they start the L2 acquisition process. The FDH is predicated on the analysis of salient differences between L1 acquisition among children and L2 acquisition among adults. Bley-Vroman argues that L1 acquisition happens rapidly and efficiently because the process is guided by UG. In contrast, L2 acquisition is typically variable and incomplete because adult learners no longer have access to UG (presumably due to a critical period). Thus, Bley-Vroman contends that in L1 acquisition, language learning is controlled by a modular domain-specific process, whereas in L2 acquisition among adults, learning is guided by a non-modular general-domain problem-solving process. Bley-Vroman further stipulated nine characteristics that distinguish L1 from L2 acquisition:

1. Lack of complete success (which is also the norm for learning in general)
2. The effect of age on proficiency
3. Variation in success, course and strategy
4. Variation in goals
5. Fossilization
6. Indeterminate intuitions (grammaticality judgements)
7. Influence of instruction
8. Influence of negative evidence
9. Role of affective factors

Bley-Vroman's argument has been expanded and updated in more recent proposals. For instance, Hawkins and Chan's (1997) failed functional feature hypothesis (FFFH) places the argument within the perspective of Minimalism. Hawkins and Chan argue that even though the principles of UG are still available to guide the development of the L2 among adults, parameterized formal features are no longer accessible for development (i.e., there is a critical period). More specifically, the formal features not selected during L1 acquisition become inaccessible to cognitively mature adult learners learning a second language. Adult learners can, however, process L2 morphology productively by mapping features from their L1 functional categories (i.e., there is L1 transfer). Among the studies that empirically support the FFFH, Hawkins and Liszka (2003) argue that temporality features not instantiated in a learners' L1 will not be part of the L2 grammar. Their claim is based on the analysis of data from L2 English past tense marking produced by two L1 Chinese speakers in oral narratives (116 past tense tokens in total). Hawkins and Liszka point out that the L1 Chinese speakers were more successful using irregular past tense forms (approximately 84 per cent correctly inflected for past) than regular past tense (approximately 63 per cent correctly inflected for past). Given that Chinese is a language that does not mark tense (unlike English), Hawkins and Liszka regard this as preliminary evidence that the irregular forms may be processed as independent lexical items that have a different morphological status than syntactically based regular forms.

Extrapolating from their findings, Hawkins and Liszka argue that 'Chinese speakers cannot establish [+/-past] on T in English precisely because this feature is absent in their L1'. In other words, syntactic features not present in the L1 will not be modifiable during L2 development, effectively blocking the development (among adults) of an L2 system equivalent to the one that native speakers have. They further conjecture that it is possible that 'the language faculty allows some monitoring of surface strings' (p. 40). Thus, the best that learners can do at this point is to post-syntactically monitor the data and insert the past tense morphological marker whenever they deem it necessary. Another study that also focused on L1 Chinese–L2 English past tense marking is the case study of Patty (Lardiere, 1998a, 1998b). The analysis is relevant because, arguably, Patty's use of past tense marking may be regarded as representative of the final state of acquisition: Patty had significant amounts of exposure to the L2 and high motivation to learn the language. In fact, the analysis of Patty's data was based on a first interview after she had spent 10 years in the United States and then again nine years after. Interestingly,

Patty's performance shows limited marking of past tense (approximately one third of the time) and no developmental changes from time 1 to time 2 of data collection.

6.3 Summary: Modular versus general learning processes

The theoretical proposal that learning is guided by a non-modular, general-domain learning process is substantiated by important trends in the comparative analysis of findings from the L2 acquisition of tense-aspect marking across learning settings. In particular, note that most studies that have analysed data from natural language learners generally fail to show any extended use of the inflectional morphology that is associated with the marking of aspectual distinctions in the L2 (e.g., Dietrich, Klein and Noyau, 1995; Klein and Perdue, 1992; Sato, 1990; Schumann, 1987).[12] In contrast, studies that have analysed data from instructed (academic) language learners show a progressive use of inflectional morphology that is associated with the marking of aspectual distinctions in the L2 (see Chapter 3 for detailed analyses). This stark contrast of findings is supportive of the claim that instruction is influential and perhaps necessary for the acquisition of knowledge about tense-aspect meanings in the L2.

On the other hand, several studies have consistently showed that the development of form precedes the acquisition of functional knowledge of aspectual contrasts (e.g., Bardovi-Harlig, 1992a; Bergström, 1995; Giacalone-Ramat, 2002; Montrul and Slabakova, 2002; Salaberry, 2000a; Slabakova and Montrul, 2002a, 2002b, 2003). Despite this caveat, it is apparent that, unlike in L1 acquisition, instruction is essential for cognitively mature adult learners to acquire some specific grammatical meanings in a second language. More importantly, in some cases instructional procedures may lead learners to the wrong conclusion despite the fact that the target aspectual concept is already represented in the L1. For instance, how do English speakers learning Spanish acquire knowledge about the concept of iterativity?

As discussed in Chapter 3, iterativity is a concept that is already instantiated in English. On the other hand, in most instructional programmes the specific instantiation of iterativity through inflectional morphology in Spanish is not explicitly taught. Should we conclude that the simple availability of examples of iterativity (i.e., positive evidence) is enough for Spanish L2 learners to learn the realization of the concept of iterativity through formal means? Previous findings indicate that English native speakers have difficulty in appropriately marking iterativity in Spanish with the Preterite, choosing instead to mark it with the Imperfect (e.g., Pérez-Leroux et al., 2007; Salaberry and Scholes, forthcoming; Montrul and Slabakova, 2002b, 2007). Interestingly, most instructional procedures will inadvertently teach learners to use the Imperfect to mark iterativity (i.e., confusing it with habituality). In other words, the lack of appropriate marking of iterativity in L2 Spanish is the product of a 'double whammy:' not only are learners not taught to use the Preterite, but they are taught to use the Imperfect instead. Essentially, thus, instruction seems to have an important effect on the marking of aspectual distinctions.

7. Instructional Effects

Many studies make explicit reference to the role played by instruction in the development of tense-aspectual meanings. Goodin-Mayeda and Rothman (2007: 3) thus argue that it is possible that 'pedagogical conventions lead to the development of non-linguistic rules that affect L2 performance in spite of native-like competence'.[13] Along the same lines, Slabakova and Montrul (2003: 174) claim that 'the generic/specific meanings of the Preterite and Imperfect are not taught and are not very frequent in the input'. They further argue that the lack of information about the generic/specific meanings of past tense markers in Spanish in the primary linguistic input, 'present[s] a poverty of the stimulus situation for language learners'. In sum, information about instructional procedures, materials and input data in general is crucial to elucidate possible instructional effects on the development of tense-aspectual knowledge. Thus, I review the relevant findings from some of the few studies that have looked at the data and procedures represented in typical instructional methodologies (for specific pedagogical recommendations, see Blyth, 2005).

7.1 Pedagogical rules

There is a general dissatisfaction with textbook rules on the use of the Preterite–Imperfect contrast in Spanish (e.g., Delgado-Jenkins, 1990; Frantzen, 1995; Hernán, 1994; Negueruela and Lantolf, 2006; Ozete, 1988; Westfall and Foerster, 1996; Whitley, 1986). For instance, Westfall and Foerster (1996: 550) claim that textbook presentations do not address how the Preterite and the Imperfect 'interact to determine discourse dynamics'. Similarly, Frantzen (1995: 145) argues that 'textbook explanations . . . often provide confusing, unreliable and even inaccurate explanations'.

Interestingly, it appears that the concern that L2 teaching researchers may have about the use of rules of thumb on the use of the Preterite and Imperfect in Spanish is shared by theoretical researchers on the nature of aspectual distinctions. For instance, Binnick (1991: 155) summarizes the concern that researchers have about the never-ending criteria to distinguish perfective and imperfective meanings: 'We seek a system, not merely a collection of uses replete with exceptions and anomalies'. In fact, note that Frantzen's examples of what she considers to be inaccurate rules (gathered from a survey of textbooks of college Spanish) reflect the type of haphazard nature of Binnick's reference to a collection of uses:

1. The Imperfect describes emotional or mental activity,
2. the Imperfect is used to express repeated or habitual past action,
3. *would + infinitive* signals use of the Imperfect,
4. certain words and expressions are frequently associated with the Preterite and others with the Imperfect,
5. some verbs take on a special meaning in the Preterite tense and
6. when two actions occur simultaneously in the past, the Imperfect is used.

Contrary to the unsystematic nature of the previous list of rules, Frantzen mentions the use of two common translations offered by textbooks that seem to be helpful for students to understand the contrast in Spanish: the progressive (*to be + verb-ing*), and the construction with *used to + infinitive*. Note that the forms highlighted by Frantzen convey the notions of progressivity and habituality respectively. Thus, these structures are reliable predictors of the use of the Imperfect in Spanish because both progressivity and habituality are central components of the aspectual meaning conveyed by the Imperfect. In passing, note too that both these concepts can be easily transferred from L1 English. On the other hand, it should be noted that the notions of progressivity and habituality do not encompass all meanings conveyed by the Imperfect (e.g., uses typically associated with time, weather, age, etc.).

Not only are most pedagogical rules unsystematic, they are also ambiguous. Whitley (1986: 109) provides a specific example of such ambiguity:

If students wish to convey their *I slept all day*, should they opt for "what was happening", "describes physical state", "describes background", or "records, reports"? All these seem applicable and conflicting; thus, students are baffled when their teacher recommends *Dormí todo el día* over *Dormía todo el día*.

In reality, all of these interpretations are possible depending on how the target sentence is contextualized and how the speaker (or hearer) interprets the given piece of discourse. In other words, all of these descriptions are complementary although not all of them are necessarily applicable at the same time. For their part, Negueruela and Lantolf (2006: 83) claim that most pedagogical rules tend to make reference to various levels of representation of aspectual meanings at once. Thus rules

> . . . are capricious to the extent that some are semantic in referring to a complete event, others are functional as when the preterit is used for foregrounding, while others are perceptual and concrete as when the imperfect is used to tell time.

Negueruela and Lantolf further point out a second problem typically associated with most pedagogical rules about the use of the Preterite and Imperfect:

> Simplified and reductive rules of thumb have the potential to do more harm than good, because for one thing, they depict language as a sedimented entity that appears to have a life of its own independent of people. Rules of thumb easily lead students down a garden path of confusion and frustration (p. 83).

In other words, many pedagogical rules fail to guide learners towards a more conceptual-based approach to learning aspectual distinctions. This conclusion is in line with the notion of a highly contextualized definition of aspectual distinctions. For instance, concepts such as iterativity and habituality and how to distinguish them represent a valid instructional target that is not typically included in most pedagogical treatments.

Aside from the pedagogical rules, there are different approaches with regards to the process typically used to introduce the topic of tense-aspect meanings. For instance, many instructional treatments start with a focus on the most prototypical uses of past tense aspectual distinctions with texts that reflect a clear narrative line and where the overall context does not override the inherent lexical aspectual value of the verb (e.g., Bergström, 1995 for French; García and van Putte, 1988 for Spanish). In contrast, Bull (1965: 166–71) recommends that the pedagogical presentation of the Preterite–Imperfect contrast be based on the discrimination of the three aspectual values (i.e., inceptive, imperfective and terminative) through English examples. He points out that the student does not need to distinguish between inceptive and terminative values, only to discriminate whether an event is imperfective or not (i.e., a dichotomous contrast).

For his part, Guitart (1995) suggested the use of a movie analogy to teach the Preterite–Imperfect contrast: the frame showing the event one is talking about is the key frame and the situation before the main event represents the previous frame (see also Hernán, 1994). In passing, note that key and previous frame may correspond to Klein's (1994) theoretical constructs of target and source state, respectively. Finally, Blyth (1997, 2005) argues for a process-oriented, constructivist approach towards the conceptualization of aspectual contrasts. Blyth further highlights the important role of foreground/background contrasts in narratives, arguing specifically for the use of first person narratives to better focus learners on the notion of perspective. Blyth points out that film-based narratives are especially useful to pedagogically focus learners on the effects of first and third person narratives.

7.2 Mapping concepts to form

Among the pedagogical procedures used to teach tense-aspect phenomena, an important point of reference is Negueruela and Lantolf's (2006: 86) Concept Based Instruction (CBI): 'an integrated approach to instruction whose purpose is to help learners develop new meaning-making resources, a different thinking for speaking framework, as Slobin (1996) might put it'. Their claim is especially interesting considering that we discussed how Slobin's thinking for speaking proposal may be a useful framework to analyse how L2 learners map tense-aspectual meanings onto language form. Negueruela and Lantolf's approach to grammar instruction is predicated on the Vygotskyan principle that 'schooled instruction is about developing control over theoretical concepts that are explicitly and coherently presented to learners as they are guided through a sequence of activities designed to prompt the necessary internalization of the relevant concepts'.

In terms of specific pedagogical intervention, Negueruela and Lantolf propose that the understanding of the meaning potential of tense aspect in L2 Spanish is through the 'construction of appropriate *didactic models* that learners can use to guide their performance and *ultimately internalize* as a means of regulating their meaning-making ability in the L2'. (p. 80, stress added). It is unfortunate, however, that the didactic model used by Negueruela and Lantolf is based on an outdated model of aspectual meanings (i.e., Bull's (1965), distinction between cyclic and non-cyclic events). As a consequence,

Negueruela and Lantolf's definition of lexical aspect is predicated on whether the meaning of the verb is cyclic or not (p. 85).

There are at least two theoretical problems with the selection of a dated model of aspectual meanings as the target of instruction of CBI. First, Bull's proposal is incomplete both in terms of lexical aspectual classes and semantic features (see Bull, 1960 for an extended discussion of the topic of tense and aspect). Bull claims that cyclic events are the ones that 'cannot be observed or reported until they are terminated', whereas non-cyclic events are the ones 'whose characteristics are all observable at the instant of their initiation' (1965: 168). Bull further specifies that cyclic events are represented by telic events (accomplishments and achievements), whereas non-cyclic events correspond to atelic events (activities). Thus, Bull concludes that the 'Preterite regularly indicates the initiative aspect of non-cyclic events and the terminative aspect of cyclic events' (pp. 168–9). Thus, *Julián caminó* (Julian walked) signals the inception of the activity, whereas *Julián caminó hasta la estación de tren* (Julian walked to the train station) focuses on the completion of the activity of walking. In essence, Bull's distinction between cyclic and non-cyclic events is focused solely on the factor of telicity. Furthermore, Bull's model is further restricted to the description of dynamic verbs only (i.e., states are not included).

Second, the subdivision of dynamic verbs according to telicity does not seem to correlate well with initiative and terminative aspects of verbs. Guitart (1978: 142), for instance, claims that 'the contrast between PRET and IMP is the same in speaking of completive (cyclic) occurrences as it is in speaking of extendable (non-cyclic) occurrences'. In Guitart's example '*Ayer el presidente habló (PRET) por televisión* (The president spoke on television yesterday)' ... there is no reason to suppose that the President's speech continued until the next day and every reason to suppose that it ended yesterday' (p. 139). In other words, contrary to Bull's claim, the use of Preterite signals the terminative value of a non-cyclic verb. In fact, as we mentioned in Chapter 2, when analysing data in context, it is difficult not to assign a *telos* to almost every atelic verb (cf. Dowty, 1986). Thus, when analysed in context, dynamicity is a major division of verb types that overrides the distinction according to telicity.

The use of a more updated model of tense-aspect meanings in the procedure of pedagogical intervention proposed by Neguerulea and Lantolf would provide very important information about the acquisition of tense-aspect markers. For instance, the distinct meanings conveyed by iterativity versus habituality discussed in Chapters 2 and 3 represent a dependent variable that should be explicitly analysed in future studies. In fact, the representation of iterativity and habituality according to Cognitive Grammar (Doiz-Bienzoibas, 1995, 2002; Langacker, 1987) seems to be particularly appropriate for an analysis within the CBI model.

7.3 Acquiring target rules

Despite the limitations of the theoretical model used by Neguerulea and Lantolf to delimit the meaning of lexical aspect, the results of their investigation are useful to the extent that they describe in significant detail some of the changes in the working hypotheses entertained by students during the process of learning tense-aspect meanings. For instance, the following definition of aspect provided by one of their learners was collected prior to the pedagogical intervention proposed in the CBI model:

> The idea behind imperfect and preterit is for expressing things in the past. I use preterit when it wants to express something that is finished, or that it has a definitive time. The imperfect is used to describe things that happened with frequency in the past, or general things. The imperfect is used in the past to describe characteristics of people, to tell age of a person, and also to tell time.

Obviously, the student had received prior instruction on the uses of the Preterite and Imperfect. In line with the discussion so far, however, the student's account is inaccurate or incomplete at best. Subsequent to receiving instruction according to the model proposed in CBI, the same learner provided the following descriptions:

> The imperfecto is used to describe a point in the past that isn't specific. It is also used when describing the background of a story. The pretérito is used when you are talking about a recalled point in the past, something specific that happened at a specific time.

The selected samples excerpted from Neguerulea and Lantolf's chapter indicate that during the first time of data collection, both Preterite and Imperfect are perceived as two past tense forms on an equal footing. During the second time of data collection, in contrast, the Imperfect is associated with a secondary function (i.e., conveys the background of a story) whereas the Preterite becomes identified with a more archetypal past tense (i.e., recalled point in the past). At first blush, it is striking how close this student's definitions approximate the theoretical analysis of the meanings of Preterite and Imperfect provided by Doiz-Bienzobas (1995). In essence, it appears that pedagogical treatments may have some potential effect that future studies, using a more updated definition of aspectual concepts, would be able to tease out more precisely.

8. Conclusion

I have argued that tense-aspect meanings cannot be properly represented at the level of the verb-phrase alone because tense-aspect is an inherently contextualized concept instantiated on a lexico-discursive continuum (i.e., a single construct as opposed to the two-component theory of Smith, 1997 among others). A single-construct theory is essential to address outstanding issues related to the so-called shifting of lexical aspectual classes. On the other hand, a contextual definition of tense-aspect meanings does not necessarily entail that there are no basic aspectual meanings that are essentially invariant concepts (e.g., boundedness, iterativity, genericity). The latter have been the primary dependent variables addressed by syntactic approaches to the analysis of tense-aspect phenomena. In essence, the nature of the theoretical framework proposed in this chapter straddles the boundaries previously established between discursive and syntactic frameworks.

A second theoretical claim advanced in this chapter is that L1 English speakers understand the use of aspect-bearing past tense inflectional morphology in L2 Spanish with reference to aspectual distinctions that they are already familiar with in their native language. Given that English speakers have a distinct conceptualization of past-tense aspectual meanings already 'moulded' on their L1 representational system of tense-aspectual knowledge, their main challenge is to match aspectual concepts with formal carriers of those meanings. In this respect, Slobin's thinking-for-speaking proposal is a very enticing argument to assess the status of the development of tense-aspectual knowledge in a second language. Contrary to the strong interpretation of Slobin's proposal, however, the most plausible account is that English speakers may have difficulty not necessarily with the conceptual understanding of aspectual distinctions in the L2 per se, but rather with the representation of aspectual contrasts through inflectional endings (i.e., mapping concepts onto forms).

Chapter 5

Final Thoughts

1. Introduction

Despite the fact that there is a significant body of research on the topic of tense-aspect acquisition, an increasing number of studies seem to be conducted within the boundaries of isolated 'research islands'. Thus, in order to effectively harness the power of such a research database, it is important to widen our point of view and take into account findings from a variety of research perspectives, even if only as a point of reference. On that point, it would be presumptuous to assume that the theoretical framework proposed in this book should become an overarching theoretical foundation for future studies. The theoretical framework herein proposed is, however, based on the analysis of both theoretical analyses and empirical findings (cf. Chapters 2 and 3) that span more than one single theoretical paradigm. Even though I ultimately favoured one specific line of research, I believe I have made the case for that claim based on the findings of studies conducted within more than one research strand. The assessment and critique of the present framework will hopefully lead to a productive exchange of ideas across theoretical models, and ultimately to a better understanding of the phenomenon of tense-aspect acquisition.

The arguments presented so far are, nevertheless, preliminary given that additional empirical data will be needed to substantiate them. In the present chapter, I discuss possible lines of research that can help us refine, modify and expand the present specific proposal in order to subsume it within a comprehensive model of L2 acquisition. In that context, I discuss some of the theoretical and methodological factors that can be taken into account towards the elaboration of a research agenda that will advance the analysis of the L2 acquisition of tense-aspect knowledge.

2. Theoretical Issues

2.1 Temporal versus extensional meanings

I start with a brief description of the 'larger picture' in which the notion of temporal aspectual meanings are situated. The conceptual meaning of aspect may be quite broad or very narrow depending on the scope of the definition of aspectual knowledge that one chooses. At the broad end of the spectrum of definitions, Fleischman (1990: 5–6) claims that the grammatical category past conveys multiple oppositional properties at various levels of analysis: referential meaning based on truth conditionals especially related to temporality, textual meaning related to the organization of discourse (foreground versus background), expressive, conative, affective and social functions, and metalinguistic information that signals styles, registers or types of language. Of particular importance is the pragmatic function of tense-aspect marking motivated by the extension of the concept of temporal distance along other axes such as modal distance (e.g., counterfactual statements expressed with past tense) or social distance (e.g., assertiveness and politeness). For example, with respect to social distance, Fleischman (1989: 9) argues that 'by removing these speech acts from "actuality" the PAST tense serves a pragmatic function of distancing the speaker from what are perceived to be assertive speech acts (requests, questions, invitations) or acts of assertive behavior (an unannounced visit)'.

Making specific reference to Spanish, Doiz-Bienzobas (1995: 3ff) agrees with Fleischman insofar that the imperfective past tense form (e.g., the Spanish Imperfect) is used in the apodosis of counterfactuals (1), and to express politeness (2).

1. Si tuviera dinero me compraba (IMP)/*compré (PRET) la casa.
   If I had money, I would buy the house.
2. Quería (IMP)/*Quise (PRET) pedirle un favor.
   I wanted to ask you for a favour.

In this respect, the fact that the Preterite is not appropriate in these examples poses a learning challenge for learners and a language acquisition question for researchers. In fact, Doiz-Bienzobas expands the list of extensional meanings conveyed by the Imperfect, making specific reference to the expression of irrealis (3), the highlighting of specific events in a sequence (4), and the expression of future reference in the context of a past time description (5).

3. Ayer soñé (PRET) que ganaba (IMP)/*?gané (PRET) la lotería.
   Yesterday I dreamt that I won the lottery.
4. Juan cayó (PRET) enfermo, dos años después se arruinó (PRET), y
   poco después moría (IMP)/?murió (PRET).
   Juan became ill, two years later he went into bankruptcy and sometime
   later he died.
5. Al día siguiente tenía (IMP)/?tuve (PRET) un examen.
   The following day I had an exam.

The same argument about the extension of the meanings of the Preterite and the Imperfect in Spanish has been made for the Progressive in English. Ziegeler (2007) argues that the use of the English Progressive may convey meanings other than progressivity. Thus, if sentence (6) were used during the last lap of a race, 'the progressive would refer to a prediction rather than an on-going situation extending over speaker-time' (p. 1020).

6. She is winning the race.

The previous examples from Doiz-Bienzobas and Ziegeler show that verbal morphology typically used to express tense and aspect meanings has extensional meanings that go beyond the basic notion of temporality that has been the traditional target of most studies of tense-aspect marking. By definition, however, these extensional meanings are related to the basic notion of temporality that represents their core meaning.

In fact, within the framework of some theories, the analysis of these extensional meanings is unavoidable. For instance, Cognitive Grammar (e.g., Langacker, 1987, 1999) makes no categorical distinction between core and extensional meanings insofar that all are based on the same cognitive conceptualizations. Within Cognitive Grammar, the expression and cognitive processing of meaning result in particular conceptualizations of linguistic information. Thus, the analysis of the use of the Preterite and Imperfect for the expression of extensional meanings represents a valid research objective. Despite its obvious importance, however, the analysis of the extensional meanings of tense-aspect morphology has been almost completely neglected in L2 acquisition. Future studies on this topic should be crucial for the development of an overall model of tense-aspect representational meanings.

2.2 A broad contextual definition of temporal aspectual meanings

I have argued that the need to rely on extralinguistic knowledge about the world is necessary to understand, for instance, habituality and iterativity.

As an example, Arche (2006) proposes that the definition of a habitual requires (1) the iteration of an event, (2) a high proportion of the event relative to a reasonable context, and (3) a minimum level of systematicity or regularity. More specifically, Arche (2006: 163) argues that 'whereas the progressive and the perfective (in the absence of adverbial modification) refer to a singular occasion, the habitual viewpoint refers to a plural number of occasions by itself'. Arche adds that contextual information is relevant to establish whether the plurality of occasions is proportionally valid to convey habituality. Thus, it is conventionally accepted (cf. Smith, 1997) that *four times a year* would be proportionally valid to speak of *traveling to New York* as a habitual event (7). In contrast, *four times a year* would not be enough to assume that someone habitually engages in *smoking* (8) (examples are from Arche (2006)).

7. Juan va a Nueva York habitualmente.
   Juan habitually goes to New York.
8. Juan fuma habitualmente.
   Juan habitually smokes.

In essence, Arche points out that to determine proportionality, we need to have some notion of average as a point of reference. In turn, 'the number of times considered "average" is established taking into account extralinguistic information' (164). Similarly, extralinguistic information is also necessary to understand why the Preterite, and not the Imperfect, may be used to convey the semantic notion of simultaneity, which is normally conveyed with the imperfective form. Thus, Silva-Corvalán (1986) points out that in the following sentence, the use of the Preterite in the second clause does not necessarily convey the idea (nor do native speakers interpret) that the two verbs (i.e. *to asolearse = sunbathe* and *conversar = to talk*) are sequentially ordered as normally expected from a series of events in the Preterite

9. Fuimos (PRET) a la playa. Nos asoleamos (PRET) y conversamos (PRET) toda la tarde.
   We went to the beach. We sunbathed and we talked all afternoon.

Silva-Corvalán argues that although both events are presented as single events – and thus are potentially sequentially ordered – knowledge of the world leads us to consider that both events occurred simultaneously. In principle, the analysis of extra-linguistic information (i.e., world knowledge) lies beyond the analysis of the basic conceptual meanings of temporality expressed by past tense markers. Nevertheless, as the previous discussion shows, it is difficult to ignore the effect of some conventional ways of interpreting the use of past tense markers. At a minimum, the identification of the specific independent variables that underlie the selection of aspectual markers, as in the example provided by Silva-Corvalán, can be essential to understanding particular developmental trends among L2 learners.

The examples from Arche and Silva-Corvalán summarize the benefits of using a broad contextualization framework to define most conventional meanings of tense-aspect representation. What I have not discussed in detail thus far, is the relevance of a single construct of tense-aspect to analyse non-conventional choices of tense-aspect marking, both among native and non-native speakers. On this point, Waugh (1990) argues that there are two types of use of past tense grammatical markers. The first type is represented by the traditional functions accorded by language academies, reference and pedagogical grammars, and grammar experts in general (including teachers, I add). There is, however, Waugh argues, a second type of use of grammatical markers, those uses whose

> presence has not been recognized by the academy or traditional grammarians, except insofar as they are looked on as curiosities, are referred to as exceptional or puzzling, and are deemed to be merely stylistically marked and even at times of doubtful grammaticality (pp. 159–60).

The analysis of less conventional ways of marking temporality represents an important object of study that may provide useful information to analyse how tense-aspectual meanings are conveyed in different languages. In particular, non-conventional ways of expressing aspectual meanings may represent the 'entry-points' of a grammaticalization process that will introduce new conventional meanings in due time (cf. Ziegeler, 2007).

2.3 Theoretical frameworks

Slabakova's (2002: 186) assertion that the last three decades of research on the L2 acquisition of tense-aspect has produced an embarrassment of riches in terms of data leaves open the question as to whether researchers have actually analysed previous findings from alternative models to evaluate the representations they proposed. Shirai (2007: 61), for one, argues that the studies conducted within different research paradigms have not benefited from a more open dialogue. For instance, comparing the studies conducted by researchers testing the LAH and the ones conducting studies within the generative framework of analysis, Shirai claims that '[d]espite the overlap in the target phenomenon, however, the two approaches have virtually ignored each other'. In line with Shirai's argument, I believe that, irrespective of theoretical framework, the overall review of empirical findings can be very important in building an adequate model of tense-aspect acquisition.[1]

The potential value of building a comprehensive model of tense-aspect acquisition based on multiple theoretical 'points of entry', so to speak, has been, nevertheless, challenged. Slabakova (2002: 175), for instance states:

> I disagree with Bardovi-Harlig, who on pp. 191–93 of her book states that the primacy of aspect is a 'theory-driven inquiry' and 'is based on a theory of lexical, or inherent, aspect'. Nothing in the theoretical semantic description of lexical classes of predicates makes any predictions about how they are going to be acquired.

I agree with Slabakova insofar as the theoretical semantic description of lexical aspectual classes does not offer any prediction about the acquisition of past tense markers. In fact, it is the LAH that makes the prediction that lexical aspect is an independent variable that has an effect on the dependent variable of L2 morphological marking of tense-aspect contrasts. Thus, from this point of view, the LAH does represent a theory-driven inquiry as originally proposed by Bardovi-Harlig. As a matter of fact, the theoretical hypotheses favoured by Slabakova in her article parallel the conditions just described for the LAH with regard to theoretical generalizability. For instance, nothing in the linguistic theory of Minimalism makes any (direct) prediction about the acquisition of knowledge about tense-aspect meanings (e.g., Ellis, 2001; Gregg, 2001). Thus, Ellis posits that 'UG is neither a prescription nor a program for development, but rather it is a partial and a posteriori description of the phenotypic product of the developmental system. In this view, UG is a consequence, not a condition of development' (2001: 67). Despite this clarification, Slabakova's point is well taken: using a comprehensive language theory (e.g., Minimalism) is beneficial for the overall enterprise of hypothesis-posing and hypothesis-testing. That is, a comprehensive theory provides a larger framework against which we can assess the significance of a given hypothesis about tense-aspect knowledge.

As I have argued in previous chapters, however, there is more than one comprehensive language theory that we can use for the purpose of analysing tense-aspect meanings. An alternative theoretical framework that has not been as commonly used as the one provided by strictly syntactic theories is the one provided by Cognitive Grammar, (e.g., Langacker, 1982, 1987, 1999). The latter is ideally suited to describe the representation of knowledge about tense-aspect marking in which contextual factors larger than the verb and the sentence are crucial in explaining the choices of tense-aspect grammatical markers. For instance, Doiz-Bienzobas (1995: 259) argues that the 'understanding of grammar and meaning rely on viewing, where the latter represents a conceptualization of perception'. Doiz-Bienzobas' argument brings together the two separate components of Smith's (1997) framework: a general cognitive factor (i.e., situation aspect), along with a discursive-pragmatic component (i.e., viewpoint aspect), by making the argument that viewpoint aspect is, essentially, a basic cognitive phenomenon (see also Lunn, 1985). That is, there is a lexically based continuum ranging from lexical aspect to narrative grounding that serves to contextualize and ultimately define tense-aspect meaning at a conceptual level (i.e., how to define a situation). In particular, Cognitive Grammar represents a good theoretical framework for describing iterativity as opposed to habituality (e.g., Doiz-Bienzobas, 1995, 2002; Langacker, 1987). Unfortunately, it is not possible to assess the relevance of this theoretical framework to account for the acquisition of tense-aspect given that, to the best of my knowledge, there have been no studies on this topic conducted within a Cognitive Grammar perspective.

2.4 Form precedes meaning

Despite the ongoing debate on several central components of a definition of aspect, as discussed in the previous sections, there are also significant points of agreement across research paradigms. In particular, studies from a wide variety of perspectives show that, at least among tutored learners, the development of form precedes the acquisition of functional knowledge of grammatical contrasts (e.g., Bardovi-Harlig, 1992a; Bergström, 1995; Giacalone-Ramat, 2002; Montrul and Slabakova, 2002; Salaberry, 2000a; Slabakova and Montrul, 2002a, 2002b, 2003). For instance, Montrul and Slabakova (2002) conclude that their results suggest that at least in instructional settings, correct morphology is acquired before the semantic entailments of these tenses. Along the same lines, Schell (2000: 114) describes how one of the learners she studied (i.e., Mitch) demonstrated almost total *accuracy* with the use of Spanish past tense morphology before his study-abroad semester. Schell points out, however, that Mitch's aspectual selection of Preterite–Imperfect was only 58% (aspectually) *appropriate.*

Thus, there seems to be a dissociation between the acquisition of the morphological paradigm of past tense marking and the functional category of past tense aspectual distinctions. Bardovi-Harlig (1992a) surmises that instructed learners have an advantage with use of morphology simply because instruction focuses on form and meaning at the same time, possibly giving more emphasis to form. Buczowska and Weist (1991: 548) phrase it succinctly in the following way: 'Adults are capable of processing the morphology, and given typical pedagogical practices, tutored L2 learners are not permitted to avoid doing so'.

That learners develop control of verbal morphology before they develop a good grasp of the semantic-discursive meanings of tense-aspect markers has significant theoretical consequences. Thus, Montrul and Slabakova rightfully point out that because instructed learners first learn tense/aspect morphology and only later learn the appropriate use and semantic function, we cannot infer complex semantic knowledge just from observing correct or incorrect morphological production. Interestingly, researchers working with a radically different model of language agree on this point. For instance, Negueruela and Lantolf (2006: 82), working within the framework of sociocultural theory, argue that '[t]he key task for the learner is not so much to master the suffixes, but to understand the meaning potential made available by the concept of aspect and to learn to manipulate this in accordance with particular communicative intentions'. Regarding the role of central concepts conveyed by tense-aspect markers, some of the more recent studies (e.g., Slabakova and Montrul, 2002b, 2007; Salaberry & Scholes, forthcoming) point in the direction of specific aspectual concepts (e.g., iterativity versus habituality) that will require a more focused analysis in future studies. In sum, this is an area of investigation of the acquisition of tense-aspect phenomena that seems to be ripe for the development of a research agenda that cuts across theoretical frameworks of analysis.

2.5 Competence versus performance

The distinction between competence and performance is represented in most analyses of the acquisition of tense aspect meanings in L2 development. For instance, Shirai (2004) proposes that the distinct outcome of some L2 empirical studies seemingly contradicting the theoretical claim advanced by the LAH can be accounted for by a competence-performance distinction prompted by methodological factors. Shirai specifically argues:

> In contrast to production data, discrete-point paper-and-pencil tests of verb form manipulation yielded results consistent with the AH. In

paper-and-pencil tests, it is not likely that a high-frequency, rote-learned form is haphazardly produced because the communicative pressure is much weaker and the learner has much more time and the attention is not on meaning, but on form. Thus the results may reflect the learners' semantic representations of tense-aspect morphology more directly (p. 103).

The assumption made by Shirai is that more controlled tasks can more faithfully (i.e., more directly) access the representational nature of the learners' evolving interlanguage (i.e., competence). That is, in more controlled tasks learners are less prone to use memorized forms, especially irregular forms. On the other hand, contrary to Shirai's assertion, most previous studies have proposed that monitored data are more likely to be affected by learned rules (e.g., Ellis, 1987; Skehan, 1998; Tarone, 1988). Thus, discrete-point paper-and-pencil tests would not reflect the 'true' competence of the learner. Obviously, this is a debate that, although difficult to settle on empirical grounds, brings up an important theoretical distinction that future studies can openly address.

The distinct effect of competence and performance contrasts is most evident in the proposal advanced by generative linguistic approaches. Herschensohn (2000: 23, stress added), for instance, argues that '[a] strictly cognitive approach furnishes no theoretical framework for examining either expert or intermediate knowledge *as grammatical competence*'. Herschensohn adds that a '[g]enerative theory can thus isolate the area of investigation and provide a falsifiable model that can be tested' (p. 24). There are, however, alternative perspectives on this topic. For instance, although Ayoun (2005: 100), shares the view that L2 grammars are constrained by Universal Grammar (UG), she claims that processing difficulties may prevent L2 learners from successfully mapping abstract functional features or feature values to the appropriate L2 surface morphology. Thus, Ayoun (2004) indicates that adult L2 learners could have access to UG without necessarily achieving native-like knowledge in the more cognitively demanding tasks.

Finally, in line with the argument advanced in Chapter 4, approaches that leave the selection of perfective/imperfective marking that contradicts lexical aspectual marking out of the analysis of grammatical competence are not comprehensive enough to depict the type of native speaker knowledge about tense-aspect. To relegate the non-prototypical cases to a realm that is not deemed to be part of the scope of analysis of a theory is a valid methodological choice. It is not, however, without theoretical consequences. Most notably, the representation of native speakers' intuitions about the selection of past tense markers in, for instance, Spanish cannot be done without taking into account non-prototypical choices. Essentially, knowledge of tense-aspect meanings cannot be represented as simple prototypical associations (distributional tendencies) of lexical aspectual classes and grammatical markers. Similarly, aspectual information instantiated in the inner Aspect Phrase cannot be all there is to the representation of aspectual meanings. In fact, the representation of grammatical aspect is fully represented at the level of the Outer Aspect Phrase. As discussed by Andersen (1994), native speakers of Spanish go beyond simply matching up the lexical aspectual class of verbs with their prototypical markers of past tense (e.g., Preterite with telic events and Imperfect with atelic events). In addition, as shown in previous studies (e.g., García and van Putte, 1988; Granda, 2004) native speakers may select radically different responses than the ones selected by non-native speakers. Any theoretical account must take into consideration a definition of tense-aspect meanings that includes non-prototypical choices.

2.6 Developmental stages

Most previous studies have proposed that tense-aspect acquisition occurs in a stage-wise progression and previous empirical data on the L2 acquisition of tense-aspect phenomena in the Romance languages support this contention. Thus, learners show signs of stage-like systemic reorganization of tense-aspect knowledge according to narrative grounding (i.e., foreground versus background). What is not entirely clear is whether the apparent stage-wise progression of tense-aspect development is mostly a gradual process, or whether, there are major reorganizational stages. Sharwood Smith and Truscott (2005: 237) argue that developmental stages will be noticeable at some point or another 'as the learner system evolves, grammatical principles dictate uneven patterns of growth: there will be periods of accelerated change where certain thresholds are crossed and this, in turn, will then trigger some form of wider reorganization'.

Some theoretical proposals are supportive of the claim of major restructuring stages. For instance, the discussion of findings of researchers working within the theory of Minimalism makes specific reference to the fact that learners are 'resetting' feature values in the process of learning the L2. Early on, however, the idea that clusters of properties of a language are 'reset' all at once started to become less empirically plausible. Liceras (1986), for instance, raised serious questions about the possibility of resetting all properties of the pro-drop parameter once triggering had occurred.

In contrast, more recent versions of generative linguistics focus on the notion of gradual changes that reflect an accretion-based, piece-meal process of second language acquisition. For instance, Schell (2000) uses the framework of Constructionism to account for the data gathered from study abroad students. Similarly, Pérez-Leroux et al. (2007) discount the view that learners acquire feature values across the board, favouring instead a selectional approach that allows for the learning of the Preterite or the Imperfect independently and at different rates of development. It is still too early to ascertain whether learners' development of tense-aspectual knowledge is based mostly on gradual accretion, or perhaps gradual accretion in addition to some major thresholds of system restructuring.

On the other hand, it is possible to define developmental stages according to the distinct effect of specific independent variables that become prevalent at different points in time. Ayoun and Salaberry (2005), for instance, argue that L1 English learners go through three distinct stages in the acquisition of the Romance languages. The three stages are defined by the effect of specific factors that become most relevant at specific times. These factors are (1) the L1 transfer of tense marking instantiated in English as a default past tense marker, (2) the effect of the distribution of lexical aspectual classes in the input data, and (3) discursive factors as represented in narrative grounding. Furthermore, Ayoun and Salaberry claim that some of the discrepancies among various theoretical hypotheses are due to the fact that different hypotheses tend to focus on particular stages of development and, concomitantly, on specific independent variables. Finally, in contrast with the idea of system-wide developmental stages (inherent in the notion of parameter resetting), some studies have provided evidence in favour of the acquisition of an L2 system of tense-aspect meanings based mostly on accretion. Buck's (2007) findings, in particular, show that although irregular forms may be the prevalent marker of past tense in the earlier stages of acquisition in L2 English, this tendency does not diminish in association with higher levels of proficiency. In fact, more advanced learners rely on the guidance of irregular inflectional endings even more than less proficient learners. Interestingly, the unexpected outcome of Buk's study is correlated with a similarly unexpected effect of the use of default past tense markers among more advanced learners as shown in the analysis of data of Antonio (2007), Granda (2004), Liskin-Gasparro (2000) and other more recent studies. Arguably, the findings associated with the use of irregulars and default past tense markers may be indicative of possible "ceiling effects" in the acquisition of past tense marking.

2.7 Default tense markers

As I discussed in Chapter 3, there are significant empirical findings that although not enough to categorically substantiate the claim of the DPTH, do raise intriguing questions about the potential use of the Preterite as a default past tense marker (but see Comajoan, 2005a for an alternative perspective). From a theoretical standpoint, the specific description of the invariant meanings of the Preterite and Imperfect advanced by Cognitive Grammar provides theoretical substance to support the claim of the DPTH. Doiz-Bienzobas, in particular, proposes that whereas the Imperfect does not necessarily provide a temporal specification of the situation, the Preterite always does. In essence, the Preterite acts as a true tense marker, whereas the imperfective is anaphoric: it requires an overt specification of the temporal argument of the predicate. One consequence of this theoretical claim is that sentences with the Imperfect sound odd if no context is provided. Furthermore, the findings from various studies reviewed in Chapter 3 provide initial empirical support for the notion of a default past tense marker.

In fact, even studies that did not set out to identify possible default values seem to point in that direction. Schell's (2000) study is especially relevant for the evaluation of the default past tense hypothesis, because although she does not set out to test it, her analysis presents explicit evidence in its favour. More specifically, Schell analysed her data in terms of the POA (Primacy of Aspect) hypothesis and concluded that this hypothesis 'does not adequately account for the early stages of L2 aspect, nor does it explain the variability found in intermediate L2 production' (pp. 140–41). Schell further claimed that it is only by the late intermediate to early advanced stages of acquisition that L2 learners have become 'aware of lexical aspect and match it with its corresponding grammatical aspect'. More importantly, Schell concluded that during the initial stages of acquisition learners were very much affected by L1 transfer in the form of a generalized use of the perfective marker across lexical aspectual classes. One interesting possibility to be addressed by future studies is whether the role of a default past tense marker is relevant among advanced learners as well. In this respect, studies that use retrospective protocols about specific language selections may prove useful in investigating this possibility.

Finally, it is important to emphasize that the claim about the use of a default past tense marker can be regarded as an extension of claims already advanced within the framework of analysis of previous hypotheses, most notably the LAH. In particular, Li and Shirai (2000) use Prototype theory (Rosch, 1973; Rosch and Mervis, 1975) to account for the attested developmental stages of acquisition of past tense morphology. Their account is, however, mostly focused on the analysis of the effect of proto-types represented through lexical aspect (thus directly applicable to account for the findings supporting the LAH). For example, Li and Shirai propose that the prototype for past tense meaning is best represented in predicates that convey telic and punctual lexical aspectual meanings (i.e., achieve-ments). As we can see, these prototypes are mostly restricted to the level of lexical aspect. The notion of a prototype, however, can be extended to the level of grammatical aspect. Effectively, this allows learners to make a con-nection between, for instance, Simple Past in English and Preterite in Spanish as two equivalent prototypical past tense grammatical markers. The latter argument falls in line with basic theoretical assumptions that lead us to believe that the Simple Past and the Preterite are the default past tense markers in English and Spanish respectively (e.g., Ziegeler, 2007 for English and Doiz-Bienzobas, 1995, 2002 for Spanish). In fact, Shirai (2004: 1) seems to take into account the effect of L1 transfer proposing that the 'prototype past (i.e., past tense with telic events) is frequent in the input, and the learners' L1s tend to have a similar prototype'. Shirai goes on to contend that, in principle, both the effects of input and native language could account for the bias towards using perfective morphology, especially during the beginning stages of acquisition.

3. Methodological Issues

3.1 Interpretation and production data

Undoubtedly, there are major differences in the research design adopted by the studies that have tested the acquisition/development of tense-aspect marking. For instance, studies differ along the lines of the use of oral data versus written data, controlled versus spontaneous tasks and so on. These methodological differences are likely to account for some of the different outcomes among studies. Nowhere is this discussion more salient than in the debate over the use of interpretation versus production tasks. Herschensohn (2000: 24), for instance, argues that we should 'put aside the performance deficiencies of L2ers in order to determine the systematic aspects of interlanguage'. It appears, however, that Herschensohn is mak-ing a methodological point given that she also states that '[t]he near native speaker of an L2 . . . has gained the major parametric values for the L2 and is able to use these values *in both production and grammaticality judgment*' (p. 221, stress added). The latter statement entails that, at least in principle, we should be able to investigate the knowledge representation of non-native speakers in both interpretation and production tasks.

Making specific reference to studies focused on the analysis of tense-aspect research, Montrul (2004: 155) argues that studies that tested the effect of lexical aspect and grounding 'draw conclusions about what possible meanings learners associate with morphological markers solely on the evidence of USING certain morphemes with different verb classes in some discourse contexts'. Montrul further argues that L2 learners are more likely than native speakers to show variable behaviour with inflectional morphology especially in production. Montrul, thus, suggests that if learners do not initially produce certain verbal endings (e.g., the Preterite with statives), it does not necessarily mean that they cannot interpret stative verbs as telic or that they do not know the difference between a state in the present and a state in the past. Montrul further extends the previous argument to conclude that the study of the acquisition of tense and aspect needs to rely on other experimental methodologies, in particular, the type of interpretations used in Montrul and Slabakova (2002, 2003) and Slabakova and Montrul (2002a, 2002b, 2003).

I think Montrul's argument is correct insofar as her claim does not entail that interpretation tasks are to be used instead of production tasks. Interpretation-based methodologies (e.g., grammaticality judgements, conjunction tests) are obviously complementary to production-based methodologies (e.g., film retells, multiple choice tests). More specifically, while interpretation-based methodologies are useful in constraining the effect of some performance limitations, they also introduce other no less spurious effects. For instance, even in fairly controlled environments, interpretation-based tasks increase the likelihood that learners will monitor their use of language form, perhaps leading them to overanalyse particular structures. For instance, the findings from Güell (1998) reviewed in Chapter 3 show that in comprehension tasks, learners may be affected by their biases stemming from explicit rule formation. Durational adverbs, in particular, seemed to trigger the use of the imperfective based on the application of rules of thumb. Furthermore, sentence-based interpretation tasks affect the choices of aspectual morphology through the de-contextualization of language data. The latter appears to be an important factor to consider in light of the context-sensitive nature of tense-aspect marking in Spanish.

In fact, as discussed in Chapter 3, some studies (e.g., Slabakova and Montrul, 2002a) acknowledge that the ambiguous interpretations introduced by the lack of contextual support may lead control groups of native speakers to be less accurate in their selections of past tense marker.

Furthermore, most of the methodological factors that affect production tasks also affect comprehension tests. For instance, both the effect of L1 transfer and previous pedagogical instruction affect all types of tasks. The proper methodological control of these intrusive effects should include the implementation of measures such as time constraints in any type of task we use, whether production or interpretation. Narratives, especially oral narratives, constitute one way through which time demands are easily implemented. Thus, if anything, we could argue that production tasks have inherent time processing constraints given that learners do not have time to pause and think about what forms to use. Granted, time constraints may also introduce an additional effect to be aware of for our theoretical analyses.

Finally, there are also important theoretical issues associated with the use of a limited set of methodological procedures. For instance, let us assume that non-natives were capable of providing the correct interpretation of tense-aspectual contrasts, and at the same time, they were not able to use that interpretive knowledge during productive, spontaneous tasks. In that situation we would need to theoretically account for this outcome. Correlating the different outcomes between interpretive and productive tasks to competence and performance respectively is a speculative proposition that would need to be substantiated, not simply asserted tautologically. In fact, there are several alternative proposals that would be equally valid from a speculative perspective. For instance, given that interpretive tasks tend to be based on sentence-level propositions and that productive tasks tend to be based on a larger contextualization of verbal predicates, the contrast in outcome may be due to the fact that interpretive tasks do not adequately tap into the actual competence about tense-aspect morphology. Similarly, another possibility is that the definition of tense-aspect knowledge shows up in the dissimilar outcome of more demanding tasks such as production ones. Indeed, given that both natives and non-natives are subject to the same performance constraints (assuming this is adequately controlled through methodological procedures), we need to account for the fact that native speakers are more homogeneous than non-natives in their judgements of tense-aspectual contrasts (cf. Coppieters, 1987).

3.2 The analysis of data

The use of a common metric to code data is especially relevant for studies that deal with semantic-discursive phenomena like tense-aspect. For instance, as discussed in Chapter 2, the classification of verbs according to lexical aspectual classes is subject to numerous problems. This is particularly important in the case of data collected from learners of a second language. Thus, Lardiere (2003: 137) argues that the following use of the verb *wear* in Patti's oral data does not parallel the meaning assigned to this verb by English native speakers.

> even I just *wear* it, it's not hurt
> [speaking about brand new shoes:] 'even though I've just put them on/ just started wearing them for the first time, they don't hurt'

Lardiere argues that 'the intended meanings include an inchoative or inceptive sense that is likely quite different from native speakers' semantic representations of the verbs in question . . .' (p. 137). In sum, we cannot be certain that 'the contents of [Patti's] lexical entries for English verbs exactly match those of English native speakers'. Lardiere speculates that it is likely that the inceptive use of the verb *wear* in Patti's data is due to transfer of semantic features from her L1 because the Chinese equivalent verb 'is ambiguous in meaning between "to wear" (atelic) and "to put on" (telic)'. It should be noted that in a response article, Shirai (2007: 58) agreed with Lardiere in that 'This is an important methodological and theoretical issue that needs to be addressed in L2 aspect research'. Shirai argued further that:

> since we cannot be sure about learners' intentions or their semantic representations, it is probably more reasonable to be agnostic about them to some degree. But at the same time we need rigour in classification to ensure some level of replicability across studies (p. 59).

The discussion of Bley-Vroman's (1983) 'Comparative Fallacy' between Lardiere (2003) and Shirai (2007) is informative in this regard. Essentially, the Comparative Fallacy states that the analysis of L2 data with reference to the target grammar may fail to provide an adequate characterization of the learners' interlanguage. In his conclusion, Shirai (2007: 57) argues that '[t]he only way to avoid the comparative fallacy in morpheme acquisition studies is to look at all uses of the linguistic form being investigated: and even then the comparative fallacy is hard to avoid, since our analysis is always coloured by the target norm'.

The importance of the application of a common procedure is also relevant for the analysis of other independent variables. For instance, the classification of sentences in a narrative text according to grounding (backgrounded and foregrounded clauses) does not always take into account the criteria discussed in Chapter 2. Güell (1998), for instance, classified the first seven predicates in the following narrative as the background of the story. The remainder 25 predicates were taken to represent the foregrounded events. Arguably, Güell's classification of clauses in terms of narrative grounding may not necessarily be accurate. For instance, items 14 and 16–18 in the following excerpt from the story used in Güell should probably be considered part of the background instead of the foreground of the story.

Entonces, (13) VER lo que (14) PARECER un platillo volante. Todos (15) QUEDARSE inmóviles con la boca abierta, menos el perro que (16) CONTINUAR su "persecución", y la vieja María, que no (17) ENTERARSE de nada, (18) CAMBIARSE de sitio buscando el sol.

Then, [everybody] (13) SEE what (14) SEEM a UFO. Everybody (15) REMAIN still in complete surprise, except for the dog who (16) CONTINUE its chase, and the old lady María, who (17) NOT REALIZE anything, (18) MOVE from her place looking for the sun.

That is, items 14, and 16–18 do not seem to move the story line forward, and should, instead be regarded as clauses providing background information about the scene (cf. Bardovi-Harlig, 2000; Comajoan, 2001). Thus, any categorical classification of foreground versus background clauses in large 'chunks' of clauses, although efficient, risks mischaracterizing one of the independent variables.

The specific procedures to carry out the data analysis are also very important. One clear example is the distinction made by Bardovi-Harlig (2000: 252–65; 2002) with regards to the contrasting conclusions researchers can gather doing a within- versus an across-analysis of tokens of past tense morphology categorized into lexical aspectual classes. Bardovi-Harlig explains that open-ended narratives bring about an unequal distribution of tokens of verbal morphology within each lexical aspectual category. This unequal distribution, in turn, leads to important differences in conclusions gathered from *an across-category analysis* of data versus *a within-category analysis*. The across-category analysis focuses on the distribution of the past tense marker (as opposed to the lexical aspectual classes). In other words, this analysis draws our attention to the distribution of the overt marker of past tense (e.g., Spanish Preterite or imperfect) across different lexical aspectual classes (e.g., achievements, states). For instance, we can investigate the use and distribution of the Imperfect across all lexical aspectual classes. The alternative approach, a within-category analysis, focuses our attention on the distribution of inflectional morphology within a given lexical aspectual class. That is, we focus, for instance, on the proportion of use of Preterite and Imperfect within the category of statives.

Importantly, Bardovi-Harlig argues that the type of analysis of the effect of lexical aspect on verbal morphology (whether it is an across-category or within-category analysis), 'could lead us to support or reject the aspect hypothesis on the basis of the very same data' (p. 252). On this point, Bardovi-Harlig, echoing Robison's insight, argues that the within-category analysis is not influenced by the unbalanced distribution across lexical aspectual categories. For instance, in the extreme case that out of a 100 tokens, 90 are classified as achievements and the rest are equally divided into activities and states, the within-category analysis gives us percentages of use of verbal morphology that are controlled within categories. On the other hand, an across-category analysis may be useful to investigate the initial entry of specific morphological markers into the system (e.g., first uses of the Imperfect), or the possible spreading of markers across categories. In passing, note that both of these examples would be very useful to assess the validity of the LAH. Thus, it is important to point out that neither one of these classifications (i.e., within- and across-analysis) is inherently superior to the other one with regard to the evaluation of empirical data.

4. Conclusion

One of the significant challenges identified in the theoretical framework proposed in this book is represented by the larger contextualization framework regarded as necessary for a complete and adequate definition of tense-aspect. That is, it is necessary to look beyond the verb phrase (defined by the verb and its argument only) in order to offer a more realistic account of tense-aspect meanings. On the other hand, a discursive contextual definition of tense-aspect meanings does not necessarily entail that there are no basic aspectual meanings that are essentially invariant concepts (e.g., boundedness, iterativity, genericity). Interestingly, the latter have become the primary dependent variables addressed by syntactic approaches, whereas the contextualized tense-aspect meanings represented in inflectional morphology have been the primary dependent variable of discourse approaches. The proposed theoretical framework also points to the fact that L1 speakers may not need to learn any new conceptual knowledge if, as is the case of the

L1 English–L2 Spanish pairing, aspectual concepts are already represented in the L1. These aspectual concepts are, however, sometimes represented with a different range of formal devices. Future studies will have to continue expanding this and other lines of research, keeping in mind that findings from studies conducted within various research paradigms provide complementary answers.

Notes

Chapter 1

[1] In keeping with the convention proposed by Comrie (1976) and Andersen (2002), I use capitals to refer to grammatical markers (e.g., Preterite and Imperfect) and lower case to refer to semantic categories (e.g., perfective and imperfective).

[2] The examples are taken from de Swart and Verkuyl (1999).

[3] The lowest proficiency group was, however, represented primarily by English speakers.

[4] As I discuss in Chapter 5, there are some methodological shortcomings in García and van Putte's and Güell's studies that need to be taken into account in our analysis (for a critique of Coppieter's study, see Birdsong, 1992). The main findings from those studies are, nevertheless, indicative of significant trends that need to be studied in detail and replicated in future studies.

[5] Given that I will concentrate primarily on the form-oriented studies, I am leaving out of this discussion the analysis of meaning-oriented hypotheses such as the ones researched by the ESFP.

[6] There are, however, some volumes that have provided an integrative account of the findings within a large area of studies as done, for instance, by Ayoun and Salaberry (2005) with regard to the acquisition of tense-aspect in the Romance languages.

Chapter 2

[1] To be clear, Smith (1997: 7) does argue that '[t]he speaker, not the situation, determines aspectual choice.' The statement, however, is restricted to viewpoint aspect only.

[2] We will see, however, that the use of Preterite with the verb *saber* is not necessarily restricted to conveying the notion of inception of a state (see Chapter 4).

[3] In keeping with Depraetre's (1995) principled distinction between boundedness and telicity, Doiz-Bienzobas is really referring to telicity and not boundedness.

[4] Smith (1997) also includes the category of semelfactives that I discuss in more detail in subsequent sections.

[5] For reasons of space, I will not review studies that have focused on the analysis of the specific aspectual meanings conveyed by individual- and stage-level predicates. Luján (1981) is one of the early works on this topic.

[6] Tatevosov (2002: 19) argues that: 'Inchoative' is taken to denote the beginning of a state, 'ingressive' refers to the beginning of an atelic process and 'inceptive' is

associated with telic process. These terms are, however, used interchangeably in several studies.

[7] One may argue that the ungrammaticality of sentence (37b) may be attributed to the [−agentive] value of the subject *the road* as compared to the [+agentive] value of the subject *Sally*. This explanation, however, is not adequate because it does not explain the grammaticality of sentence (37a) with the same nonagentive subject.

[8] Some researchers consider these secondary modifications of basic verb meanings through aspectual particles as part of lexical aspect (e.g., de Miguel, 1992; Shirai, 1991).

[9] I am leaving out of the summary of Binnick's list, the exemplary meaning of the Preterite because it is not relevant for the discussion of the distinction in Spanish or English past tenses.

[10] See Klein's (1994) classification of lexical contents into 0-state, 1-state and 2-state.

[11] Other authors have proposed an even longer list of type-shifters. Filip (1999: 63), for instance, claims that adverbials, phasal verbs (Smith's superlexical morphemes and Binnick's aspectualizers), mood (e.g., imperative), grammatical aspect (e.g., progressive) and tense are all eventuality type shifters.

[12] Fleischman (1990: 22), Sebastian and Slobin (1994: 257–8) also discuss the classification of so-called aspectual verbs into inchoative verbs (e.g., *empezar*, to start), protractive verbs (e.g., *quedarse*, to remain), cumulative verbs (e.g., *continuar*, to continue) and completive verbs (e.g., *acabar de*, to finish).

[13] Extending this analysis to other categories of lexical aspect, Depraetre (1995: 1) argues that in Dowty's imperfective paradox 'the use of the progressive form seemingly has the effect of taking away the built-in endpoint in sentences such as *John was drawing a circle*. Accordingly, this raises the question whether there is still reference to an accomplishment'.

[14] In the first edition of her book, Smith (1991) argued that both marked focus (brought about by morphological marking) as well as the effect of superlexical morphemes '[a]ll enable the speaker to present a situation from several points of view. Although the point of view changes in marked focus, the situation talked about does not change' (p. 80).

[15] Piñango et al. (1999: 398) define coercion as a process of 'enriched semantic composition' necessary 'to achieve aspectual compatibility between the verbal head and its temporal modifier'.

[16] In a subsequent publication (de Swart and Verkuyl, 1999: 112), de Swart clarified her position on the type of duration adverbial to be considered as a valid explicit aspectual operator: 'coercion is of the same semantic type as an aspectual operator such as the Perfect, the Progressive or *an aspectual adverbial introduced* by *in* or *for*'. The latter modification already evinces a significant theoretical change. This revision, however, does not address the question prompted by the use of the aspectual adverbial in sentences (95b–d), given that the adverbials used in those sentences are, in fact, introduced by the preposition *for*. Furthermore, the limitation of the classification of aspectual adverbials to the ones introduced by *in* or *for* seems an ad hoc solution.

[17] Caudal and Rossarie (2005: 262) points out that neither de Swart necessarily opposes the idea that viewpoint operators may exist in a model of tense-aspect

semantics nor does Smith reject the idea of aspectual shift operators as evidenced by her analysis of derived lexical classes.

[18] Some authors equate boundedness with telicity. Doiz-Bienzobas (1995: 90ff.) argues that the fact that telic events may be used with the Imperfect shows that it is not unboundedness that the Imperfect conveys. That is, contrary to Depraetre, Doiz-Bienzobas assumes that telicity is equivalent to boundedness.

[19] Twenty-seven of the thirty respondents spoke the Chilean variety of Spanish.

[20] Of the six categories, however, the abstract was not very frequent in the narratives from Silva-Corvalán because the stories she analysed were not purposely elicited, but rather arose during the conversation.

[21] Bhatt (1999: 54ff.) presents examples from Indo-Aryan languages that show a similar close association between the imperfective and perfective with habituals and iteratives/frequentatives, respectively.

[22] Note, however, that the position expressed by Pérez-Leroux et al. posits that both the habitual and the iterative refer to nonquantized events. As it will be discussed later, Comrie (1976) and Doiz-Bienzobas argue that iteratives are quantized.

[23] We note though that the examples use stative verbs to avoid iterativity.

[24] However, Chung and Timberlake also consider the possibility of a different type of the basic iterative event in which subevents are indefinite both in terms of their number and also in the position they are placed along the temporal dimension.

[25] For an alternative interpretation of Langacker's characterization of repetitive and habitual sentences, see Michaelis (2004), who argues that the structural–actual (or, equivalently, generic–episodic) distinction is irrelevant for aspectual coding.

[26] Among studies conducted within Minimalism, there are some differences in the use of labels to refer to features of the aspectual phrase. For instance, whereas Montrul and Slabakova adhere to the use of the labels [+perfective] and [−perfective] as originally proposed by Giorgi and Pianesi, Schell (2000: 41) also uses the terms [+FINAL] and [−FINAL], borrowed from Zagona's analysis. As Schell explains, however, Zagona's [+FINAL] is equivalent to Montrul and Slabakova's [+perfective].

[27] The progressive in English can be used to accomplish the same effect.

Chapter 3

[1] With respect to the possible distinction among these labels, Yasuhiro Shirai (personal communication, 10 August 2007) points out that the aspect hypothesis can be regarded as broader in scope than the other definitions, given that it may encompass both lexical and grammatical aspects.

[2] As pointed out by Comajoan (personal communication, 13 August 2007), the LAH may be defined as a categorical hypothesis (i.e., only aspectual information is conveyed through verbal morphology) or a relative hypothesis (i.e., there are other factors other than lexical aspect at play). Both versions propose that lexical aspect has a preponderant role at the beginning of the acquisition process. Thus, the argument that lexical aspect plays an increasingly important

role as L2 proficiency increases (e.g., the DPTH) stands in contrast with the basic claim advanced by either the categorical or the gradual version of the LAH.

3 In more recent research, the term *motherese* has been replaced by CDS (child directed speech).

4 Andersen collected data from both learners on two occasions separated by a two-year gap.

5 Some studies of the acquisition of L2 English, however, have shown an advantage for regular over irregular past tense morphology (e.g., Birdsong and Flege, 2001).

6 Although the latter statement is speculative, it is an empirically verifiable assertion. In fact, analysis of data from French classroom teacher talk (Kaplan, 1987), Spanish textbook presentations (Ramsay, 1990) and the author's own analysis of classroom talk provide some tentative support about the preponderant use of the imperfective with states.

7 Additional supporting evidence for beginning stages of acquisition of L2 Spanish among Dutch learners can be found in González (2003).

8 There are also several studies from L2 English acquisition showing that Progressive morphology may first appear with both atelic and telic events at the same time and sometimes competing with past tense in the marking of achievements (e.g., Robison, 1995; Rohde, 1996).

9 Shirai's position on the possible lack of evidence for the LAH is discussed in more detail in Chapter 5.

10 It is possible, however, as Camps proposed, that there is indirect evidence for such developmental spread of the Preterite and Imperfect if we compare the findings from his study with other studies that gathered data from other developmental levels. For that purpose, Camps uses as a reference point the findings from Cadierno (2000). The latter study was discussed in previous sections.

11 The selected passages were cited by Lunn (1985: 58–59) as the types of narratives that contain examples of nonprototypical marking of aspect (viewpoint aspect).

12 The exam consisted of 15 items focusing on oral comprehension of Spanish and 85 items focusing on grammatical knowledge.

13 That is, almost all of the students in the highest level of proficiency belonged to the group of exchange students in the translation programme. Students from this group also represented about 60 per cent of the informants in levels 2 and 3: 23 out of 38 in level 3 (NN3) and 9 out of 15 in level 2 (NN2).

14 The native languages of Güell's subjects are also worthy of note. About half of her subjects were Anglophones (more precisely, 44 out of 86 informants). Furthermore, ten of her informants were French native speakers and among 14 'others', there were also speakers of Italian (although the exact number is not mentioned). The inclusion of Romance speakers in the group of non-native speakers is relevant because we cannot rule out the strong effect of transfer from one Romance language to another. In sum, the informants in Güell's study were fairly proficient in Spanish due to the combined effect of their previous academic experience with Spanish, and their knowledge of another Romance language.

15 The results from the narrative task did not include the lowest level of proficiency (i.e., NN1), because the latter did not do this task.

16 Table 2 from Martínez Baztán presents some conflicting information. The table shows that the number of states in the Imperfect is 79. However, that figure does not add up when we consider there are 79 other states marked with the Preterite for a total of 253 tokens of statives (i.e., we are short 95 tokens). I calculated, however, that the 21 per cent of errors listed on that table for statives marked with the Imperfect would correspond to 174 tokens (instead of 79), a figure that would reconcile the total number of tokens for statives. That is, the total of 253 tokens corresponds to 79 plus 174.

17 The test did not include activities because sentences with activities were illogical with Preterite and Imperfect.

18 The results of the individual data did not reveal any type of clustering of data that would signal that, for instance, half the learners were accurate and the other half were inaccurate. The latter finding would have contradicted the claim that, by and large, learners were noncommitted in their judgements.

19 An alternative interpretation of the meaning of the Imperfect and Preterite in this context as proposed by Doiz-Bienzobas is presented in Chapter 4.

20 Also note there is an interesting trend prompted by the methodological design of the test: in all three types of lexical aspectual classes tested, the illogical outcomes are all rendered by a telic event with the Preterite.

21 The Slabakova and Montrul (2007) chapter is a longer version of the same study published in the Boston University Conference on Language Development (BUCLD) Proceedings.

22 Note that iterativity is not the same as habituality (see Chapter 2 for extended discussion).

23 In a previous publication, Slabakova (2001: 111) argued that semelfactives do not really belong to the atelic class of verbal predicates (reaffirmed in Slabakova, 2002: 178). Thus, one could claim that the results from Piñango et al. are immaterial for the argument advanced by Slabakova and Montrul.

24 Nevertheless, the possibility of L1 transfer as an added factor cannot be ruled out. That is, through transfer from their native language, L2 learners may initially assume that Simple past tense corresponds to the Preterite and that use of the periphrastic Progressive are largely equivalent to the Imperfect. Learners of course would use these generalizations as rules of thumb, quickly realizing there are exceptions to them. Nevertheless, as a first crude approximation they do a good job of providing learners with a usable heuristic. Similarly, instruction tends to focus on prototypical combinations of lexical and grammatical aspects that, by and large, mirror and confirm the rules of thumb that the students may develop through their L1 knowledge.

25 Note that there is a significant degree of variation in favour of the accurate selection of the Preterite over the accurate selection of the Imperfect across all groups (except for the case of generic sentences). In fact, even native speakers tended to be up to 10 per cent more accurate in their selections associated with the Preterite instead of the Imperfect. As Slabakova and Montrul acknowledge in their analysis, this trend raises concerns about the possible intervening variable of test effects on the measurement of the dependent variable.

[26] The previous caveats of the research design are relevant given that the success of learners in their correct assessment of generic versus habitual meanings that is argued to substantiate the argument about the domain-specific nature of the acquisition of aspectual semantics: 'Crucially, we do not expect to find individuals who know how habitual meaning is encoded but who do not know that a generic subject reading results' (p. 180).

[27] Schell also obtained four writing samples from each learner, that by and large confirm the results of the cloze-test summarized here.

Chapter 4

[1] The distinction between the Perfect and the Progressive as aspectual operators on the one hand, and the *Imparfait* and *Passée Simple* as non-aspectual operators (but rather as aspectually sensitive tenses) on the other hand, may not be as significant as de Swart would argue given that what the *Imparfait* and the *Passée Simple* do is to 'impose a general aspectual constraint on the eventuality description they apply to, *which must be satisfied, if necessary, by means of coercion*'. We should remember, however, that coercion, by definition, is an eventuality description modifier (p. 360). Therefore, we may have a distinction without a difference.

[2] Indeed, Depraetre (1995: 12) points out that a habit or repetitive situation is not inherently atelic and unbounded. A repetitive situation can also be telic, that is, the situation holds a predetermined number of times.

[3] Ziegeler specifies that the phenomenon of coercion can be analysed as part of the process of metonymy (i.e., contiguity) relating 'two concepts within one cognitive domain'.

[4] The examples are an expansion of test sentences from Slabakova and Montrul (2002b, 2007).

[5] In this respect, both the LAH and Minimalism are constrained in their predictions to the prototypical match-ups of grammatical aspect and lexical aspect (e.g., Preterite with telic events, Imperfect with states, etc.).

[6] Slabakova (2001: 111) claims that semelfactives do not really belong to the atelic class of verbal predicates. In a later publication (Slabakova, 2002: 178), however, she accepts that semelfactives may be regarded as atelic in nature.

[7] Dalila Ayoun (personal communication 31 July 2007) comments that the sentence with the perfective form leads us to believe that Marie was waiting for Pierre to arrive with some important information that had to be relayed by phone later on. In other words, the choice of the past tense marker (perfective or imperfective) brings about a distinct difference in meaning.

[8] Example (27) is borrowed from Slabakova and Montrul (2002b) and example (28) is adapted from García and van Putte (1988).

[9] The stress on the qualification of *initial* effect should make this claim uncontroversial given that most proposals favouring the modular effect of UG are not necessarily against that claim.

[10] There are, however, some discrepancies in previous analyses. For instance, Schell (2000) argues that states are marked with the Preterite due to transfer of the feature [+perfective] from the L1 over to the L2.

[11] It must be noted that there is not enough evidence yet to substantiate the prevalent effect of any one of the above-mentioned effects on the acquisition of the Preterite–Imperfect contrast in Spanish.

[12] Nevertheless, we have yet to clearly extricate the effect of possible intervening variables that are typically associated with natural learners (e.g., guest workers with little or no academic training and in some cases exhibiting low levels of literacy).

[13] I will discuss the relevance of Goodin-Mayeda and Rothman's proposed contrast between competence and performance effects of instruction in more detail in Chapter 5.

Chapter 5

[1] Not surprisingly, the empirical findings gathered by each theoretical strand of analysis of tense-aspect phenomena have been the result of the search for answers to specific questions regarded as important for each theoretical approach. This is not only theoretically coherent, but also practical. It bears repeating that central factors of the research design of most studies (e.g., choice of dependent and independent variables) are inherently defined by central tenets of the specific theoretical approach. Moreover, research methodologies used by different studies have also been designed in response to specific theoretical conditions regarded as relevant. For instance, studies on the acquisition of tense-aspect conducted within a Minimalist approach tend to discount the findings gathered through the collection of the open production of language, favouring instead the use of controlled grammaticality judgement tasks.

References

Andersen, R. (1986). El desarrollo de la morfología verbal en el español como segundo idioma. In *Adquisición del Lenguaje – Aquisição da Linguagem*, ed. J. Meisel, 115–38. Frankfurt: Klaus-Dieter Vervuert Verlag.

Andersen, R. (1991). Developmental sequences: The emergence of aspect marking in second language acquisition. In T. Huebner and C. A. Ferguson (Eds), *Crosscurrents in Second Language Acquisition and Linguistic Theories* (pp. 305–324). Amsterdam: John Benjamins.

Andersen, R. (1994). The insider's advantage. In A. Giacalone-Ramat and M. Vedovelli (Eds), *Italiano Lingua Seconda/Lingua Straniera [Italian: Second language/foreign language: Acts of the 26th Congress of the Italian Linguistic Society]* (pp. 1–26). Rome: Bulzoni.

Andersen, R. (2002). The dimensions of "pastness". In R. Salaberry and Y. Shirai (Eds), *The L2 Acquisition of Tense-Aspect Morphology* (pp. 79–105). Philadelphia: Benjamins.

Andersen, R., and Shirai, Y. (1994). Discourse motivations for some cognitive acquisition principles. *Studies in Second Language Acquisition, 16*, 133–156.

Andersen, R., and Shirai, Y. (1996). The primacy of aspect in first and second language acquisition: The pidgin-creole connection. In B. Laufer and W. Ritchie (Eds), *Handbook of Second Language Acquisition* (pp. 527–570). New York: Academic Press.

Antinucci, F., and Miller, R. (1976). How children talk about what happened. *Journal of Child Language, 3*, 169–189.

Antonio, T. (2007). 'Aspectual performance and selection by advanced speakers of Spanish'. (Unpublished manuscript. Austin, TX: University of Texas-Austin).

Arche, M. (2006). *Individuals in Time: Tense, Aspect and the Individual/Stage Distinction*. Amsterdam/Philadelphia: Benjamins.

Ayoun, D. (2004). The effectiveness of written recasts in the second language acquisition of aspectual distinctions in French: A follow-up study. *Modern Language Journal, 88*, 31–55.

Ayoun, D. (2005). The acquisition of tense and aspect in L2 French from a Universal Grammar perspective. In D. Ayoun and R. Salaberry (Eds), *Tense and Aspect in the Romance Languages: Theoretical and Applied Perspectives* (pp. 79–127). Amsterdam and Philadelphia: John Benjamins.

Ayoun, D., and Salaberry, R. (2005). *Tense and Aspect in the Romance Languages: Theoretical and Applied Perspectives*. Amsterdam and Philadelphia: John Benjamins.

Bache, C. (1982). Aspect and aktionsart: Toward a semantic distinction. *Journal of Linguistics, 18*, 57–72.

Bardovi-Harlig, K. (1992a). The relationship of form and meaning: A cross sectional study of tense and aspect in the interlanguage of learners of English as a second language. *Applied Psycholinguistics, 13*, 253–278.

Bardovi-Harlig, K. (1992b). The telling of a tale: Discourse structure and tense use in learner's narratives. In L. Bouton and Y. Kachru (Eds), *Pragmatics and Language Learning* (Vol. 3, pp. 144–161). Urbana-Champaign, IL: Division of English as an International Language.

Bardovi-Harlig, K. (1994). Anecdote or evidence? Evaluating support for hypotheses concerning the development of tense and aspect. In E. Tarone, S. Gass and A. Cohen (Eds), *Research Methodology in Second-Language Acquisition* (pp. 41–60). Hillsdale, NJ: Lawrence Erlbaum.

Bardovi-Harlig, K. (1995). A narrative perspective on the development of the tense/aspect system in second language acquisition. *Studies in Second Language Acquisition, 17*, 263–289.

Bardovi-Harlig, K. (1998). Narrative structure and lexical aspect: Conspiring factors in second language acquisition of tense aspect morphology. *Studies in Second Language Acquisition, 20*, 471–508.

Bardovi-Harlig, K. (1999). From morpheme studies to temporal semantics. *Studies in Second Language Acquisition, 21*, 341–382.

Bardovi-Harlig, K. (2000). *Tense and Aspect in Second Language Acquisition: Form, Meaning, and Use.* Ann Arbor, MI: Blackwell.

Bardovi-Harlig, K. (2005). Tracking the elusive imperfect in adult L2 acquisition. In P. Kempchinsky and R. Slabakova (Eds), *Aspectual Inquiries* (pp. 397–419). Dordrecht: Springer.

Bardovi-Harlig, K., and Bergström, A. (1996). Acquisition of tense and aspect in second language and foreign language learning: Learner narratives in ESL and FFL. *Canadian Modern Language Review, 52*, 308–330.

Bardovi-Harlig, K., and Reynolds, D. (1995). The role of lexical aspect in the acquisition of tense and aspect. *TESOL Quarterly, 29*, 107–131.

Barner, D., Wagner, L., and Snedeker, J. (2008). Events and the ontology of individuals: Verbs as a source of individuating mass and count nouns. *Cognition, 106*, 805–832.

Bates, E., and Goodman, J. (1997). On the inseparability of grammar and the lexicon: Evidence from real acquisition, aphasia and real-time processing. *Language and Cognitive Processes, 12*(5/6), 507–584.

Bates, E., Elman, J., Johnson, M., Karmiloff-Smith, A., Parisi, D., and Plunkett, K. (1998). Innateness and emergentism. In W. Bechtel and G. Graham (Eds), *A Companion to Cognitive Science* (pp. 590–601). Oxford: Basil Blackwell.

Bates, E., and Goodman, J. (1999). On the emergence of grammar from the lexicon. In B. MacWhinney (Ed.), *The Emergence of Language* (pp. 29–79). Mahwah, NJ: Lawrence Erlbaum.

Bayley, R. (1994). Interlanguage variation and the quantitative paradigm: Past tense marking in Chinese-English. In E. Tarone, S. Gass and A. Cohen (Eds), *Research Methodology in Second-Language Acquisition* (pp. 157–181). Hillsdale, NJ: Lawrence Erlbaum.

Bergström, A. (1995). 'The expression of past temporal reference by English-speaking learners of French'. (Unpublished PhD dissertation, Pennsylvania State University, State College, PA).

Bertinetto, P. (1994). Stative, progressives, and habituals: Analogies and differences. *Linguistics, 32*, 391–423.

Bhatt, D. N. S. (1999). *The Prominence of Tense, Aspect and Mood*. Amsterdam/ Philadelphia: John Benjamins.

Binnick, R. (1991). *Time and the Verb*. Oxford: Blackwell.

Birdsong, D. (1992). Ultimate attainment in second language acquisition. *Language, 68,* 706–755.

Birdsong, D., and Flege, J. (2001). Regular–irregular dissociations in L2 acquisition of English morphology. In *BUCLD 25: Proceedings of the 25 Annual Boston University Conference on Language Development* (pp. 123–132). Boston, MA: Cascadilla Press.

Bley-Vroman, R. (1983). The comparative fallacy in interlanguage studies: The case of systematicity. *Language Learning, 33,* 1–17.

Bley-Vroman, R. (1989). What is the logical problem of foreign language learning? In S. Gass and J. Schachter (Eds), *Linguistic Perspectives on Second Language Acquisition* (pp. 41–68). Cambridge: Cambridge University Press.

Bloom, L., Lifter, K., and Hafitz, J. (1980). Semantics of verbs and the development of verb inflection in child language. *Language, 56,* 386–412.

Blyth, C. (1997). A constructivist approach to grammar: Teaching teachers to teach aspect. *Modern Language Journal, 81*(i), 50–66.

Blyth, C. (2005). From empirical findings to the teaching of aspectual distinctions. In D. Ayoun and R. Salaberry (Eds), *Tense and Aspect in Romance Languages: Theoretical and Applied Perspectives* (pp. 211–252). Amsterdam/Philadelphia: John Benjamins.

Bronckart, J. P., and Sinclair, H. (1973). Time, tense, and aspect. *Cognition, 2,* 107–130.

Brown, R. (1973). *A First Language: The Early Stages*. Cambridge, MA: Harvard University Press.

Buck, M. (2007, April 18–21, 2007). *Irregular verbs as Formulaic exemplars in second language acquisition*. Paper presented at the Linguistics Symposium on formulaic Language, University of Wisconsin-Milwaukee.

Buck, M. (forthcoming). The roles of cognitive saliency, lexical aspect and narrative structure in the development of past tense morphology in English L2. *IRAL.*

Buczowska, E., and Weist, R. (1991). The effects of formal instruction on the second language acquisition of temporal location. *Language Learning, 41,* 535–554.

Bull, W. (1960). *Time, Tense and the Verb*. Berkeley: University of California Press.

Bull, W. (1965). *Spanish for Teachers: Applied Linguistics*. New York: The Royal Press Company.

Bybee, J. (1985). *Morphology: A Study of the Relation between Meaning and Form*. Philadelphia: John Benjamins.

Bybee, J. (1995a). Spanish tense and aspect from a typological perspective. In P. Hashemipour, R. Maldonado and M. van Naerssen (Eds), *Studies in Language Learning and Spanish Linguistics*. New York: McGraw-Hill.

Bybee, J. (1995b). Regular morphology and the lexicon. *Language and Cognitive Processes, 10*(5), 425–455.

Bybee, J., and Dahl, O. (1989). The creation of tense and aspect systems in the languages of the world. *Studies in Language, 13,* 51–103.

Cadierno, T. (2000). The acquisition of Spanish grammatical aspect by Danish advanced language learners. *Spanish Applied Linguistics, 4*(1), 1–53.

Cadierno, T. (2004). Expressing motion events in a second language: A cognitive typological approach. In M. Achard and S. Neimeier (Eds), *Cognitive Linguistics, Second Language Acquisition and Foreign Language Pedagogy* (pp. 13–49). The Hague: Mouton de Gruyter.

Cadierno, T., and Ruiz, L. (2006). Motion events in Spanish L2 acquisition. *Annual Review of Cognitive Linguistics, 4,* 183–216.

Camps, J. (2002). Aspectual distinctions in Spanish as a foreign language: The early stages of oral production. *International Review of Applied Linguistics, 40,* 179–210.

Camps, J. (2005). The emergence of the imperfect in Spanish as a foreign language: The association between imperfective morphology and state verbs. *International Review of Applied Linguistics, 43,* 163–192.

Caudal, P., and Roussarie, L. (2005). Aspectual viewpoints, speech act functions and discourse structure. In P. Kempchinsky and R. Slabakova (Eds), *Aspectual Inquiries* (pp. 265–290). Dordrecht: Springer.

Chierchia, G. (1995). Individual-level predicates as inherent generics. In G. Carlson and F. Pelletier (Eds), *The Generic Book* (pp. 176–223). Chicago: Chicago University Press.

Chung, S., and Timberlake, A. (1985). Tense, aspect, and mood. In T. Shopen (Ed.), *Language Typology and Syntactic Description III: Grammatical Categories and the Lexicon* (pp. 202–258). Cambridge: Cambridge University Press.

Clarke, M. (1980). The short circuit hypothesis of ESL reading - or when language competence interferes with reading performance. *The Modern Language Journal, 64,* 203–209.

Collins, L. (2002). The roles of L1 influence and lexical aspect in the acquisition of temporal morphology. *Language Learning, 52*(1), 43–94.

Collins, L. (2004). The particulars on universals: A comparison of the acquisition of tense-aspect morphology among Japanese- and French-speaking learners of English. *Canadian Modern Language Review, 61*(2), 251–274.

Comajoan, L. (2001). 'The acquisition of Catalan L2 past morphology: Evidence for the aspect and discourse hypotheses'. (Unpublished PhD dissertation, Indiana University, Bloomington, IN).

Comajoan, L. (2005a). The early L2 acquisition of past morphology: Perfective morphology as an aspectual marker or default tense marker? In D. Eddington (Ed.), *Selected Proceedings of the 6th Conference on the Acquisition of Spanish and Portuguese as First and Second Languages* (pp. 31–43). Somerville, MA: Cascadilla Proceedings Project.

Comajoan, L. (2005b). The acquisition of perfective and imperfective morphology and the marking of discourse grounding in Catalan. In D. Ayoun and R. Salaberry (Eds), *Tense and Aspect in Romance Languages: Theoretical and Applied Perspectives* (pp. 35–78). Amsterdam/Philadelphia: John Benjamins.

Comajoan, L. (2006). The aspect hypothesis: Relationship between use of morphology and appropriateness of use. *Language Learning, 56*(2), 201–268.

Comajoan, L., and Pérez Saldanya, M. (2005). Grammaticalization and language acquisition: Interaction of lexical aspect and discourse. In D. Eddington (Ed.), *Selected Proceedings of the 6th Conference on the Acquisition of Spanish and Portuguese as First and Second Languages* (pp. 44–55). Somerville, MA: Cascadilla Proceedings Project.

Comrie, B. (1976). *Aspect.* Cambridge: Cambridge University Press.

Comrie, B. (1985). *Tense.* Cambridge: Cambridge University Press.

Coppieters, R. (1987). Competence differences between native and near-native speakers. *Language, 63*, 544–573.

Croft, W. (1998). The structure of events and the structure of language. In M. Tomasello (Ed.), *The New Psychology of Language* (pp. 67–92). Mahwah: Erlbaum.

Dahl, O. (1985). *Tense and Aspect Systems.* Oxford: Basil Blackwell.

Delgado-Jenkins, H. (1990). Imperfect vs. preterit: A new approach. *Hispania, 73*, 1145–1146.

Depraetre, I. (1995). On the necessity of distinguishing between (un)boundedness and (a)telicity. *Linguistics and Philosophy, 18*, 1–19.

Dietrich, R., Klein, W., and Noyau, C. (1995). *The Acquisition of Temporality in a Second Language.* Philadelphia, PA: John Benjamins.

Dinan, M. (2007). 'Influence of narrative type on past tense aspect in Spanish'. (Unpublished Manuscript. Austin, TX: University of Texas-Austin).

Doiz-Bienzobas, A. (1995). 'The Preterite and the Imperfect in Spanish: Past situation vs. past viewpoint'. (Unpublished PhD dissertation, University of California-San Diego, San Diego).

Doiz-Bienzobas, A. (2002). The preterit and the imperfect as grounding predications. In F. Brisard (Ed.), *Grounding: The Epistemic Footing of Deixis and Reference* (pp. 299–347). Berlin: Mouton de Gruyter.

Dowty, D. (1972). *Studies in the Logic of Verb Aspect and Time Reference in English.* Austin: University of Texas.

Dowty, D. (1979). *Word Meaning and Montague Grammar.* Dordrecht: D. Reidel.

Dowty, D. (1986). The effects of aspectual class on the temporal structure of discourse: Semantics or pragmatics? *Linguistics and Philosophy, 9*, 37–61.

Dry, H. (1983). The movement of narrative time. *Journal of Literary Semantics, 12*, 19–53.

Duffield, N. (2003). Measures of competence gradience. In R. van Hout, A. Hulk, F. Kuiken and R. Towell (Eds), *The Lexicon-Syntax Interface in Second Language Acquisition* (pp. 97–128). Amsterdam-Philadelphia: Benjamins.

Ellis, N. (2001). Memory for language. In P. Robinson (Ed.), *Cognition an Second Language Instruction* (pp. 33–66). Cambridge: Cambridge University Press.

Ellis, N. (2002). Frequency effects in language processing: A review with implications for theories of implicit and explicit language acquisition. *Studies in Second Language Acquisition, 24*, 143–188.

Ellis, R. (1987). Interlanguage variability in narrative discourse: Style shifting in the use of the past tense. *Studies in Second Language Acquisition, 9*, 1–20.

Filip, H. (1999). *Aspect, Eventuality Types and Nominal Reference.* New York: Garland Publishing.

Fleischman, S. (1989). Temporal distance: A basic linguistic metaphor. *Studies in Language, 13*, 1–50.

Fleischman, S. (1990). *Tense and Narrativity.* London: Routledge.

Frantzen, D. (1995). Preterite/Imperfect half-truths: Problems with Spanish textbook rules for usage. *Hispania, 78*, 145–158.

Frawley, W. (1992). *Linguistic Semantics.* Hillsdale, NJ: Lawrence Erlbaum.

Gabriele, A., Martohardjono, G., and McClure, W. (2005). Evaluating the role of the L1 in the L2 acquisition of aspect: A study of Japanese learners of English. In J. Cohen, K. McAlister, K. Rolstad and J. MacSwan (Eds), *Proceedings of the 4th*

International Symposium on Bilingualism (pp. 808–826). Somerville, MA: Cascadilla Press.

García, E., and van Putte, F. (1988). The value of contrast: Contrasting the value of strategies. *International Review of Applied Linguistics, 26,* 263–281.

Gass, S., and Selinker, L. (2001). *Second Language Acquisition: An Introductory Course* (2nd ed.). Hillsdale, NJ: Erlbaum.

Giacalone-Ramat, A. (1992). Grammaticalization processes in the area of temporal and modal relations. *Studies in Second Language Acquisition, 14,* 297–322.

Giacalone-Ramat, A. (2002). How do learners acquire the classical three categories of temporality? Evidence from L2 Italian. In R. Salaberry and Y. Shirai (Eds), *The L2 Acquisition of Tense-aspect Morphology* (pp. 221–247). Philadelphia: Benjamins.

Giorgi, A., and Pianesi, F. (1997). *Tense and Aspect: From Semantics to Morphosyntax.* Oxford: Oxford University Press.

Givón, T. (1982). Tense-aspect-modality: The Creole prototype and beyond. In P. J. Hopper (Ed.), *Tense-Aspect: Between Semantics and Pragmatics* (pp. 115–163). Amsterdam: John Benjamins.

Goldsmith, J., and Woisetschlaeger, E. (1982). The logic of the English progressive. *Linguistic Inquiry, 13,* 79–90.

González, P. (2003). *Aspects on Aspect: Theory and Applications of Grammatical Aspect in Spanish.* Utrecht, The Netherlands: LOT.

Goodin-Mayeda, C., and Rothman, J. (2007). The acquisition of aspect in L2 Portuguese and Spanish. Exploring native/non-native performance differences. In S. Baauw, F. Drijkoningen and M. Pinto (Eds), *Romance Languages and Linguistic theory* (pp. 131–148). Amsterdam: John Benjamins.

Granda, B. (2004). 'La expresión de la temporalidad en textos narrativos en español como segunda lengua por anglohablantes'. (Unpublished Master's thesis, Universidad Nacional Autónoma de México, Mexico, DF).

Gregg, K. (2001). Learnability and second language acquisition theory. In P. Robinson (Ed.), *Cognition an Second Language Instruction* (pp. 152–181). Cambridge: Cambridge University Press.

Güell, L. (1998). 'La adquisición del tiempo verbal en el aprendizaje del español como lengua extranjera'. (Unpublished PhD dissertation, Universitat Autònoma de Barcelona, Barcelona).

Guitart, J. (1978). Aspects of Spanish aspect: A new look at the preterit/imperfect distinction. In M. Suñer (Ed.), *Contemporary Studies in Romance Linguistics* (pp. 132–168). Washington, DC: Georgetown University Press.

Guitart, J. (1995). 'Preterit and imperfect in a nutshell'. (Unpublished Manuscript. Buffalo, NY: SUNY Buffalo).

Harley, B. (1989). Functional grammar in French immersion: a classroom experiment. *Applied Linguistics, 10,* 331–359.

Hasbún, L. (1995). 'The role of lexical aspect in the acquisition of the tense/aspect system in L2 Spanish'. (Unpublished PhD dissertation, Indiana University, Bloomington).

Hawkins, R., and Chan, C. (1997). The partial availability of Universal Grammar in second language acquisition: The 'failed functional features hypothesis'. *Second Language Research, 13*(3), 187–226.

Hawkins, R., and Liszka, S. (2003). Locating the source of defective past tense marking in advanced L2 English speakers. In R. van Hout, A. Hulk, F. Kuiken and R. Towell (Eds), *The Lexicon–Syntax Interface in Second Language Acquisition* (pp. 21–44). Amsterdam: John Benjamins.

Hernán, L. (1994). VIPI, Visualización del pretérito y del imperfecto. *Hispania*, 77–2, 280–286.

Herschensohn, J. (2000). *The Second Time Around: Minimalism and L2 Acquisition.* Amsterdam: Benjamins.

Hinrichs, E. (1986). Temporal anaphora in discourses of English. *Linguistics and Philosophy*, 9, 62–82.

Hopper, P. (1979). Aspect and foregrounding in discourse. In T. Givón (Ed.), *Syntax and Semantics. Vol. 12* (pp. 213–241). New York: Academic Press.

Hopper, P. (1982). *Tense-Aspect: Between Syntax and Pragmatics.* Philadelphia: John Benjamins.

Housen, A. (1994). Tense and aspect in second language learning: The Dutch interlanguage of a native speaker of English. In C. Vet and C. Vetters (Eds), *Tense and Aspect in Discourse* (pp. 257–291). Berlin: Mouton de Gruyter.

Housen, A. (2002). The development of Tense-Aspect in English as a second language and the variable influence of inherent aspect. In R. Salaberry and Y. Shirai (Eds), *The L2 Acquisition of Tense-Aspect Morphology* (pp. 155–197). Philadelphia: Benjamins.

Jakobson, R. (1957). Shifters, verbal categories, and the Russian verb. In R. Jakobson (Ed.), *Selected Writings, Volume 2: Word and Language.* The Hague: Mouton.

Kamp, H., and Rohrer, C. (1983). Tense in texts. In R. Bäuerle, C. Schwarze and A. von Steechow (Eds), *Meaning, Use and Interpretation of Language* (pp. 250–269). Berlin: Walter de Gruyter.

Kaplan, M. (1987). Developmental patterns of past tense acquisition among foreign language learners of French. In B. VanPatten (Ed.), *Foreign Language Learning: A Research Perspective* (pp. 52–60). Rowley, MA: Newbury House.

Karmiloff-Smith, A. (1992). *Beyond Modularity: A Developmental Perspective on Cognitive Science.* Cambridge, MA: MIT Press.

Kempchinsky, P. (2000). Aspect projections and predicate type. In H. Campos, E. Herburger, A. Morales-Front and T. Walsh (Eds), *Hispanic Linguistics at the Turn of the Millennium: Papers from the 3rd Hispanic Linguistics Symposium* (pp. 171–187). Somerville, MA: Cascadilla Press.

Kenny, A. (1963). *Action, Emotion and Will.* New York: Springer.

Kihlstedt, M. (2002). Reference to past events in dialogue: The acquisition of tense and aspect by advanced learners of French. In R. Salaberry and Y. Shirai (Eds), *The L2 Acquisition of Tense-Aspect Morphology* (pp. 323–361). Amsterdam and Philadelphia: John Benjamins.

Klein, W. (1994). *Time in Language.* London: Routledge.

Klein, W., Dietrich, R., and Noyau, C. (1995). Conclusions. In R. Dietrich, W. Klein and C. Noyau (Eds), *The Acquisition of Temporality in a Second Language* (pp. 261–280). Philadelphia, PA: John Benjamins.

Klein, W., and Perdue, C. (Eds). (1992). *Utterance Structure: Developing Grammars again.* Amsterdam: John Benjamins.

Krasinski, E. (1995). The development of past marking in a bilingual child and the punctual–nonpunctual distinction. *First Language*, 15, 239–276.

Krifka, M. (1998). The origins of telicity. In R. Rothstein (Ed.), *Events and Grammar* (pp. 197–235). Dordrecht: Kluwer Academic Publishers.

Labeau, E. (2005). *Beyond the Aspect Hypothesis: Tense-aspect Development in Advanced L2 French.* New York: Peter Lang.

Lafford, B. (1996). *The development of tense/aspect relations in L2 Spanish narratives: Evidence to test competing theories.* Paper presented at the Second Language Research Forum 96, Tucson, AZ.

Langacker, R. (1982). Remarks on English aspect. In P. Hopper (Ed.), *Tense-Aspect: Between Syntax and Pragmatics* (pp. 265–304). Philadelphia: John Benjamins.

Langacker, R. (1987). *Foundations of Cognitive Grammar, Vol 1: Theoretical Perspectives.* Stanford, CA: Stanford University Press.

Langacker, R. (1999). *Grammar and Conceptualization.* Berlin: Mouton de Gruyter.

Lardiere, D. (1998a). Case and tense in the "fossilized" steady state. *Second Language Research, 14*(1), 1–26.

Lardiere, D. (1998b). Dissociating syntax from morphology in a divergent end-state grammar. *Second Language Research, 14*, 359–375.

Lardiere, D. (2003). Revisiting the comparative fallacy: A reply to Lakshmanan and Selinker, 2001. *Second Language Research, 19*(2), 129–143.

Larsen-Freeman, D. (2003). *Teaching Language: From Grammar to Grammaring.* Boston: Thomson/Heinle.

Li, P., and Shirai, Y. (2000). *The Acquisition of Lexical and Grammatical Aspect.* Berlin: Mouton de Gruyter.

Liceras, J. (1986). On some properties of the 'pro-drop' parameter: Looking for missing subjects in non-native Spanish. In S. Gass and J. Schachter (Eds), *Linguistic Perspective on Second Language Acquisition* (pp. 109–133). Cambridge, MA: Cambridge University Press.

Liskin-Gasparro, J. (2000). The use of tense-aspect morphology in Spanish oral narratives: Exploring the perceptions of advanced learners. *Hispania, 83*(4), 830–844.

López-Ortega, N. (2000). Tense, aspect, and narrative structure in Spanish as a second language. *Hispania, 83*(3), 488–502.

Lubbers-Quesada, M. (1999). *The acquisition of aspectual distinction in Spanish: A look at learners in an immersion program.* Paper presented at the 6th International Cognitive Linguistics Conference, Stockholm, Sweden.

Lubbers-Quesada, M. (2006). L2 Acquisition of temporal reference in Spanish and the interaction of adverbials, morphology and clause structure. In N. Sagarra and A. Toribio (Eds), *Selected Proceedings of the 9th Hispanic Linguistics Symposium* (pp. 157–168). Somerville, MA: Cascadilla Press.

Lubbers-Quesada, M. (2007). La percepción de las propiedades semánticas y la adquisición de la morfología verbal en el español como L2. *Estudios de Lingüística Aplicada, 44*, 11–36.

Lucy, J. (1992). *Grammatical Categories and Cognition: A Case Study of the Linguistic Relativity Hypothesis.* Cambridge: Cambridge University Press.

Luján, M. (1981). The Spanish Copulas as aspectual indicators. *Lingua, 54*, 165–210.

Lunn, P. (1985). The aspectual lens. *Hispanic Linguistics, 2*, 49–61.

Lyons, J. (1968). *Introduction to Theoretical Linguistics.* Cambridge: Cambridge University Press.

Maingueneau, D. (1994). *L'Enonciation en Linguistique Française.* Paris: Hachette.

Martínez-Baztán, A. (1994). Análisis transversal del uso de los tiempos indefinido/ imperfecto por estudiantes holandeses de español L2. In J. Slagter (Ed.), *Aproximaciones a cuestiones de adquisición y aprendizaje del español como lengua extranjera o lengua segunda* (pp. 31–48). Atlanta, GA: Rodopi.

Michaelis, L. (1998). *Aspectual Grammar and Past-time Reference.* New York: Routledge.

Michaelis, L. (2004). Type shifting in construction grammar: An integrated approach to aspectual coercion. *Cognitive Linguistics, 15,* 1–67.

de Miguel, E. (1992). *El Aspecto en la Sintaxis del Español: Perfectividad e Imperfectividad.* Madrid: Ediciones de la Universidad Autónoma de Madrid.

Mitchell, R., and Myles, F. (2004). *Second Language Learning Theories.* New York: Arnold.

Montrul, S. (2002). Incomplete acquisition and attrition of Spanish tense/aspect distinctions in adult bilinguals. *Bilingualism: Language and Cognition, 5*(1), 39–68.

Montrul, S. (2004). *The Acquisition of Spanish: Morphosyntactic Development in Monolingual and Bilingual L1 Acquisition and Adult L2 Acquisition.* Amsterdam and Philadelphia: Benjamins.

Montrul, S., and Salaberry, R. (2003). The development of Spanish past tense morphology: Developing a research agenda. In B. Lafford and R. Salaberry (Eds), *Studies in Spanish Second Language Acquisition: State of the Science* (pp. 47–73). Washington, DC: Georgetown University Press.

Montrul, S., and Slabakova, R. (2002). The L2 acquisition of morphosyntactic and semantic properties of the aspectual tenses Preterite and Imperfect. In A. T. Pérez-Leroux and J. Liceras (Eds), *The Acquisition of Spanish Morphosyntax: The L1/L2 Connection* (pp. 115–151). Dordrecht: Kluwer.

Montrul, S., and Slabakova, R. (2003). Competence similarities between native and near-native speakers: An investigation of the Preterite/Imperfect contrast in Spanish. *Studies in Second Language Acquisition, 25*(3), 351–398.

Morales, A. (1989). Manifestaciones de pasado en niños puertorriqueños de 2-6 años. *Revista de Lingüística Teórica y Aplicada, 27,* 115–131.

Mourelatos, A. P. (1981). Events, processes, and states. In P. J. Tedeschi and A. Zaenen (Eds), *Syntax and Semantics, vol. 14: Tense and Aspect* (pp. 191–212). New York: Academic Press.

Negueruela, E., and Lantolf, J. (2005). Concept-based instruction and the acquisition of L2 Spanish. In R. Salaberry and B. Lafford (Eds.), *Spanish Second Language Acquisition: From research findings to teaching applications* (pp. 79–102). Washington, DC: Georgetown University Press.

Nishida, C. (1994). The Spanish reflexive clitic *se* as an aspectual class marker. *Linguistics, 32,* 425–458.

Noyau, C. (1990). The development of means for temporality in the unguided acquisition of L2: Cross-linguistic perspectives. In H. Dechert (Ed.), *Current Trends in European Second Language Acquisition Research* (pp. 143–170). Clevedon: Multilingual Matters.

Olsen, M. (1997). *A Semantic and Pragmatic Model of Lexical and Grammatical Aspect.* New York: Garland Publishing.

Ozete, O. (1988). Focusing on the preterit and imperfect. *Hispania, 71,* 687–691.

Pérez-Leroux, A., Cuza, A., Majzlanova, M., and Sánchez-Naranjo, J. (2007). Non-native recognition of the iterative and habitual meanings of Spanish preterite and imperfect tenses. In J. Liceras, H. Zobl and H. Goodluck (Eds), *Formal Features in Second Language Acquisition* (pp. 432–451). Amsterdam: John Benjamins.

Pienemann, M., Di Biase, B., Kawaguchi, S., and Håkansson, G. (2005). Processability, typological distance and L1 transfer. In M. Pienemann (Ed.), *Cross-Linguistic Aspects of Processability Theory* (pp. 85–116). Amsterdam: Benjamins.

Piñango, M., Zurif, E., and Jackendoff, R. (1999). Real-time processing implications of enriched composition at the syntax–semantics interface. *Journal of Psycholinguistic Research, 28(4)*, 395–414.

Potowski, K. (2005). Tense and aspect in the oral and written narratives of two-way immersion students. In D. Eddington (Ed.), *Selected Proceedings of the 6th Conference on the Acquisition of Spanish and Portuguese as First and Second Languages* (pp. 123–136). Somerville, MA: Cascadilla Proceedings Project.

Ramsay, V. (1990). 'Developmental stages in the acquisition of the perfective and the imperfective aspects by classroom L2 learners of Spanish'. (Unpublished PhD dissertation, University of Oregon, Eugene, OR).

Reid, W. (1980). Meaning and narrative structure. *Columbia University Working Papers in Linguistics, 5*, 12–20.

Reinhart, T. (1984). Principles of Gestalt perception in the temporal organization of narrative texts. *Linguistics, 22*, 779–809.

Rispoli, M., and Bloom, L. (1985). Incomplete and continuing: Theoretical issues in the acquisition of tense and aspect. *Journal of Child Language, 12*, 471–474.

Robison, R. (1990). The primacy of aspect: Aspectual marking in English interlanguage. *Studies in Second Language Acquisition, 12*, 315–330.

Robison, R. (1995). The aspect hypothesis revisited: A cross sectional study of tense and aspect marking in interlanguage. *Applied Linguistics, 16*, 344–371.

Rocca, S. (2005). Italian tense-aspect morphology in child L2 acquisition. In D. Ayoun and R. Salaberry (Eds), *Tense and Aspect in the Romance Languages: Theoretical and Applied Perspectives* (pp. 129–178). Amsterdam and Philadelphia: John Benjamins.

Rohde, A. (1996). The aspect hypothesis and the emergence of tense distinctions in naturalistic L2 acquisition. *Linguistics, 34*, 1115–1137.

Rosch, E. (1973). On the internal structure of perceptual and semantic categories. In T. Moore (Ed.), *Cognitive Development and the Acquisition of Language* (pp. 111–144). New York: Academic Press.

Rosch, E., and Mervis, C. (1975). Family resemblances: Studies in the internal structure of categories. *Cognitive Psychology, 7*, 573–605.

Rothstein, S. (2004). *Structuring Events: A Study in the Semantics of Lexical Aspect.* Malden, MA: Blackwell.

Salaberry, R. (1998). The development of aspectual distinctions in classroom L2 French. *Canadian Modern Language Review, 54(4)*, 504–542.

Salaberry, R. (1999). The development of past tense verbal morphology in classroom L2 Spanish. *Applied Linguistics, 20(2)*, 151–178.

Salaberry, R. (2000a). *The Development of Past Tense Morphology in L2 Spanish.* Amsterdam, The Netherlands: John Benjamins.

Salaberry, R. (2000b). The acquisition of English Past tense in an instructional setting: Irregular and frequent morphology. *System, 28*, 1–18.

Salaberry, R. (2002). Tense and aspect in the selection of past tense verbal morphology. In R. Salaberry and Y. Shirai (Eds), *Tense-Aspect Morphology in L2 Acquisition* (pp. 397–415). Amsterdam and Philadelphia: John Benjamins.

Salaberry, R. (2003). Tense aspect in verbal morphology. *Hispania, 3(86)*, 559–573.

Salaberry, R. (2004). El uso de las distinciones aspectuales del español en tres actividades con diferentes grados de control. In M. Lubbers-Quesada and R. Maldonado (Eds), *Estudios sobre la Adquisición del Español* (pp. 102–127). México: Universidad Nacional Autónoma de México.

Salaberry, R. (2005). Evidence for transfer of knowledge about aspect from L2 Spanish to L3 Portuguese. In D. Ayoun and R. Salaberry (Eds), *Tense and Aspect in the Romance Languages: Theoretical and Applied Perspectives* (pp. 179–210). Amsterdam and Philadelphia: John Benjamins.

Salaberry, R. (forthcoming). Assessing the effect of lexical aspect and grounding on the acquisition of L2 Spanish Preterit and Imperfect among L1 English speakers.

Salaberry, R., and Scholes, J. (forthcoming). Assessing instructional effects on the acquisition of iterativity.

Salaberry, R., and Shirai, Y. (2002). *Tense-Aspect Morphology in L2 Acquisition.* Amsterdam and Philadelphia: John Benjamins.

Sato, C. (1990). *The Syntax of Conversation in Interlanguage Development.* Tübingen: Gunter Narr Verlag.

Schell, K. (2000). 'Functional categories and the acquisition of aspect in L2 Spanish: A longitudinal study'. (Unpublished PhD dissertation, University of Washington, Seattle, WA).

Schmitt, C. (2001). Cross-linguistic variation and the Present Perfect: The case of Portuguese. *Natural Language and Linguistic Theory, 19*, 403–453.

Schumann, J. (1987). The expression of temporality in basilang speech. *Studies in Second Language Acquisition, 9*, 21–41.

Schwartz, B., and Sprouse, R. (1996). L2 cognitive states and the Full Transfer/Full Access hypothesis. *Second Language Research, 40*, 40–72.

Sebastian, E., and Slobin, D. (1994). Development of linguistic forms: Spanish. In R. Berman and D. Slobin (Eds), *Relating Events in Narrative* (pp. 239–284). Hillsdale, NJ: Lawrence Erlbaum.

Sharwood Smith, M., and Truscott, J. (2005). Stages or continua in second language acquisition: A MOGUL solution. *Applied Linguistics, 26(2)*, 219–240.

Shirai, Y. (1991). 'Primacy of aspect in language acquisition: Simplified input and prototype'. (Unpublished PhD Dissertation, UCLA, Los Angeles, CA).

Shirai, Y. (2002). The prototype hypothesis of tense-aspect acquisition in second language. In R. Salaberry and Y. Shirai (Eds), *The L2 Acquisition of Tense-aspect Morphology* (pp. 455–478). Philadelphia: Benjamins.

Shirai, Y. (2004). A multiple-factor account for the form-meaning connections in the acquisition of tense-aspect morphology. In J. Williams, B. VanPatten, S. Rott and M. Overstreet (Eds), *Form-Meaning Connections in Second Language Acquisition* (pp. 91–112). Mahwah, NJ: Erlbaum.

Shirai, Y. (2007). The Aspect Hypothesis, the comparative fallacy and the validity of obligatory context analysis: A reply to Lardiere, 2003. *Second Language Research, 23*(1), 51–64.

Shirai, Y., and Andersen, R. (1995). The acquisition of tense-aspect morphology: A prototype account. *Language, 71*(4), 743–762.

Shirai, Y., and Kurono, A. (1998). The acquisition of tense-aspect marking in Japanese as a second language. *Language Learning, 48*(2), 245–279.

Silva-Corvalán, C. (1983). Tense and aspect in oral Spanish narrative: Context and meaning. *Language, 59,* 760–780.

Silva-Corvalán, C. (1986). A speech event analysis of tense and aspect in Spanish. In P. Baldi (Ed.), *Papers from the 12th Linguistic Symposium on Romance Languages* (pp. 229–251). Amsterdam: Benjamins.

Silva-Corvalán, C. (1994). *Language Contact and Change: Spanish in Los Angeles.* Oxford: Clarendon.

Skehan, P. (1998). *A Cognitive Approach to Language Learning.* Oxford: Oxford University Press.

Slabakova, R. (1997). *The L2 acquisition of telicity in English: A parametric approach.* Paper presented at the SLRF 97, Michigan State University, East Lansing, MI.

Slabakova, R. (2001). *Telicity in the Second Language.* Amsterdam: John Benjamins.

Slabakova, R. (2002). Recent research on the acquisition of aspect: An embarrassment of riches? *Second Language Research, 18*(2), 172–188.

Slabakova, R., and Montrul, S. (2002a). On viewpoint aspect interpretation and its L2 acquisition. In R. Salaberry and Y. Shirai (Eds), *The L2 Acquisition of Tense-Aspect Morphology* (pp. 363–395). Amsterdam and Philadelphia: John Benjamins.

Slabakova, R., and Montrul, S. (2002b). On aspectual shifts in L2 Spanish. In Skarabela (Ed.), *BUCLD 26 Proceedings* (pp. 631–642). Sommerville, MA: Cascadilla Press.

Slabakova, R., and Montrul, S. (2003). Genericity and aspect in L2 acquisition. *Language Acquisition, 11*(3), 165–196.

Slabakova, R., and Montrul, S. (2007). L2 acquisition at the grammar-discourse interface: Aspectual shifts in L2 Spanish. In J. Liceras, H. Zobl and H. Goodluck (Eds), *Formal Features in Second Language Acquisition* (pp. 452–483). Mahwah, New Jersey: Lawrence Erlbaum.

Slobin, D. (1996a). From 'thought and language' to 'thinking for speaking'. In J. Gumperz, J. John and S. Levinson (Eds), *Rethinking Linguistic Relativity* (pp. 70–96). Cambridge: Cambridge University Press.

Slobin, D. (1996b). Two ways to travel: Verb motion in English and Spanish. In M. Shibatani and S. Thompson (Eds), *Grammatical Constructions: Their Form and Meaning* (pp. 95–219). Oxford: Clarendon Press.

Smith, C. (1983). A theory of aspectual choice. *Language, 59,* 479–501.

Smith, C. (1991/1997). *The Parameter of Aspect.* Dordrecht: Kluwer Academic Press.

Smith, C., and Weist, R. (1987). On the temporal contour of child language: A reply to Rispoli & Bloom. *Journal of Child Language, 14,* 387–392.

Sorace, A. (2000). Gradients in unaccusative and unergative syntax. *Language, 76,* 859–890.

Studerus, L. (1989). On the role of Spanish meaning changing preterites. *Hispanic Linguistics, 3,* 131–145.

de Swart, H. (1998). Aspect shift and coercion. *Natural Language and Linguistic Theory, 16*(2), 347–385.

de Swart, H. (2000). Type, tense and coercion in a cross-linguistic perspective. In M. Butt and T. King (Eds), *Proceedings of the Berkeley Formal Grammar Conference Workshops* (pp. 1–20). Stanford: CSLI Publications.

de Swart, H., and Verkuyl, H. (1999). *Tense and Aspect in Sentence and Discourse: Lecture Notes of the 11th European Summer School in Logic, Language, and Information.* Utrecht: Utrecht Institute of Linguistics OTS.

Tarone, E. (1988). *Variation in Interlanguage.* London: Edward Arnold.

Tatevosov, S. (2002). The parameter of actionality. *Linguistic Typology, 6,* 317–401.

Tenny, C. (1994). *Aspectual Roles and the Syntax–Semantics Interface.* Dordrecht: Kluwer Academic Press.

Tracy, N. (2007). '*Testing the distributional bias hypothesis: A corpus-based study of lexical and grammatical aspect in Spanish*'. (Unpublished manuscript).

Travis, L. (1994). Event phrase and a theory of functional categories. In P. Koskinen (Ed.), *Proceedings of the 1994 Annual Conference of the Canadian Language Association* (pp. 559–570). Toronto: Toronto Working Papers in Linguistics.

Trévise, A. (1987). Toward an analysis of the (Inter)language activity of referring to time in narratives. In C. Pfaff (Ed.), *First and Second Language Acquisition Processes* (pp. 225–251). Cambridge, MA: Newbury House.

Ungerer, F., and Schmidt, H.-J. (1996). *An Introduction to Cognitive Linguistics.* New York: Longman.

Vainnika, A., and Young-Scholten, M. (1996). Gradual development of L2 phrase structure. *Second Language Research, 12,* 7–39.

Vendler, Z. (1967). *Linguistics in Philosophy.* Ithaca, NY: Cornell University Press.

Verkuyl, H. (1989). Aspectual classes and aspectual composition. *Linguistics and Philosophy, 12,* 39–94.

Verkuyl, H. (1993). *A Theory of Aspectuality: The Interaction between Temporal and Atemporal Structure.* Cambridge: Cambridge University Press.

Verkuyl, H. (1999). *Aspectual Issues: Studies on time and quantity* (Vol. 12). Stanford, CA: CSLI Publications.

Véronique, D. (1987). Reference to past events and actions in narratives in L2: Insights from North African workers' French. In C. Pfaff (Ed.), *First and Second Language Acquisition Processes* (pp. 252–272). Cambridge, MA: Newbury House.

Vet, C., and Vetters, C. (1994). *Tense and Aspect in Discourse.* Berlin: Mouton de Gruyter.

von Stutterheim, C., and Klein, W. (1987). A concept-oriented approach to second language studies. In C. Pfaff (Ed.), *First and Second Language Acquisition Processes* (pp. 191–205). Cambridge, MA: Newbury House.

Wagner, L. (2001). Aspectual influences on early tense comprehension. *Journal of Child Language, 28,* 661–681.

Wagner, L. (2006). Aspectual bootstrapping in language acquisition: Transitivity and telicity. *Language Learning and Development, 2,* 51–77.

Wallace, S. (1982). Figure and ground: The interrelationships of linguistic categories. In P. Hopper (Ed.), *Tense-Aspect: Between Syntax and Pragmatics* (pp. 201–233). Philadelphia: John Benjamins.

Waugh, L. (1990). Discourse functions of tense-aspect in French: Dynamic synchrony. In N. Thelin (Ed.), *Verbal Aspect in Discourse* (pp. 159–187). Philadelphia: John Benjamins.

Weist, R. (1983). Prefix versus suffix information processing in the comprehension of tense and aspect. *Journal of Child Language, 10,* 85–96.

Weist, R., Wysocka, H., Witkowska-Stadnik, K., Buczowska, E., and Konieczna, E. (1984). The defective tense hypothesis: On the emergence of tense and aspect in child Polish. *Journal of Child Language, 11,* 347–374.

Westfall, R., and Foerster, S. (1996). Beyond aspect: New strategies for teaching the preterite and the imperfect. *Hispania, 79,* 550–560.

Whitley, S. (1986). *Spanish/English contrasts: A course in Spanish linguistics.* Washington, DC: Georgetown University Press.

Wiberg, E. (1996). Reference to past events in bilingual Italian–Swedish children of school age. *Linguistics, 34,* 1087–1114.

Wolfram, W. (1985). Variability in tense marking: A case for the obvious. *Language Learning, 35*(2), 229–253.

Zagona, K. (1994). Compositionality of aspect: Evidence from Spanish aspectual se. In C. Parodi, C. Quicoli, M. Saltarelli and M. Zubizarreta (Eds), *Aspects of Romance Linguistics: Selected Papers from the Linguistic Symposium on Romance Languages XXIV* (pp. 475–488). Washington, DC: Georgetown University Press.

Ziegeler, D. (2007). A word of caution on coercion. *Journal of Pragmatics, 39,* 990–1028.

Index

Introductory Note

References such as "178–9" indicate (not necessarily continuous) discussion of a topic across a range of pages, whilst "254n" indicates one or more notes on page 254. Wherever possible in the case of topics with many references, these have either been divided into sub-topics or the most significant discussions of the topic are indicated by page numbers in bold. Because the entire volume is about the second-language past tense acquisition, which results in "past tense", "imperfect", "preterite", "tense-aspect" and a number of related terms occurring constantly throughout, the use of these terms as entry points has been minimized. Information should be sought under the corresponding detailed topics.

Index